If Your Adolescent Has Bipolar Disorder

If Your Adolescent Has Bipolar Disorder

An Essential Resource for Parents

Dwight L. Evans, MD, Tami D. Benton, MD, and Katherine Ellison

THE ANNENBERG
PUBLIC POLICY CENTER
OF THE UNIVERSITY OF PENNSYLVANIA

The Adolescent Mental Health Initiative of the Annenberg
Public Policy Center and the Sunnylands Trust

The Annenberg Foundation Trust at
SUNNYLANDS

OXFORD
UNIVERSITY PRESS

OXFORD
UNIVERSITY PRESS

Oxford University Press is a department of the University of Oxford. It furthers
the University's objective of excellence in research, scholarship, and education
by publishing worldwide. Oxford is a registered trade mark of Oxford University
Press in the UK and certain other countries.

Published in the United States of America by Oxford University Press
198 Madison Avenue, New York, NY 10016, United States of America.

© Oxford University Press 2023

First edition published as *If Your Adolescent Has Depression or Bipolar Disorder: An Essential
Resource for Parents*, by Dwight L. Evans, MD, and Linda Wasmer Andrews (Oxford
University Press, 2005)

Library of Congress Cataloging-in-Publication Data
Names: Evans, Dwight L., author. | Benton, Tami, author. |
Ellison, Katherine, 1957– author.
Title: If your adolescent has bipolar disorder : an essential resource for parents /
Dwight L. Evans, Tami D. Benton, and Katherine Ellison.
Description: New York, NY : Oxford University Press, [2023] |
Series: The adolescent mental health initiative of the Annenberg
Public Policy Center and the Sunnylands Trust |
Includes bibliographical references.
Identifiers: LCCN 2022053506 (print) | LCCN 2022053507 (ebook) |
ISBN 9780197636015 (hardback) | ISBN 9780197636022 (paperback) |
ISBN 9780197636046 (epub) | ISBN 9780197636053
Subjects: LCSH: Bipolar disorder in adolescence—Popular works. | Bipolar disorder in
adolescence—Treatment—Popular works. | Parent and teenager—Popular works.
Classification: LCC RJ506.D4 E927 2023 (print) | LCC RJ506.D4 (ebook) |
DDC 616.89/500835—dc23/eng/20230210
LC record available at https://lccn.loc.gov/2022053506
LC ebook record available at https://lccn.loc.gov/2022053507

DOI: 10.1093/med-psych/9780197636015.001.0001

Paperback printed by Sheridan Books, Inc., United States of America
Hardback printed by Bridgeport National Bindery, Inc., United States of America

Contents

Six

Seven

Eight

Nine

Introduction

Unnerving Highs and Lows

One of the few predictable things about raising a child with bipolar disorder is that you will be constantly surprised. One day your son or daughter may seem spirited and energetic. The next: driven and consumed. One morning, a bit peevish. Three hours later: raging. There may be times when you will find it hard to recognize the child you thought you knew.

> "I wanted to grab her and bring her back, but there was no turning back," writes the journalist Michael Greenberg, recounting how he'd chased his manic, 15-year-old daughter down a New York City street in his memoir, *Hurry Down Sunshine: A Father's Story of Love and Madness.* "Suddenly every point of connection between us had vanished. It didn't seem possible. She had learned to speak from me; she had heard her first stories from me . . . and yet from one day to the next we had become strangers."

This illness, which used to be called manic depression, is a *mood disorder*: a potentially harmful variety of the ordinary course of shifting attitudes and behavior. It most often consists of some degree of mania—a giddy, overconfident, or irritable "high"— alternating with cycles of depression, or pervasive sadness.

Until just a few decades ago, most doctors believed children were immune. Yet today "early onset bipolar disorder" is diagnosed in kids as young as 6, with the average age of onset between 15 and 19. This is the heart of adolescence, which the World Health Organization defines as between 10 and 19 years of age.

The symptoms of bipolar disorder in children often differ from those in adults, making it harder to diagnose. It is estimated to affect roughly 3% of US adolescents, or about 1 in 33, which is similar to the rate for adults. That makes it considerably rarer than depression, which today affects nearly 1 in 8 youth. Yet it suggests that roughly 1.3 million adolescents— and, by extension, their families—are suffering the fallout from this major, often dangerous, and almost always lifelong problem. It is for you that we have written this book. Our goal is to empower you with the information and confidence you'll need to best support your child. As many a parent can tell you, you can't start too soon.

"I wish I'd known even half of what I know today about bipolar disorder back when Andrew was first showing symptoms," says Nancy. "In retrospect, I feel like it took way too long for us to understand and then accept that this was what it was."

The Company You Keep

As the parent of a child with mental illness, you've probably already realized you're not alone. The rates of adolescent anxiety and depression have climbed sharply in recent years—even before the COVID-19 pandemic brought its traumas, frustrations, and social isolation. From 2019 to 2021, symptoms of anxiety and depression doubled among US youth. In early 2021, emergency room visits for suicide attempts rose 51% for adolescent girls, over the same period in 2019. (For boys, the increase was 4%.) In a survey taken during the pandemic, 46% of US parents said their children's mental health had deteriorated.

By the end of the second year of the pandemic, mental health care professionals who treat young people were reporting a huge increase in demand. One psychiatrist described an "avalanche" of severely depressed and anxious youth. While the new stresses didn't *create* more bipolar disorder, they have certainly aggravated the illness in many young people.

COVID-19 upended Paula's teenage son's life. Before the pandemic, Andy was a state-ranked swimmer and Eagle Scout. But after swim practices and scout meetings were canceled, Andy spiraled down. He spent hours alone in his room. He started cutting and burning his arms. Then one afternoon, he drove more than an hour away to a store where he shoplifted a pair of leather pants that cost $1,000. He was charged with a felony and jailed, yet when Paula tried to get him help, she faced a five-week wait for therapy.

In 2021, several leading US health groups sounded alarms. The American Academy of Pediatrics, the American Academy of Child and Adolescent Psychiatry, and the Children's Hospital Association joined in declaring "a national emergency" in youth mental health.

Welcome to Your New Job

Having a child with bipolar disorder means the normal work of parenting expands. Your job now includes trying to understand what you're dealing with, tracking down effective treatment—and finding ways to afford it—and advocating for your child outside your home. Most importantly, you will need to manage your own justifiably heated emotions as you seek to protect your child and the rest of your family from the fallout of the illness.

"I am becoming used to an overwhelming, grinding mixture of anger and worry," writes David Sheff, whose son Nic was diagnosed with bipolar disorder, in *A Beautiful Boy: A Father's Journey Through His Son's Addiction.*

All this may demand a lot more energy and time than you'd anticipated, or even imagine you can muster. But there are many ways to lighten the load. We've written this book to acquaint you with them, to be your straight-talking companion and practical guide. We understand how much you may need a nonjudgmental friend.

In the meantime, however, we strongly encourage you also to seek out real-life friends among other parents. There is nothing like the camaraderie of other adults who understand what it feels like to be coping with these challenges.

"We all knew that tunnel," writes Dorothy O'Donnell, whose daughter was diagnosed with bipolar disorder at age 5. "We knew how the strain of raising a child with a mental illness could chip away at the most solid marriage. We had seen our girls flounder in school and lose friends. We'd seen the looks of skepticism from our friends and relatives when we tried to explain 'pediatric bipolar disorder.'"

Life Between the Extremes

Mental illness—just like physical illness—occurs on a continuum. On one end lies optimum mental health, allowing people to process thoughts and feelings in ways that help them succeed in school or work, have fulfilling relationships, and cope with change and adversity. The opposite pole represents severe mental illness, which interferes with these behaviors. Most of us live somewhere between the extremes, with good days and bad days and no clear cutoff line between health and illness. Your goal is to help your child move closer to the healthiest position, with many more good days than bad ones.

"We got a psychiatrist, psychologist, and counselor involved," says Stephanie, an educator and mother in Utah. "We found the right medication. And now Gary is no longer cutting himself, and he doesn't speak so darkly anymore. He occasionally feels depressed, but he's gone from not having any interests in life to liking Legos, building Nerf guns, doing CrossFit, and playing with friends. Occasionally he will tell us when he doesn't have a lot of hope and feels like everything is wrong. And then there are days when he seems really happy."

There Is No Magic Bullet

No book can substitute for individual professional diagnosis and treatment. If you think your child may have bipolar disorder, we urge you to have him or her evaluated as soon as possible by a qualified mental health professional. At the same time, know that there is no magic bullet—a surefire pill or therapeutic technique—to treat a mood disorder. Nor, alas, is it likely you'll find a Dr. Right to lead you and your child swiftly out of distress. You may end up consulting many therapists and trying many strategies before your lives start to improve.

Many parents who have walked this road before you—including many with professional research skills and wealth—have despaired of a system that by many accounts is broken.

Horror stories are common. Yet many parents have also found compassionate, effective help from individual mental health professionals who go well beyond the basic job expectations, even offering cellphone numbers for help with crises after office hours. Some have also found insurance-plan managers willing to work to make sure they're getting all the help they need.

Along the way, you may be frustrated by the big differences in treating mental illness versus problems like a broken bone or high blood pressure. Even as illnesses involving the mind may have physical symptoms, there is much more variation, subjectivity, and controversy surrounding the approaches to treat them. That's why you need to educate yourself as much as possible. A basic understanding of diagnoses and treatments can help you choose a clinician more confidently, know the right questions to ask, and better understand the recommendations you receive. Without wishing to distress you, we do want to emphasize the stakes involved.

Risks You Can't Ignore

Bipolar disorder is a serious mental illness with potentially serious consequences. It tends to get worse when left undiagnosed and untreated. Episodes may become more frequent and severe. Children may lose precious time for academic and social growth.

The dangers include every parent's nightmare: when a child takes his or her own life. People with bipolar disorder have an unusually high risk of attempting suicide—more than 10 times that of the general population. As many as half of all people with bipolar disorder will attempt suicide over a lifetime. More than 1 in 12 will die that way.

In Chapter 9, we'll tell you what you can do if your child has attempted or is threatening suicide, a danger that has sadly been growing among all US youth. In recent years, suicide has become the second leading cause of death for youth aged 10 to 24. The death rate from suicide for this age group rose by more than 57% from 2007 to 2018—up to nearly 11 youth per 100,000.

Bipolar disorder also makes it likelier that children will injure themselves short of suicide, by cutting or burning their skin or becoming addicted to cigarettes, alcohol, or illegal drugs. When manic, people also tend to indulge in risky, often self-harmful behaviors, from gambling to jumping from heights. You will need to stay vigilant about your child's comings and goings and the company he or she keeps.

Using This Book

In the following pages, we'll advise you how to recognize bipolar disorder, what treatments are available, how to find therapists and clinicians, and what to do in an emergency. We'll provide up-to-date guidance on how to be a smart health care consumer, including information on the safety and side-effects of common medications, how to figure out the right kind of medical insurance, and how to find financial support if you can't afford insurance. We'll explain the heightened risks of consuming too much alcohol, recreational drugs, and social media. We'll also suggest ways to reduce stress at home, explain how to get accommodations at school, and advise you how best to prepare your child for life as an adult. Finally, we'll give you language to speak openly about mental illness and health with your child and anyone else in your world who needs to know what's going on.

Throughout the book, you'll hear from credentialed experts and from many ordinary parents throughout America who have walked this road before you and learned from their experience. We found our parents' brain trust through a variety of means. Some were active on social media; others were personal acquaintances. Still others were authors who have written about their children's struggles. Some were interviewed while still amid heart-breaking struggles. Others, with their children grown, were able to look back more calmly on the choices that helped them endure and offer hard-earned practical advice. We follow several of their stories all the way through the book.

In all but a few cases, we changed their names. In all cases, however, we used quotes verbatim. The one question we asked everyone was: "What have you learned?"

"Jason is 'out' with close friends and family, and that feels like a miracle," said Meg, who has been diagnosed with bipolar disorder along with her 27-year-old son. "At this point, to my knowledge, the only people who are 'out' on a broad public level are actors, writers, and musicians. So, yes, please use a pseudonym. The stigma, fear, and misunderstanding about bipolar disorder is still too strong."

Don't Lose Hope

By now, you're probably ready for some good news.

Consider this: We know so much more about mental illness today than ever before. Long gone are the days when people with bipolar disorder were thought to be possessed by evil spirits, and "treated" with exorcisms or blood-letting. Gone, too, is the old consensus among psychiatrists that parents were solely to blame for their children's mental illnesses. And no longer do most Americans choose to suffer in silence rather than seek treatment for a mood disorder for themselves or their children.

In the place of all that misinformation and stigma has come a cultural sea-change, including recent national campaigns, with mottos like "Make It OK," "Bring Change to Mind," and "Kicking the Stigma," the latter aligned with the Indianapolis Colts football team.

Many popular artists with bipolar disorder have used their fame to try to help others who are struggling. Among them are singer-songwriter Mariah Carey, comedian Russell Brand, and actresses Catherine Zeta-Jones and Carrie Fisher. Fisher, best known for her portrayal of Princess Leia in *Star Wars*, stepped up heroically, launching the magazine *bphope* and openly discussing her addictions to drugs and alcohol—frequent companions to the disorder.

"Being bipolar can be an all-consuming challenge, requiring a lot of stamina and even more courage," Fisher has said. "So if you're living with this illness and functioning at all, it's something to be proud of, not ashamed of. They should issue medals along with the steady stream of medication."

The celebrity confessions have a sobering side. Fisher died of cardiac arrest at age 60, in 2016, after which an autopsy found traces of heroin, cocaine, and MDMA ("Ecstasy") in her blood. The rock group Nirvana's Kurt Cobain, who wrote a song called "Lithium," famously died by suicide at the age of 27.

There is still no ignoring the hopeful messages of so many who have not only survived the illness but managed to lead successful lives.

"There is no need to suffer silently and there is no shame in seeking help," Zeta-Jones told *People* magazine.

Knowledge Is Power

The better you understand your child's disorder, the greater his or her chances will be of getting—and taking full advantage of—effective treatment and an appropriate education, and of living a healthier, happier life. *You* can make the critical difference. And while from time to time you may feel frustrated, confused, or even overwhelmed, take heart in knowing how far we've come. Our awareness, understanding, and compassion for people with all kinds of mental illnesses is growing every day.

The Authors

This guide has three coauthors.

Coauthor Dwight L. Evans, MD, sadly passed away as this book was going to press. He was the Joseph and Madonna DiGiacomo Professor of Psychiatry and Professor of Psychiatry, Medicine, and Neuroscience at the Perelman School of Medicine at the University of Pennsylvania. He was Chair of the Depression and Bipolar Commission of the Annenberg Adolescent Mental Health Initiative and past President of the American Foundation for Suicide Prevention and the American College of Psychiatrists.

Tami D. Benton, MD, is Psychiatrist-in-Chief, Executive Director, and Chair of the Department of Child and Adolescent Psychiatry and Behavioral Sciences at the Children's Hospital of Philadelphia. She is the Fredrick Allen Professor of Psychiatry, and Professor of Psychiatry and Pediatrics at the Perelman School of Medicine at the University of Pennsylvania. She is the Chair of the Board of the Juvenile Law Center and serves on the board of Friends Central School. In 2021, Dr. Benton was elected President of the American Academy of Child and Adolescent Psychiatry (AACAP).

Coauthor Katherine Ellison is a Pulitzer Prize–winning former foreign correspondent and author and coauthor of 10 nonfiction books, who has specialized in reporting on mental health issues for the past two decades. Her articles on mental health (and other topics) have appeared in leading publications, including the *New York Times*, the *Washington Post*, *Scientific American*, and *Knowable Magazine*.

We are grateful to veteran science writer Linda Wasmer Andrews for her contributions to the book's first edition in 2005. Katherine would additionally like to thank the psychiatrists Michelle Guchereau, Kiki Chang, Jean Milofsky, and James Ellison; the psychologist Stephen Hinshaw; Jeanne Blake; and education expert Patricia Howey for their important contributions.

All of us are also especially indebted to the many parents of children with bipolar disorder throughout the country who contributed their experienced voices in interviews. A special thanks to the writers Dorothy O'Donnell and Michael Greenberg, who were particularly generous with their time and insights.

No pharmaceutical funding was used in the development or marketing of this book. Dr. Tami Benton has nothing to disclose. Katherine Ellison has nothing to disclose.

The following pages include guidance on best practices for parents and descriptions of medical treatments that may be useful if your child is depressed without mania. For more thorough information on depression, please see our companion book, *If Your Adolescent Has Depression*.

Chapter One

Understanding Bipolar Disorder

Raising a child with bipolar disorder can take over your world. You may stay awake at night worrying about the latest call from school. Family dinners may end in chaos. Former friends may give you a wide berth, as if your child's struggles are contagious. Your marriage may be battered by the stress, while your life savings are running low to pay for help. Perhaps you're terrified by your child's threats to end his or her life. And you may agonize over the fact that bipolar disorder is a serious, lifelong illness with no cure.

This is no job for the weak of heart. Still, for ages, other parents have endured—and survived—the challenges you're now facing, and more.

"Last week my son punched three holes in his wall," says Mark, whose child is 15.

"My whole life has come to a standstill as I wait for her next crisis," says Ellen, the mother of a 14-year-old daughter.

"The stereo's on; the TV's on; the computer's on, and he's talking on the phone," says Robin. "He could do everything all at once and know what was going on everywhere—*and* hear voices in the basement, or so he told me."

Like most parents, you yearn to keep your child healthy and safe. But this bewildering illness may be making you feel powerless. We hope this book can help you feel more in control. If your child is experiencing symptoms of bipolar disorder or has already been diagnosed, you can start being more helpful by learning about the symptoms, causes, and consequences. The first thing you should know is that millions of children with bipolar disorder have grown up to be independent and stable, with families, jobs, and a decent shot at happiness. At the same time, there's no avoiding that the symptoms must be managed.

What Is Bipolar Disorder?

"Soon you don't register day versus night because you don't need sleep," writes award-winning scientist Hope Jahren, in her best selling 2017 memoir, *Lab Girl*. "You don't need food or water or a hat against the frigid weather, for that matter, either. You need to run. You need to feel the air on your skin. You need to take off your shirt and run so you can feel the air and you explain this to the person holding you that it's okay it's okay it's okay to do this but he doesn't get it and his face looks worried like someone died and you feel pity for him because he doesn't realize how wonderful and okay and okay and okay everything is. . . ."

Looking back on your own adolescence, you may wistfully remember the physical energy and emotional intensity you had during that time. Bipolar disorder is different. Its defining characteristic is mania, the overpowering sensation that Jahren so well describes. Mental health professionals describe mania as an "abnormally and persistently elevated, expansive, or irritable mood accompanied by excessive energy or activation." In its milder form, "hypomania," it's a "somewhat high, expansive, or irritable mood."

In some cases, mania alternates with depression. In others, depression isn't present—or obvious. Adolescents often experience mania and depression at the same time, resulting in what might seem like chronic, extreme crankiness.

As is true with any illness, the symptoms of bipolar disorder may be stronger or weaker, more damaging or more tolerable, and more or less requiring intensive treatment, depending on the person. That's why you may hear references to "bipolar *spectrum* disorder."

Mania makes some people elated and hyperproductive—a feeling that many people with bipolar disorder understandably miss once it's gone. In others, however, it brings tremendous suffering, causing painful restlessness, irritability, and even rage. Mania also sometimes leads to psychosis, with delusions (beliefs that aren't true) and hallucinations (sensations that aren't real). Delusions might include grandiosity, such as a child believing he or she has superpowers or expecting to become an Instagram sensation overnight. Hallucinations might include hearing imaginary voices or feeling as if something is crawling on your skin.

Some degree of grandiosity exists in nearly 90% of adolescents with bipolar disorder, creating a major dilemma for parents. Most parents don't want to—and shouldn't—discourage realistic ambition or confidence in their children. There's always a time and place for dreaming big, sticking to one's guns, and even challenging authority. Still, it's wise to keep watch if your son or daughter seems *unrealistically* overconfident in his or her abilities. Or if a teacher or siblings warn you that your child has become atypically resistant or unusually rejecting of feedback or criticism, insisting that he or she is always right. These could be signs that you need to address the mania.

Children Aren't Immune

One of the biggest frustrations for parents of children with bipolar disorder—and many doctors who treat it—is the enduring and considerable confusion and misinformation about this illness, specifically whether it affects children under the age of puberty.

"It is ridiculous that we still have to have debates, even with colleagues, about whether bipolar disorder in kids exists!" says clinical psychiatrist Kiki Chang, a leading expert in pediatric bipolar disorder who has taught and run related research programs and clinics at Stanford University.

As we've noted, only in the last few decades have doctors begun diagnosing this disorder in children. Yet today you may still hear—even from your child's doctor—that bipolar disorder never occurs before late adolescence. Or that your child can't have bipolar disorder if there's no classic pattern of distinct highs and lows. Or that there's nothing wrong that stricter rules and discipline won't cure. Most people, and alas, also many clinicians, are still catching up to what clinicians have observed for decades.

Here's the bottom line: Even young children can and do have bipolar disorder. Indeed, the illness frequently first appears in adolescence or, somewhat less frequently, in childhood. Still, bipolar disorder often looks different in children and teens than it does in adults (see Box 1.1).

Box 1.1 Red Flags

If you suspect your child is unreasonably moody, even for an adolescent, ask yourself if one or more of these behaviors fit. If they do, consider seeking professional help:

- Bouts of explosive rage, often directed at family members
- Speech that is too much, too fast, changes topics too quickly, or cannot be interrupted
- Overly silly, irritable, or elated behavior, without reason
- An unrealistically high opinion of oneself or one's abilities
- A sudden increase in energy and ability to go for days with little or no sleep
- Attention that darts constantly from one thing to the next
- Repeated high-risk behavior, such as harmful use of drugs and alcohol, reckless driving, or sexual promiscuity

Just like adults, many adolescents may be whipsawed between extreme moods, unable to sleep or think clearly, without any apparent reason for the changes. But for many kids, the symptoms may be more continuous, with what's known as a "rapid cycling" of emotions jumbled together and fewer distinct ups and downs. This pattern of symptoms means such kids get little or none of the occasional relief between cycles experienced by older people. Children and adolescents with the disorder are also more likely to feel less euphoric when manic, but instead are more irritable, agitated, and angry.

Bipolar disorder in children often resembles—and often coincides with—other problems, most commonly attention-deficit/hyperactivity disorder (ADHD), as we'll later describe. This confusion can place an extra burden on you as a parent to seek out the most knowledgeable, up-to-date professionals and to familiarize yourself as much as possible with their language. This way you can get the most out of what all too often are hurried explanations in a brief office visit. At the same time, don't be afraid to trust your gut: You know your child better than anyone.

"Jenny was diagnosed with depression in middle school, and at the time I kept asking her doctor at our managed health care plan if it might not be bipolar disorder," says Laurel, Jenny's mother. "I'd seen some signs of what I felt might be mania, although it was quite mild. It was only after she overdosed on pills as a college sophomore that we found the right psychiatrist who told us what was really going on."

How Is Bipolar Disorder Diagnosed?

Mood disorders, including bipolar disorder, resemble purely physical illnesses in some important ways. They have biological causes and may improve with medication. One big difference is that there's no objective measuring method, like a blood test or brain scan, for diagnosing mental illness. Instead, US mental health professionals subjectively evaluate the symptoms with the help of a checklist provided in the *Diagnostic and Statistical Manual of Mental Disorders* (*DSM*), a regularly updated and commonly used guide. At this writing, the latest version of this manual is a revision of the fifth edition, the *DSM-5-TR*, released in 2022.

To diagnose bipolar disorder, a clinician must first establish that someone has experienced at least one episode of mania or hypomania (see Box 1.2). With an adult, he or she will talk directly to the patient, but with children and adolescents, it is common practice to speak both with the patient and the patients' parents or other caregivers. The parents' input is obviously indispensable if their children have trouble expressing their feelings, lack insight into them, or resist discussing them.

Box 1.2 A Checklist for Mania

During a manic period, three or more of the following symptoms, which include some of the red flags we list above, must have been present to a significant degree, representing a noticeable, persistent change in behavior:

- An overly high, expansive, or irritable mood
- Inflated self-esteem or grandiosity
- Decreased need for sleep
- Increased talkativeness
- Racing thoughts
- Distractibility
- An increase in goal-directed activity
- Excessive involvement in pleasurable activities with a high potential for painful consequences (such as buying sprees and sexual indiscretions)

Mania requires that an elevated mood last for at least one week and be present for most of the day, nearly every day, while causing significant functional impairment. Hypomania, a milder disorder which normally causes fewer problems for an adolescent's functioning, must last at least four consecutive days and be present most of the day, nearly every day.

When diagnosing young people, mental health professionals must determine that the symptoms exceed those expected for the patient's age and developmental phase. As with adults, they also must make sure they're not due to harmful use of alcohol or drugs, a general medical condition, or the side-effects of a medication. Several commonly misused drugs can produce symptoms of mania. They include anabolic steroids, amphetamines, cocaine, phencyclidine (PCP), inhalants, and MDMA (Ecstasy).

Source: Adapted from the *Diagnostic and Statistical Manual of Mental Disorders* (5th ed.). Arlington, VA: American Psychiatric Association, 2013.

How Is Depression Diagnosed?

In addition to evaluating mania, your child's clinician will want to identify and treat symptoms of depression, including feelings of sadness or emptiness or a loss of interest or pleasure in life. For a valid diagnosis, these symptoms must also be causing significant distress or impairment at home, school, or work, and not be directly due to self-destructive use of alcohol or drugs, another medical condition, or the side-effects of medication. The *DSM-5* requires that a person must experience five or more of the symptoms listed below for two weeks or longer to be diagnosed with a major depressive episode:

- A depressed mood most of the day, nearly every day. (In adolescents, this may manifest as irritableness.)
- A marked loss of interest or pleasure in all, or almost all, activities
- Significant weight loss or decrease or increase in appetite
- Behavior that seems overly keyed up or unnaturally slowed down
- Fatigue or loss of energy
- Feelings of worthlessness or guilt
- Diminished ability to think or concentrate, or indecisiveness
- Recurrent thoughts of death or suicide
- Insomnia or excessive sleeping

What Is a Mixed Episode?

A "mixed episode," which is common in children and adolescents, is just what it sounds like: a mix of mania and depression at the same time, instead of one after the other. For some with bipolar disorder, a mixed episode is a transitional state on the way from mania to depression. But for others, it's the way the disorder manifests most or all the time.

This state is usually extremely uncomfortable, akin to an energetic, restless sadness. Often it makes it hard to sleep. To be diagnosed as a mixed episode, just as with mania, it must have lasted every day for at least a week, not be the result of harmful use of drugs or alcohol, and be causing a marked impairment in functioning or relationships.

What Are the Different Bipolar Illnesses?

Bipolar disorder comes in four main varieties. Your child's mental health care provider may specify one of these:

Bipolar I, requiring at least one manic or mixed episode

Bipolar II, characterized by at least one episode of hypomania combined with episodes of depression

Cyclothymia, which causes long-lasting cycling between hypomania and relatively mild depressive symptoms, without a full manic or depressive episode. For an adolescent to be diagnosed with cyclothymia, the pattern must have lasted for at least a year. Any intermittent periods of normal mood during the illness must last less than two months. There is at least a 15% chance that a person with cyclothymia will later develop bipolar I or bipolar II.

Bipolar "other specified" or "unspecified"—which is a catch-all for illness involving altered mood states that resembles bipolar disorder but doesn't fit the previous criteria (for instance, with mania that lasts less than a week). This diagnosis, which used to be called BD-NOS, for "bipolar not otherwise specified," is common in children and adolescents who often don't quite meet the standards for adults. In youth, it can indicate an emerging bipolar I or II disorder.

What Is Disruptive Mood Dysregulation Disorder?

Disruptive mood dysregulation disorder (DMDD) describes a child who has an irritable or angry mood most of the day, nearly every day. Symptoms typically begin before the age of 10 and may include severe and otherwise inexplicable temper tantrums on average three or more times a week, together with trouble functioning at home or at school. To be diagnosed, a child must be under 18 years old and have these symptoms steadily for 12 or more months. Studies suggest between 2 and 5% of adolescents may have this disorder.

DMDD first became a diagnosis in 2013, with the publication of the *DSM-5*. It arose out of concerns that too many children with this problem were being misdiagnosed with bipolar disorder and possibly given the wrong medications. Indeed, between 1994 and 2003, the number of children diagnosed with bipolar disorder rose 40-fold, from 20,000 to 800,000.

DMDD remains controversial among experts who think normal childhood behavior is being excessively medicalized. Some clinicians also complain that the explosive outbursts at its core are more of a symptom, like a fever or sore throat, than a unique disorder. While children diagnosed with DMDD may resemble children with bipolar disorder, more will go on to develop depression and anxiety than bipolar disorder.

The shifting perspectives on bipolar disorder, combined with brand-new illnesses like DMDD, have frustrated parents and clinicians alike, further clouding an already subjective diagnostic process. Our hope is to help you learn about this illness as easily as possible, but we can't promise you that you won't later need to learn more.

"Your child's diagnosis can change," writes Dorothy O'Donnell, in her memoir about her daughter's bipolar disorder. She calls her daughter "Sadie," not her real name, in the book, which at this writing was unpublished. "Sadie's first doctor diagnosed her with bipolar II," O'Donnell writes. "Her current doctor believes she has BP-NOS. As psychiatry continues to evolve and science reveals more about mental illness, diagnosis and treatment options continue to change as well."

What If It's Really ADHD?

Bipolar disorder in adolescents is often mistaken for ADHD—for some good reasons. Both disorders can make kids distractible, hyperactive, fast-talking, impulsive, and oppositional.

At the same time, there are some important differences between the two illnesses, and it's key that your child's clinician understand them to make sure the treatment is appropriate.

Children with ADHD usually show symptoms before the age of 10, and it is more commonly diagnosed in boys than in girls. Other differences include the following:

- *Sustained angry outbursts*—Like anyone else, adolescents with ADHD may get angry, but they generally calm down within half an hour. In those with bipolar disorder, however, the anger may last for much longer.
- *Extreme mood swings*—Children with ADHD alone generally don't have the dramatic fluctuations as those with bipolar disorder.
- *Destructiveness*—Adolescents with ADHD may break things, but it's usually an accident caused by

inattentiveness. In contrast, those with bipolar disorder may destroy property intentionally in a fit of rage.

Both disorders can have serious consequences. If you suspect your child has either one, seek help sooner than later. If possible, make sure your child's clinician is experienced in diagnosing bipolar disorder.

Could It Be Schizophrenia?

Bipolar disorder is also sometimes confused with schizophrenia or schizoaffective disorder, an illness combining some of the symptoms of schizophrenia with those of a mood disorder, since any of these conditions can produce delusions and hallucinations. In addition, both bipolar disorder and schizoaffective disorder involve major mood swings. One key difference is that in bipolar disorder psychotic symptoms tend to occur only during the worst periods of the altered mood, vanishing when the moods settle down.

Extra Baggage: Common "Comorbidities" With Bipolar Disorder

As in the case of ADHD, bipolar disorder often exists side by side with other emotional and behavioral issues, known as "comorbid conditions" or "comorbidities." As many as 80% of youth with bipolar disorder will have some comorbidity. These coexisting problems can complicate diagnosis and treatment, but it's far better to find them and treat them than ignore them. At some point, if you can afford it and find an appropriate expert, you may want to seek out a neuropsychological workup, involving several hours of tests of cognitive and emotional abilities. Sometimes schools will pay for these. The exam detects not only comorbidities but learning issues, such as dyslexia and slow processing speed.

If you can't get this kind of extensive exam, however, insist that the doctor diagnosing your child check for comorbidities.

After ADHD, these are the most common coexisting conditions, any one of which can aggravate bipolar disorder and contribute to setting your child back in school:

- *Anxiety disorders*, which one large study found in nearly 45% of bipolar disorder patients. For most of the subjects, the anxiety appeared before the bipolar disorder and seemed to make it worse, with longer mood symptoms and higher depression scores.

(Anxiety disorders come in several varieties. They include separation anxiety, which causes distress when the child is away from home or relatives; social anxiety, causing extreme shyness; panic disorder, which leads to panic attacks; obsessive-compulsive disorder, which may include repetitive behaviors such as washing hands or checking to make sure a door is locked; generalized anxiety disorder, involving worries about *everything*, from schoolwork to the state of the world; and posttraumatic stress disorder, in which someone is haunted by memories of a terrible event, such as a car accident or assault.)

- *Substance use disorder* (previously known as substance abuse disorder), which researchers have found is a common risk for adolescents with bipolar disorder.

Many clinicians and parents suspect that adolescents struggling with mental illness will seek to "self-medicate" problems with alcohol and drugs, which throughout the United States today are alarmingly easy to obtain. Just as with adults, this can lead to a cascade of other problems, including not only addiction but unwanted pregnancies, suicide attempts, and run-ins with police.

"Nic finally got the help he needed when a psychiatrist determined that he didn't only suffer from addiction, but co-occurring mental illnesses," writes David Sheff, about his then-teenage son. "He began treatment for addiction, bipolar disorder and depression."

- *Oppositional defiant disorder (ODD)*, which describes an uncooperative and sometimes hostile pattern of behavior that can include angry outbursts, excessive arguing with adults, refusal to comply with requests, and deliberate attempts to annoy people.
- *Conduct disorder*, which is similar but more severe than ODD and often includes criminal conduct. Children may threaten others, get into fights, set fires, vandalize property, lie, steal, stay out all night, or run away from home. Researchers have found that up to two-thirds of young people with mania may also have conduct disorder. A key difference is that kids with conduct disorder alone rarely express remorse, whereas those with both disorders do. Either way, such youth are frequently labeled "bad" or delinquent rather than mentally ill, and some may wind up being written off as lost causes rather than getting the help they need.
- *Eating disorders*, including bulimia nervosa, anorexia nervosa, and binge-eating disorder. While these have been studied less than the other comorbidities in people with bipolar disorders, many researchers think there's a significant overlap. In one recent study, nearly 15% of patients with bipolar disorder also had an eating disorder.

What Role Does Biology Play?

Doctors may have your best interests at heart and still lapse into unnecessarily arcane explanations when you're anxiously trying to figure out how to help your child. During a rushed office visit, it's too much to expect that your doctor would offer—or you'd be able to absorb—a tutorial on the anatomy and chemistry involved in this vexing diagnosis. But you won't need a medical degree to understand the following explanation, and it's worth taking the time. A basic understanding of the physical aspects of bipolar disorder may help you appreciate how at least some of your child's behavior is beyond his or her control. It may also make you more comfortable with a doctor's recommendation to use medication to treat a condition that has both medical and psychological components. If you want to delve deeper, check out the Resources section at the end of this book, where among other things we recommend two excellent lay-readers' books on the brain.

Meanwhile, here's a condensed explanation:

Scientists using sophisticated imaging techniques have found that the brains of people with bipolar disorder tend to differ from those of healthy individuals, both structurally and functionally. The differences include the following:

- Small, abnormal areas of white matter, which connects important brain structures
- Fewer and thinner specialized brain cells and reduced activity, during the depressive phase, in the prefrontal cortex, the brain structure involved in "executive function," including complex thought, problem-solving, and planning

This difference could help explain why many people with bipolar disorder tend to be impulsive and disorganized.

Another important difference, particularly in children who suffer both mania and depression, relates to neurotransmitters: the chemicals that neurons use to communicate with each other. In healthy brains, neurotransmitters ferry messages across synapses, the gaps between cells. But in the brains of people with mood disorders, including bipolar disorder, something interferes with this process.

Five neurotransmitters are believed to play a part in various mood disorders when their levels in the brain are not optimal. *Serotonin* helps regulate sleep, appetite, anxiety, and sexual drive. *Norepinephrine* influences the body's response to stress and helps maintain alertness, sleep, and blood pressure. *Dopamine* is essential for physical movement, while also influencing a person's sense of pleasure, motivation, and perception of reality. *GABA* (gamma-aminobutyric acid) plays a role in anxiety, and *glutamate* is key to overall brain functioning.

Discoveries relating to these differences in brain structure and function beg the question of whether people with bipolar disorder start off with different brains or whether the illness changes their brains over time. Future improvements in diagnostic technology may bring clearer answers, but at this writing, most experts believe in the latter explanation.

Many more years may pass before we truly understand the physiology and biochemistry underlying bipolar disorder. Yet it's abundantly clear that it's a genuine illness affecting the brain.

Does Gender Matter?

Bipolar disorder is equally prevalent in males and females, both adolescents and adults, but there are some important differences. One large study showed that women with bipolar disorder are more likely than men to be predominantly depressed and to have a higher lifetime history of suicide attempts, while bipolar men are more likely to engage in harmful use of drugs or alcohol.

What About Race?

Bipolar disorder also appears to be equally prevalent among different ethnic groups, although, as we'll later explain further, members of minority groups with the disorder on average receive less and worse care, and are more likely to be misdiagnosed with schizophrenia, conduct disorder, or antisocial behavior instead.

How Hereditary Is Bipolar Disorder?

Genes play a major role in determining who develops bipolar disorder. The offspring of parents with bipolar disorder have up to a 10-fold increased rate of the illness, compared to family members of control groups. Other research suggests that the risk could be as high as 70% for those with a bipolar identical twin. Yet genes don't tell the whole story. If they did, the identical twin of someone with the disorder would *always* also develop it. In fact, some identical twins and others whose genetic risk seems high never do, and indeed, most people with a family history of bipolar disorder won't develop it. It's obviously important to be aware of family history, even as relatives may resist discussing it.

As with other illnesses, having a particular genetic variant doesn't automatically mean you'll develop the condition. Environmental factors play a significant role in determining to what extent a genetic tendency becomes reality.

Since other people are a major part of any child's environment, it's important to understand their influence. Given that bipolar disorder is so hereditary, many adolescents with the disorder will have relatives who share the illness. This can be a hardship if one or more parents are struggling with their own mood disorders while raising the child. But relatives can also serve as positive role models.

"I grew up with a sister with bipolar disorder," says Candace. "During our childhood and teens, she drove everyone crazy with her mania, but today she's a hospice nurse with two degrees and a great family. Since my daughter was diagnosed, I've gotten closer to her than ever before. I keep asking: How did you do it?"

How Does Stress Affect Bipolar Disorder?

Stress is the body's natural response to a perceived threat—real or imagined, physical or psychological. In response to such alarms, the brain releases hormones that prepare the body to fight or flee. A person's heart rate, blood pressure, and muscle tension increase, in a rapid response system that can save lives in a true emergency. Yet when stress is frequent or prolonged, it takes a toll on both the body and mind, sometimes leading to depression.

As far back as 1921, Emil Kraepelin, the German psychiatrist who first defined bipolar disorder as we know it today, noted that initial episodes of mania or depression were often brought on by stressful life events. As time went on, however, less and less stress was needed to trigger an episode. Eventually, episodes would occur spontaneously, with no apparent trigger.

One effort to explain this effect is known as the "kindling" hypothesis. It suggests that the first episode of mania or depression may spark long-lasting changes in the brain that make it more sensitive to future stress. It boils down to neuroplasticity: the concept that "neurons that fire together wire together"—that is, the more you engage a brain in certain behaviors, the more naturally it will engage in those behaviors in the future. This phenomenon might apply to mania and depression as much as it does to learning to play tennis or the piano.

This perspective may explain why some mood disorders, when untreated, tend to worsen over time, and why less intensive "triggers" may be needed to set off an episode. While more research is needed on the particulars, we do know it's essential to get treatment for children with bipolar disorder as early as possible to help the brain develop in healthier ways and reduce both short-term and long-term suffering.

It's also important to be aware of the role of childhood trauma, which is unfortunately surprisingly common, particularly involving children with depression and bipolar disorder. Specific psychotherapy for trauma may be helpful.

Are Parents to Blame?

Many parents' greatest fear is that they caused or aggravated their child's mood disorder.

"When I think back to my son's early years, I know I made so many mistakes," says Beth, whose grown son has bipolar disorder. "I lost my temper—a lot. I wasn't home every evening for dinner. I didn't provide much structure and rules."

If you find that you're talking to yourself this way, keep in mind that many children who grow up under severe stress and even abuse never develop mood disorders. At the same time, many children raised by loving, attentive, and competent parents can become mentally ill, just as they can develop other diseases. Bipolar disorder is complex, with multiple influences, the most important of which is family history (i.e., genetics). Yes, parents pass genes to their children, but they don't get to pick which genes! Rest assured that garden-variety parenting mistakes did not create the illness.

At the same time, we'd be misleading you by telling you that parents and the overall quality of family life don't influence children's emotional development. As we'll later explain, there are both helpful and hurtful ways that you can affect your child's emotional development. For now we'll simply stress that finding the right treatment for your adolescent can make a big difference. As a parent, this is most likely your greatest opportunity to influence the course of your child's life.

What Is Your Child's Prognosis?

At the risk of repetition, we want to remind you that bipolar disorder is a serious disease. It may be more or less severe, depending on the person and the circumstances.

About 10% of patients will have just one episode of mania during a lifetime. But the majority will have more, with some having two or three episodes in a single year. A single bout of untreated mania may last from a few weeks to several months, and bouts of major depression may hang on even longer. It can all add up to a lot of heartache and time lost to the disease. That's why, at this writing, at least, we believe most patients who have had two or more episodes or one very severe episode of this illness should continue treatment that may include medication and psychotherapy throughout their lives.

If you suspect that your adolescent son or daughter may be suffering from bipolar disorder, now is the time to consult a qualified professional for advice. The sooner you seek help, the better the outcome is likely to be. It's always upsetting to discover that your child has a serious illness, but you can take heart in knowing there are things you can do to help. You can also anticipate that things will get better. Adolescence is the hardest time for kids with mood disorders. Many become more stable as adults, as they mature and find more resources to cope with the disorder.

"A few years ago, I thought the chances that Mike would attend college were remote," says the father of a 19-year-old with bipolar disorder. Mike was first hospitalized at age 11, and the next several years were tumultuous at best. "Yet here he is, and he's not only attending college, but he's also living away from home and doing fine." This father credits his son's progress partly to the treatment he has received, and partly to his simply growing older. "As he's gotten more mature, he's gotten better at handling his illness," he says.

We'll tell you more about the treatment options for bipolar disorder in the next chapter.

Chapter Two

Treatment

Medication

By now you know the worst news. Bipolar disorder is a life-long illness which, as of this writing, has no cure. It requires careful treatment, and if left untreated, it has a high chance of leading to harm that can include suicide. Unfortunately, there's no way to deny the gravity of this prognosis. Yet there's also this big silver lining, which is that now that you've got the diagnosis, you've also got some promising paths to help your child feel and do a lot better, with a good chance of staying healthy, and even thriving. Most people with bipolar disorder who receive treatment for it are able to manage their relationships and jobs, and live successful lives.

Medication is the mainstay treatment for this illness. Psychotherapy and family therapy, which we will describe in the next chapter, are also essential to help your child learn to regulate his or her emotions. So are healthy habits with sleep and nutrition, which we'll tell you about in Chapter 5. The basic dilemma is that a child in the middle of mania or depression may not cooperate with psychotherapy or self-care. You must tackle the physical problem first. But here's more good news: Not all children with bipolar disorder—especially those on the milder side of the spectrum and who are treated as early as possible—will need to stay on medication for life. Sometimes early treatment can stop the worst symptoms in their tracks, helping the brain to develop healthier habits.

"This is not a life sentence," says bipolar disorder expert Kiki Chang. "Plenty of kids are able to wean off at least some of the medications. The most important thing is getting things stabilized, getting the child well as early as possible, and letting the brain heal and develop as healthily as possible. I'm not saying your child won't need meds in the future. But we are treating a new generation today, and there's just not enough known to say they'll have to stay on the medications forever."

Yet another consolation which we hope you'll share with your child is that this diagnosis can become an opportunity. As long as you avoid getting stuck in denial, your son or daughter may be able to develop exceptional self-awareness. Knowing your strengths and weaknesses and the way your mind works early in life can be a rare blessing if you face it bravely.

This chapter aims to help educate you about your child's best options for treatment. We can't repeat this maxim too much: Knowledge is power. You'll feel a lot more comfortable supporting your child's recovery if you learn some of the basics about your different choices and get a sense of the right questions to ask. And please don't hesitate to ask them. Each child is different, so you have a right to expect that his or her treatment won't be formulaic. Additionally, as you'll see, each type of treatment has different risks and benefits. Your child's clinician should be willing to explain why one course of action is better than another.

The two types of treatment most helpful with bipolar disorder are medication and psychotherapy (the formal term for "talk therapy"). Our position on medication for bipolar disorder is simple and clear: Your child will need it to get better—and above all to be safe—despite the many challenges involved.

We understand and share some of your concerns about starting medication. The global pharmaceutical industry's reputation has been badly tarnished, as anyone following the opioid epidemic can attest. You may also worry that we live in a time when nearly one in seven Americans over the age of 18 takes an antidepressant. We can debate all day long the relative advantages of medication for problems including mild depression and attention-deficit/hyperactivity disorder (ADHD). But if your child has been diagnosed with bipolar disorder, this is not time to embrace yoga or dietary supplements as your first line of defense. The situation is too serious to skip conventional medical treatment.

> "In the beginning I was like, 'Meds? Not for my family!' says Charlene, whose 15-year-old daughter tried to kill herself by jumping off a roof. 'Now I'm like 'What else you got?' I didn't know we needed them 'til we needed them.'

Once you've found a medication you can live with, however, psychotherapy can also be helpful and typically is necessary to improve day-to-day functioning. In fact, researchers have found that a combination of the two will give your child—and your family—the best hope of success in managing bipolar disorder. We'll say more about this later. As always, the more you know, the better equipped you'll be to minimize risks and maximize benefits as you set out on this difficult but essential path.

"It is a hard, hard road, loving someone with bipolar disease," writes the mega-best selling author Danielle Steel, in

His Bright Light: The Story of Nick Traina, about her bipolar son. "There are times when you want to scream, days when you think you can't do it anymore, weeks when you know you haven't made a difference. . . . It is their problem, not yours, and yet it becomes yours if you love the person suffering from it. You have no choice. You must stand by them. You are trapped, as surely as the patient is. And you will hate that trap at times, hate what it does to your life, your days, your own sanity. But hate it or not, you are there, and whatever it takes, you have to make the best of it."

Choosing Medication

There's a lot to learn about medications for bipolar disorder. They come in different classes, with varying risks and benefits, and may also vary in terms of the stage of treatment—that is, whether there's an acute, or emergency, need, versus keeping emotions stable over a longer term (see below). What's more, even though most doctors agree these medications are essential, there are lots of strong opinions about which ones and how many are best. Some clinicians swear by "polypharmacy"—prescribing more than one drug to treat a complex problem—and some kids, especially those with more than one disorder, will indeed need different tactics to treat different symptoms. The National Institute of Mental Health advises that children should take the smallest doses and fewest number of medications possible, following the doctrine "Start low, go slow." In spite of this, researchers have found that children with bipolar disorder often receive three or more medications at a time, especially at the start, when a clinician is seeking to stabilize symptoms.

Alas, there isn't any medication for this illness that doesn't have potentially concerning side-effects. Any parent reading the packaging inserts in a doctor's office might be excused for running out the door in tears. (Of course, the same could be said for anyone reading a consent form for surgery, right?) Take heart and keep this in mind: Manufacturers are required to list even extremely rare effects, the scariest of which are vanishingly rare.

Either way, it's essential to find a clinician you trust. Especially in the beginning, you should be working together closely and often. Make sure the process starts with a thorough evaluation of your child by someone experienced with managing bipolar disorder (which is not necessarily every psychiatrist or psychologist) and continues with a monitoring plan that inspires your confidence. Also, make sure that you and the clinician have a plan for efficient communication about any concerns.

What Is "Off-Label"?

Trust in your child's clinician will be especially important, given that finding the right medication will require clinical judgment. It's almost certain the clinician will prescribe some medications "off-label"—that is, without specific Food and Drug Administration (FDA) approval for children and adolescents. The term may sound sketchy, but it's a common and well-respected practice—and unfortunately also a needed one. At this writing, the medications specifically approved for adolescent bipolar disorder remain limited compared to those approved for adults. That's because relatively few of these medications have been thoroughly tested on youth. Some have been tested on adolescents and approved for illnesses other than bipolar disorder. In such cases, you can at least be confident that adolescents can safely take them, and some will likely be effective as well. We'll provide a list of medications and their FDA approval status in the Appendix.

The Trials of Trial and Error

Discovering the right formula and dose for your child can test your patience. In many cases your child's doctor will have to use a trial-and-error process to discover the right medication and dose for your child. What makes the process harder is that any side-effects may appear right away, weeks before benefits kick in.

> "My daughter was super-sensitive to medication, so there was a lot of playing around with different formulas," writes Dorothy O'Donnell. "There was a period during elementary school where she was trying several different ones. The tricky thing with meds is that sometimes something works for awhile and then not. I had always said I would never be the kind of parent who would experiment with drugs on my child, but I guess that's what I ended up doing."

Ideally, you'll try a medication for several weeks, while paying attention to the effect on specific symptoms your child is experiencing. The clinician should always start with the minimally effective dose and allow adequate time—usually weeks—before making a change. After that, the dose might be increased if the child's symptoms aren't improving. If side-effects are a problem, the clinician may try reducing the dose. The next option is to switch medications.

As a parent, you can contribute by keeping notes on any changes in your child's mood and behavior during the medication trials. Consider keeping a journal, or if you want to get techy, there's an app (actually several apps) for that. We provide some options in the Resources section, but you can also track one down by googling "mood" and "app." Make sure to check the price before you buy, because you don't need anything fancy, and you may not need to pay anything. It might be more than enough to note a few basic variables, such as sleep habits, appetite, focus, and, of course, mood.

Treating Mania: Mood Stabilizers, Anticonvulsants, and Antipsychotics

Medications for bipolar disorder come in three groups: mood stabilizers, anticonvulsants, and antipsychotics. The pioneer and most familiar mood stabilizer is *lithium*, which helps reduce mania in about half of adolescents with bipolar disorder.

Lithium is an alkaline substance found in trace amounts in the human body, plants, and mineral rocks. (Its name comes from the Greek *lithos*, for stone.) It's used in several industrial processes, including making batteries, and also has a long, colorful history in treating mental illness.

More than 1,800 years ago, the Greek physician Galen prescribed bathing in and drinking from alkaline springs as a treatment for manic patients. Fast-forward to the late 1800s, when doctors in the United States and Denmark prescribed lithium to treat mania in their patients. Another century would pass, however, before the Australian psychiatrist John Cade, while employed at a mental hospital in Melbourne, conducted rudimentary experiments in the hospital's kitchen that serendipitously led to the discovery of lithium as a treatment for bipolar disorder. While pursuing a treatment for patients with mania, Cade injected urine from mentally ill patients into the bellies of guinea pigs. He initially used lithium to help make uric acid more soluble in water—but soon found it was having a calming effect on the guinea pigs. He proceeded to test it on himself and then on some of his patients, who responded so strongly that he published his findings in the *Medical Journal of Australia* in 1949. By the mid-1950s, lithium had helped instigate a pharmacological revolution that liberated hundreds of thousands of US patients from asylums. In 1970, lithium carbonate became the first FDA-approved medication to treat both mania and depression. In 2019, that approval was extended to children aged 7 to 17. The medication comes in 300-mg or 450-mg tablets, with doses for a typical teen up to 1,600 mg, and it is sold under the brand names of Eskalith and Lithobid, Lithonate, or Cibalith-S. It is also available as a generic medication, making it less expensive than other available treatments.

Despite the FDA go-ahead, lithium still hasn't been as well-studied on adolescents as several newer and generally more widely used bipolar medications that we'll describe below. Yet Chang—joining many other experts on bipolar disorder—remains a devotee.

"I love lithium," he says, adding the medication is particularly effective in reducing suicidal thoughts and behaviors. "When it works, it is fantastic, with lots of protective factors for the brain. I truly feel it's underutilized."

At the same time, lithium has several well-known and possibly serious—and even potentially lethal—side-effects. Lithium toxicity risk is at its highest when dosages are too high, especially if the person taking it is dehydrated. *This is not a medication that you want to leave unsupervised for a child who is suicidal, as an overdose can be fatal.*

Your child's clinician should closely monitor your child, including checking their blood levels regularly to ensure the dose is within a narrow range that keeps it effective but prevents lithium toxicity. Too much lithium can cause problems with balance, blurred vision, trembling hands, jerky bodily movements, harm to the thyroid and kidneys, and even seizures. By affecting the kidneys, lithium can cause increased urination and even bed-wetting. More common issues are nausea and vomiting, as well as hair loss, which occurs in 12 to 19% of long-time users. Lithium can also sometimes cause acne and weight gain, which can be deal-breakers for image-conscious adolescents.

Coping With Side-Effects

We interrupt this list of medications to explain how you and your child's doctor can help avoid or reduce side-effects for lithium and its many newer competitors, including the so-called second-generation antipsychotics (SGAs) that you can read about in detail below. This is crucial, since side-effects such as weight gain are a major reason kids stop taking their medication, whether they tell you they've done so or not.

- *Try different approaches.* That trial-and-error process should help your doctor find the lowest possible effective dose with the fewest side-effects of all kinds.
- *Monitor.* If your child is taking lithium, the treatment should include mandatory blood tests beginning with at least every week or so, to check levels for efficacy and

avoid potential damage to thyroid or kidney function-ing. After the initial phase, you should get tests about every three months. These tests will also reveal whether your child is in fact taking the medicine. In all cases, the clinician should conduct a thorough initial evaluation, and then, depending on the medication, follow up with regular weigh-ins and blood pressure readings.

If your child is taking an SGA, blood tests may check for glu-cose and lipids, to guard against the risk of diabetes. Some medications may affect the heart and even the eyes, requiring tests of those as well.

- *Manage.* For daytime sleepiness, try taking pills at night. For nausea, take them with meals. Make sure to drink plenty of liquids.
- *Watch for interactions.* By no means should your child be drinking alcohol, smoking marijuana, or taking any recreational drugs while taking any psychotropic medica-tions. These at best can compromise the effectiveness of the drugs, and, at worst, cause serious side-effects. Patients taking lithium should also avoid anti-inflammatory medications, including aspirin and ibuprofen, which can increase lithium levels.
- *Don't hesitate to call the doctor or even go to the hospital emergency department* if you notice concerning symp-toms, including fever, extreme dizziness, or problems with speech or balance.
- *Add other medications.* This could include thyroid sup-plements in the case of lithium or an over-the-counter nausea aid such as ranitidine (Zantac). Vitamins with selenium or zinc may help reduce hair loss.

Anticonvulsants

Other mood stabilizers are in a class known as anticonvulsants, since they also treat seizure disorders. In some cases, they may be effective with fewer side-effects. The most commonly prescribed meds in this class are Depakote (divalproex sodium) and Lamictal (lamotrigine), either alone or in combination with another mood stabilizer. More rarely, a prescriber will recommend Depakene (valproic acid), which is closely related to Depakote, but may cause digestive problems.

Researchers have found that Depakote works just as well as lithium with this age group in preventing recurrences of mania. Some research suggests a combination of the two can work best.

Temper your expectations, however, because, alas, medications for bipolar disorder work differently for different people, and it can take time to find the right medication or combination of medications.

"Sally responded well to the medications she was taking in high school, but they stopped working for her after a few years," says Sally's father, the journalist and author Michael Greenberg.

If lithium—or any medication, for that matter—begins to lose its effectiveness, it's first important to determine if your child is taking the medication as prescribed, and then for you and your child's doctor to consider a change in dosage, or adding or changing to a new medication.

The anticonvulsants aren't as dangerous as lithium in excessive doses, may have fewer side-effects in general, and carry less stigma than that famous pioneer. Yet all have substantial downsides, including weight gain (five to six pounds in the first six weeks with Depakote), headache, nausea, anxiety, dizziness, and confusion. Girls taking Depakote must also be monitored carefully for changes in menstrual cycles and the potential for polycystic ovary syndrome (PCOS). For this reason, many clinicians simply avoid prescribing this drug to girls.

Second-Generation Antipsychotics

SGAs are the newest medications available to treat bipolar disorder. Initially intended to treat schizophrenia, they were subsequently found to also help improve mania, and some depression, in adults. The FDA has approved several of them to treat mania in adults and in youth aged 13 and older.

The SGAs may act more quickly and don't require monitoring for blood levels, which is one reason why many clinicians now use them more often than lithium. In some cases they're also more effective than lithium. Antipsychotics can help control the symptoms of bipolar disorder as a single medication or in combination with lithium or divalproex.

The five main medications in this class that are approved for use in adolescents go by the brand names Seroquel (quetiapine), Zyprexa (olanzapine), Abilify (aripiprazole), Risperal (risperidone), and Latuda (lurasidone). Clozaril (clozapine), which has been approved for resistant schizophrenia in adults, is used only rarely to treat bipolar disorder in children.

The SGAs have some potential side-effects, however, which vary depending on the patient but may be more severe for adolescents than adults. A major problem with most SGAs in youth is weight gain: as much as 10 pounds in the first three months, which is not merely problematic for a youth's self-esteem but can lead to health problems, including high blood pressure and diabetes. The weight gain occurs because the medications may affect both appetite and metabolism, which presumably means it could be avoided by reducing calories. In Europe, where diets are healthier and obesity rates lower, this side-effect has notably been less problematic.

"I peer over Sadie's shoulder in the Gap dressing room and hold my breath," writes Dorothy O'Donnell. "She's trying to squeeze into a pair of plus-sized skinny jeans. For weeks, she's begged me to buy her the trendy style all the other fourth-grade girls are wearing. But as she struggles with the zipper and snap, the excitement that filled her face on the drive to the mall disappears.

'I hate my body!' she screams, clawing at the ripple of flesh bulging over the waistband of the pants.

Gently, I pry her fingers from her belly, wincing at the scarlet welts streaking her skin. And the awful feeling that this brutal attack is my fault. A mashup of thoughts spins in my head: I've got to get her off Abilify. How did this weight thing get so out of control? She's not fat— she's adorable! The medicine's helping her . . . right? I'm calling Dr. Goldberg the second we get home."

Other side-effects of the SGAs can be more severe, including the rare danger of neuroleptic malignant syndrome (NMS), which causes a high fever and muscle stiffness. NMS is serious but easily treatable. Clozapine carries an additional rare risk of a condition called agranulocytosis, which can cause a decrease in white blood cells that can lead to infections. Although this side-effect is rare, it is concerning enough that clozapine is not used as a first-line treatment, although in some situations it can be remarkably effective.

"I had been treating one young man for years, for depression, when he came in one day and said he believed he had superpowers and was going to set himself on fire to test his invincibility," says Tami Benton. Benton immediately got her patient to the hospital. Later, she says, "After trying three of the commonly prescribed SGAs, I prescribed clozapine. Clozapine is sometimes prescribed as a last resort medication because of the requirement for frequent blood monitoring due to its potential to cause a decrease in white blood cells. With monitoring, it is a safe and effective medication. My patient has been symptom-free for several years and is now in college. The side-effects listed for clozapine sound scary, but they are extremely rare."

Treating Depression

Treating mania will often be your priority, since, as Benton's story illustrates, manic moods so often lead to self-harm. But once that's under control, your child may also need to be treated for depression.

You've probably heard about the traditional antidepressants, known as selective serotonin reuptake inhibitors (SSRIs), the most famous of these being fluoxetine (Prozac). SSRIs are rarely prescribed for people with bipolar disorder, however, and only if other treatments fail, as they risk triggering mania. They also have a small but significant risk of increasing suicidal behavior in youth, a danger that the FDA requires manufacturers to describe on their packaging, as we'll later elaborate.

The FDA has approved only two medications to treat depression in adolescents with bipolar disorder. Both work by increasing the activity of certain neurotransmitters in the brain, including serotonin. Both also have significant side-effects, although these don't include the risks of mania or suicidal behavior that come with the SSRIs.

The first is lurasidone (Latuda), the most frequent side-effects of which are nausea and drowsiness. The second is a combination of olanzapine and fluoxetine (OFC). Its most common side-effects are weight gain (a not insignificant average of about 10 pounds), drowsiness, sedation, and tremor.

Some clinicians use the anticonvulsant Lamictal off-label for treating both mania and depression in adolescents. The FDA has approved this drug for adults with bipolar disorder, for whom it is particularly effective in preventing relapses. Lamictal doesn't cause weight gain or trigger mania, but it does have side-effects, including dizziness, headache, tremor, sleepiness, nausea, cognitive slowness, and poor appetite. In rare cases—about 1% of children younger than 16—it can also produce an immune reaction known as Stevens-Johnson syndrome, a potentially fatal rash. For that reason, the FDA has issued a warning not to use the medication in that age group.

In some cases, a clinician will prescribe an SSRI, such as Prozac (fluoxetine), for your adolescent, or a non-SSRI, such as Wellbutrin (bupropion), which targets other neurotransmitters than serotonin (Wellbutrin addresses norepinephrine and dopamine). When they do, they will often combine that medication with a mood stabilizer, to avoid triggering mania.

The most common side-effects of the SSRIs are stomach upsets, including nausea and diarrhea, daytime sleepiness, vivid dreams, and headaches. Sometimes your child may grow more agitated and impulsive. One frequent effect is a change in sexual function: decreased libido and capacity to achieve orgasm. (This can be a deal-breaker for boys who find they can't get an erection but are too embarrassed to say anything about it.) You will also have to consider potential side-effects of stopping the medication, which we describe below.

An uncommon but serious risk of taking SSRIs is "serotonin syndrome," the symptoms of which may include high blood pressure and a fast heart rate, and which in rare cases requires hospitalization.

Do Antidepressants Increase the Risk of Suicide?

Of all the potential side-effects of SSRIs, the most worrisome is their well-publicized association with suicidal thoughts and behavior, known as suicidality. (This can include planning and attempting suicide.)

In 2004, after reviewing research involving more than 4,400 young people with major depression and other mental disorders, the FDA found a slightly increased risk of suicidality in young people up to the age of 25 during the first few months of treatment with antidepressants. (The average risk of such thoughts and behavior was 4% in young people taking an antidepressant, compared to 2% in young people taking a placebo.)

The FDA consequently required manufacturers of all antidepressant drugs to put strongly worded advisories—a "black box" warning—on their labeling. Pharmacists must also hand out written material about the risks to patients and families.

This warning is challenging to understand because it's so difficult to untangle the relationship between antidepressant treatment and the development of suicidality, which is already a common symptom of depression. It's worth keeping in mind that the rise in SSRI use has coincided with a *net fall* in suicide rates among adolescents. Our opinion is that on balance, and with careful support, the medications save lives.

The FDA Warning—Summarized

- Antidepressants increase the risk of suicidal thinking and behavior (suicidality) in children and adolescents with major depression and other mental disorders.
- Health care professionals considering the use of an antidepressant in a child or adolescent for any clinical purpose must balance the risk of increased suicidality with the clinical need.
- Patients starting on therapy should be observed closely for clinical worsening, suicidality, or unusual changes in behavior.
- Families and caregivers should be advised to closely observe the patient and to communicate with the prescriber.

Red Flags

If your child has started taking an SSRI, let the doctor know promptly if these symptoms develop or grow worse:

- Anxiety
- Panic attacks
- Worsening depression
- Agitation
- Irritability
- Hostility
- Impulsivity

- Extreme restlessness
- Rapid speech
- Insomnia
- Self-injurious behavior
- Suicidal thoughts

Medication for Coexisting Conditions

As we've noted, if your child has been diagnosed with bipolar disorder, it's likely that he or she will also have one or more additional psychiatric problems, whether it be ADHD, anxiety, or possibly harmful use of alcohol or drugs. Treating the bipolar disorder may help with other issues, and it is typically the first priority. But you may also need to treat the other problems concurrently, possibly with both medication and psychotherapy. If the child has ADHD, for instance, this may require taking a stimulant, such as Concerta (methylphenidate) or Adderall (amphetamine). If you are concerned about your child taking more than one medication, share your concerns with your physician and ask for more frequent monitoring to address your concerns.

How Long Will My Child Need Treatment?

Most medications for bipolar disorder can take several weeks before achieving their full effect. If your child's symptoms aren't improving by then, it's probably time to adjust the doses or try another medication. But if the medicines do their job and your child starts feeling better, don't rush to throw out the prescriptions. Unlike antibiotics for an infection, bipolar meds often must be taken for years, and sometimes over a lifetime, to reduce both recurrences of episodes and the severity of those that do recur. To repeat a common analogy, it's as if your child had epilepsy or diabetes, or needed glasses to function. Even so, you may at some point want to talk to your child's doctor about discontinuing one or more medications, using the "tapering" process we'll describe below.

A Spoonful of Sugar

No medication will help a child who isn't taking it. Yet of course this is a challenge. Researchers have found that more than 40% of kids with bipolar disorder don't take their medication as prescribed.

Your son or daughter has a mental illness that can cause oppositional behavior, and this is a big ask.

Before we offer tips to help, it's time for an empathy exercise. Imagine you're a teenage girl or boy just stepping out into the world of young romance. You're already socially awkward, and now your mom or dad wants you to take medication that may make you fat, cause your hair to fall out, give you pimples, and maybe also rob you of the only moments in your life, however manic, when you feel something like joy.

You may have resolved that the upsides of medication—like keeping your child safe—outweigh the downs. You may also trust that your child's doctor can keep side-effects to a minimum. Keep your eye on the prize: the hope that treatment will improve your son or daughter's life, and maybe save it. But try to put yourself in your kid's shoes and resist the urge to threaten or nag. Instead, try these tactics, offered by our parental brain trust.

- *Speak honestly about the pros and cons of medication treatment*—adolescents usually sense when they're not getting the full story. But downplay any misgivings you may have:

   "Once we decided to try medication, we had to put our worries aside and reflect our hopefulness that this would make a difference," says Beth. "Our son didn't need to know how difficult a decision it was for us."

- *Take responsibility for storing and supervising the medication for a child under 18*:

   "In our home, it's just known that everyone takes their medication, including me," says Vanessa. "I'm in charge of setting out all our medications at night. I put them in those little seven-day pillboxes, so we can see at a glance if anyone forgot to take their medication today."

- *Figure out what your child wants and speak to that*:

   "I recommend doing 'motivational interviewing,'" says Sally. "My goals simply aren't as meaningful to Larry as his goals are to him. So I've gotten to know the ways he thinks the medications might help him—like getting better at the guitar—and talk about that, rather than talking about his doing better in school or whatever I'm worried about."

- *Set clear expectations for older adolescents who are still living at home.*

We recommend that you not expect your child be responsible for filling his or her own prescriptions—for now, at least, you've got to take that on. Also, to the best of your ability, respect your child's need for privacy and support his or her decision about sharing treatment information in other settings, such as summer camp, sleepovers, and visits to relatives.

Tapering Off

There may come a time when your child wants to discontinue one or all of the medications, particularly for depression. If your clinician agrees to this plan—we hope—you'll most likely be advised to lower the dose gradually over several weeks. It's important not to try this during a time of unusual stress, and once you do, consider having your child start or continue with psychotherapy as an extra buffer.

Tapering can help avoid symptoms caused by a change in levels of neurotransmitters. These symptoms, which can be uncomfortable but not medically dangerous, may include flu-like symptoms, dizziness, sleep changes, and even some return to depression, any of which could emerge within days to weeks of stopping the medication or lowering the dose. Some patients have also reported strange sensations like a ringing in the ears or "zaps" that seem like electrical charges.

The bright side is that these symptoms are temporary and tapering helps. In fact, a Harvard Medical School study found that patients who reduced their dose over two or more weeks were less likely than those who stopped cold turkey to experience a relapse of depression.

The symptoms associated with stopping medication don't mean your child is "addicted"—that is, craving the medication—but they do suggest that the medication has changed your child's brain. You'll see evidence of this if your child resumes the medication for any reason. The symptoms will disappear quickly.

Some Questions for Your Child's Doctor

When medication is part of your child's treatment plan, be sure to tell the doctor about any other pharmaceuticals, including over-the-counter drugs or herbal supplements, your child may be taking since some may cause harmful interactions. Also tell the doctor if your child has allergies to any drug. Then make sure you have all the facts you need about any new medication prescribed. Here are a few questions you won't want to forget to ask:

- When and how often should my child take the medication?
- What is the plan to monitor how my child is doing with this new medication?
- Have studies been conducted using this medication in children?
- Should the medicine be taken with food or on an empty stomach?
- Can I stop the medication or adjust the dose?
- When should we expect to see results?
- What are the possible side-effects of the medication?
- Which of these side-effects are most serious?
- What should I do if these side-effects occur?
- What number should I call if I have any questions or concerns?
- How long should my child stay on the medication?

- Will my child need to limit any activities while taking the drug?
- Does the medication interact with alcohol, other drugs, or certain foods?
- Where can I get more information on the medication?

What If My Child Doesn't Respond to Mainstream Medications?

If a child's emotional crisis continues even after testing one or more medications, you may still have some options. Still, keep in mind that the ones we describe below are only very rarely used on adolescents, and only in the most critical cases.

Neuromodulation

Electroconvulsive therapy (ECT) employs electrodes positioned on the scalp that deliver a carefully controlled electrical current to the brain, producing a seizure that may last about a minute.

ECT may seem scary—especially if you watched Jack Nicholson receiving the treatment in *One Flew Over the Cuckoo's Nest*—but it's generally safe. Moreover, most patients receiving this treatment get some relief, which helps explain why the American Academy of Child and Adolescent Psychiatry concluded that ECT may be used with adolescents with severe mood disorders after at least two medications have failed or in an emergency with no time to wait for medication to work. At the same time, the conditions permitting its use—including the age of the patient and whether or how many experts must approve it—vary from state to state, so it isn't always easily accessible.

"It gave me the creeps when I first heard it, but ECT was the one treatment that turned my daughter around," says Miles, the father who'd discovered his teenage daughter

Jenny had been cutting. "The treatments made her very tired but over time helped with the self-destructive behavior."

ECT temporarily changes the brain's electrochemistry. Before treatment, patients receive a muscle relaxant, which prevents the body from convulsing, and general anesthesia. The patient awakens a few minutes later, as if having had minor surgery.

ECT typically requires 6 to 12 treatments, three times a week. Effects appear gradually over the course of the treatment. The most common side-effects are headache, muscle ache or soreness, nausea, and confusion. These usually occur within hours of a treatment and clear up quickly. Still, as the treatments go on, people also may have trouble remembering newly learned information, and some have partial and short-term loss of memories from the days, weeks, or months preceding the treatment. On the other hand, some people report that their memory *improves* after ECT, since they are no longer fighting the fog of depression.

A few other, newer methods have received enthusiastic recent media coverage, although their effectiveness and safety for youth haven't been clearly established.

Transcranial magnetic stimulation (TMS) has been studied as a possible treatment for mental illness since 1995, and some research indicates it may help with severe depression in adults. In this therapy, an electromagnetic coil is placed against the scalp, near the forehead. It delivers a pulse that stimulates cells in parts of the brain that may have reduced activity when someone is depressed. An advantage of this treatment is that it doesn't require surgery, hospitalization, or anesthesia. A physician simply applies the device during

30-minute sessions, which may be given five days per week for two to four weeks.

In studies to date, most side-effects of TMS have been relatively mild and rare. They include discomfort, headache, or lightheadedness during treatment, all of which usually go away soon after the session ends. There is also a risk that the treatment might trigger a seizure.

A big caveat here: At this writing, only one large study has examined the treatment of depressed adolescents with TMS compared to a placebo approach. The study, which was industry-sponsored, found no difference in outcomes between the two groups—that is, no perceptible benefit. More research is obviously needed to determine if TMS can help this age group. Based on what we know now, we don't recommend it at this time, and we won't unless more evidence becomes available.

Ketamine

Unless you've been on a long news fast, you've probably heard enticing news about the promise of various psychedelic drugs, including LSD, psilocybin mushrooms, and MDMA—also known as "Ecstasy"—to treat severe depression and bipolar disorder, as well as many other mental ailments. Major universities, including Yale, Johns Hopkins, and the University of California at Berkeley, have set up centers to study psychedelic therapies for all sorts of mental illnesses, and investors are pouring funds into start-ups to market them.

At this writing, the only psychedelic that a doctor may prescribe for treatment-resistant depression in anyone, including adolescents, is ketamine. The drug got its start several decades ago as an anesthesia for animals, and later it was used to help treat injured soldiers in Vietnam. Still later it was used recreationally: injected, smoked or snorted, with names like Special K and Vitamin K.

In 2019, the FDA approved Spravato (esketamine, a potent form of ketamine) nasal spray to treat depression for patients aged 18 or older who hadn't been helped by other medications. Two years later, the first study of ketamine with adolescents (just 17 subjects, aged 13 to 17) found ketamine to be well-tolerated and effective in reducing depression symptoms, at least in the short term, compared to a placebo. For these reasons, some psychiatrists have called for urgent additional research of this option for adolescents in crisis.

Unlike standard antidepressants, which may target serotonin, norepinephrine, and dopamine, ketamine acts on glutamate, another, more prevalent chemical messenger in the brain. It can cause feelings of euphoria, unreality, and sensory distortions, lasting about two hours.

Paola's son Martin was 18 when his grandmother died and Martin became so depressed that couldn't get out of bed. On the advice of a doctor and family friend, Paola brought him to a clinic for a series of six infusions of ketamine. "Because Martin has ADHD, these were like trips to the funhouse for him; he was very into it," Paola says. The sessions, which weren't covered by insurance, cost more than $3,000 altogether, and for several months it seemed the cloud had lifted. "The problem with ketamine is it doesn't last," Paola says. She suspects the benefits may have taken hold and lasted longer had a therapist been involved to help her son integrate the experience. She may try again in the future but says that for now, "We're back to where we were before the sessions."

Be advised that recreational use of ketamine is not therapeutic and carries risks including high blood pressure and dangerously slowed breathing. Ketamine should only be used in highly controlled settings, at a doctor's office, where a patient is closely watched for the two hours or so of the ketamine experience. Patients typically get the nasal spray twice a week for one to four weeks; then once a week for weeks five to nine; and then once every week or two after that. Some patients will later need boosters.

The spray carries an FDA warning about side-effects, including sedation and trouble with attention, judgment, and thinking, as well as risk for abuse or misuse of the drug and suicidal thoughts and behaviors. In some cases it has triggered psychosis, and it can also be fatal for people who misuse alcohol. For these reasons, despite the hoopla, we can't—at least not at this writing—recommend ketamine for adolescents.

Chapter Three

Treatment

Psychotherapy

As we mentioned previously, your child will need medication as part of the treatment for bipolar disorder. Yet medication is often not sufficient by itself, and adding psychotherapy will give your child the greatest chance of lifelong success. Bipolar disorder is a multifaceted illness which calls for a multidimensional treatment approach. As much as meds may help tamp down mania and lift depression, your child will still need to learn how to manage this illness and acquire skills to cope with impulsivity and mood swings. The predicament is somewhat like having diabetes: Both medication and lifestyle changes, such as maintaining a healthy diet, are essential.

Psychotherapy may seem like "just talk," but imaging studies have shown it can lead to physical changes in the brain, affecting the same regions as mood stabilizers. Potential providers include psychiatrists, clinical psychologists, clinical social workers, mental health counselors, psychiatric nurses, and marriage and family therapists.

Bipolar disorder affects not only the person who has it but the entire family. It is also, as we've described, strongly hereditary, meaning it may also affect a parent or sibling. This is why we think it's crucial, as soon as you can, to get evidence-based psychotherapy for yourself. If you haven't had the opportunity before now, don't delay. We understand that following this advice requires time, energy, and money, but it's quite likely an investment that will pay off for years. Beyond providing a customized education in how to help care for your child, it can also help you explore your own reactions and find ways to feel more in control.

We're sure by now you've heard that old saying about how when a plane starts to go down, you should put on your own oxygen mask before tending to your child. It's a bit of a cliché, but as with most clichés, there's good reason why it has caught on. Taking good care of yourself during this stressful time— including taking informed care of your own emotions—is one of the best things you can do for your child, not to mention yourself. You'll not only be a great role model, but you won't be running this marathon of stress with a heavy weight around your neck. Psychotherapy can help you better understand your child and cope with the anger, sorrow, fear, and self-blame that may besiege you.

Not least, psychotherapy may help you avoid repeating mistakes made by your own parents, who may have had mood disorders themselves. A good therapist can give you a toolkit that can help you be calmer, with more self-compassion and compassion for your child.

"When Matt got angry with me, I'd remember how terrified I was as a young girl when my father screamed at my mother," says Beth, the mother of a bipolar son. "Just understanding that reaction helped me tremendously."

Which Psychotherapies Might Be Best for My Child?

When it comes to your adolescent, several kinds of psychotherapy can be useful in treating bipolar disorder, either individually or in a mix of techniques. Overall, the benefits may include the following:

- Greater acceptance of the seriousness of the illness
- More responsibility about taking medication
- Increased ability to recognize and handle symptoms
- Better relationships at home and school

One of the best-studied psychotherapeutic approaches—and one commonly used with adolescents—is *cognitive-behavioral therapy* (CBT). A therapist using CBT challenges a patient's unhealthy thinking patterns, asking questions that can reveal misassumptions and unrealistic pessimism, while encouraging problem-solving skills and healthier choices.

In a typical conversation, a therapist might push back when a patient insists she has no friends who truly care for her. "What makes you think that?" the therapist might ask.

"I texted one of my friends yesterday and she took a whole day to answer," the patient may say.

The interchange highlights how many depressed adolescents distort reality. They may draw conclusions based on limited or no information (the friend may have had an emergency). Or they may magnify the importance of one event to make generalized assumptions. The therapist can help the young patient review the information that refutes the dire view of the world, and help identify the positives she's overlooking—such as the fact that the friend did eventually text back.

This approach is also known as "reframing." In another example, if your child says, "I'm so stupid! I always blurt out ridiculous things when I'm talking to friends," the therapist might gently call attention to the patient's habit of berating himself and consider what happened in another light, such as the way some mistakes are learning opportunities and simply part of growing up.

CBT may help adolescents with bipolar disorder learn to:

- Monitor moods
- Set and achieve goals
- Cope with social situations
- Relax and manage stress
- Solve many everyday problems

Another commonly used approach to treat bipolar disorder is *interpersonal psychotherapy* (IPT), which, unsurprisingly, focuses on interpersonal problems as triggers for the illness. This form of psychotherapy may be useful if your son or daughter is constantly getting into conflicts with you or others, lacks social skills, or is grieving over a recent loss. It's also helpful during a stressful transition, such as changing schools or coping with parents' divorce. IPT focuses on identifying the problem that triggered the episode of depression and developing the necessary social and communication skills to resolve it.

IPT can help adolescents with mood disorders learn to handle social issues such as:

- Establishing independence

- Dealing with peer pressure
- Forming healthy friendships
- Resolving family conflicts

Either CBT or IPT may be used in individual therapy, in which a person works one on one with a therapist or in a therapist-led group. Group therapy gives adolescents a chance to trade concerns and insights with peers struggling with similar issues, helping them learn from others' insights and reminding them that they are not alone. The group setting also offers kids a chance to learn and practice social skills. The relationships formed in the group can be a powerful antidote to feelings of hopelessness.

Dialectical behavior therapy (DBT), a treatment initially developed for individuals with chronic suicidal behavior, is also often used with adolescents with bipolar disorder. DBT employs mindfulness principles—teaching youth to be more present in the moment—and skill-building to help manage stress and improve relationships. The full program consists of several sessions of both group and one-on-one therapy, each once a week, with phone coaching available between sessions.

By giving kids techniques to better tolerate emotional distress, DBT can help discourage self-destructive actions, which might range from blurting out an insult to a teacher or boss to cutting or attempting suicide. One common technique is "chain analysis," which tries to show how unwanted behaviors result from a chain of interrelated events. The therapist coaxes the person receiving treatment to think back to what may have been the first, precipitating "link" in that chain: perhaps a bad night's sleep, or substance misuse, or intense emotions caused by something someone else said or did. Once the patient recognizes the sequence, the therapist can help brainstorm about ways to help prevent it from being repeated, including by coming up with healthier responses. This might include something so simple as advising a youth who has been cutting to instead stick his or her hand into a bowl of ice water or simply hold an ice cube in his or her hand. The coldness delivers a similar distracting shock to the system, but without the harm.

Family therapy can also be extremely helpful, with the benefits extending to parents and siblings as well as the patient with the initially recognized problem. Ideally, several or all family members meet with a therapist and work together to identify and change destructive patterns contributing to or arising from a child's mental illness. Family therapy can help uncover hidden issues, such as the resentment a sibling may feel because of all the attention the adolescent with bipolar disorder has been getting. It can also help open lines of communication and teach everyone better coping skills for dealing with the child's illness. Its general goals include strengthening family bonds, reducing conflict in the home, and increasing empathy among family members.

"I did some individual therapy and met regularly with my daughter's therapist, but I really think working with a qualified family therapist could have helped our family dynamic," says Dorothy O'Donnell. "I'm a naturally anxious person, and I wish I'd done a better job of hiding my anxiety at times because I know she picked up on it and internalized it."

For an adolescent with bipolar disorder, family therapy offers a chance to escape the painful feeling that he or she—as the "identified patient"—is causing all the family's problems. In fact, a single family member's depression is often a warning sign of systemic issues that, if solved, may improve everyone's lives.

Family-focused treatment (FFT) is a family therapy program tailored to bipolar disorder, which has been rigorously tested and proven to be particularly effective for adolescents and their families. Studies show it can help reduce depressive symptoms, decrease the risk of recurrence of mania, and even reduce rates of rehospitalization, partly because families and patients learn to identify signs of oncoming crises and intervene in time.

Developed by David Miklowitz, a clinical psychologist, researcher, and author of best selling books on bipolar disorder, FFT normally involves 12 to 21 family sessions, including some homework. It has three modules: psychoeducation, in which families learn about bipolar disorder and coping skills; communication enhancement training; and problem-solving to reduce situations causing conflict at home.

A key strength of FFT is that it recognizes how all members of a family are affected by this illness, encouraging them to discuss their feelings in a supportive environment. This can help kids with bipolar disorder to understand the impact their illness is having, providing more motivation for change.

Are There Any Downsides to Psychotherapy?

Overall, psychotherapy has fewer adverse impacts than medication, but it's not risk-free. By its nature, it taps into deep, sometimes disturbing, thoughts and feelings, so any therapist you choose should be prepared to handle unexpected strong reactions. It's possible that therapy could lead your child to feel worse temporarily. Assuming you trust the therapist, and he or she is offering a conventional treatment, you'll want to encourage your child to hang in there and work through those feelings.

If your adolescent is taking medication, the therapist should be knowledgeable about the effects of these drugs and willing to coordinate treatment with your child's psychiatrist or another prescriber. If your child has other mental, emotional, or behavioral disorders in addition to depression, the therapist should be well-versed in these conditions as well.

On top of these concerns are some more obvious potential problems. You want to make 100% sure your child's therapist is credentialed, experienced, and ethical, as we'll later explain further. Sometimes therapy is ineffective, resulting in wasted time and money, and potentially worsening of the illness. Therapists who violate young people's boundaries— whether physical or emotional—are fortunately rare, yet must be rigorously avoided, since they can do deep and lasting harm. Tempting as it may be, avoid engaging a therapist who is already a friend of anyone in the family. Keep an eye on the relationship and be aware that psychotherapy should not involve any physical contact other than a pat on the shoulder or handshake.

How Long Should My Child Be in Therapy?

The timeline for therapy will vary depending on what type is used, the severity of the problems, and the issues being addressed. With both CBT and IPT, good results have been achieved in anywhere from 5 to 16 sessions. The exact number of sessions needed for a particular adolescent depends on many factors, including the nature and severity of the symptoms. Unfortunately, the amount of time your child spends in therapy may also be dictated by the terms of your insurance coverage, a subject we'll tell you more about in the next chapter.

Initially, psychotherapy sessions may be scheduled once a week. But as your child starts to get better, the sessions may gradually be spaced farther apart. Even after symptoms have improved, it's often helpful if sessions are continued, even less frequently, for several months. Continuing psychotherapy provides adolescents and families with a chance to keep practicing and consolidating the new skills they have learned. It also gives kids a chance to deepen their awareness of the thoughts and behaviors that might otherwise contribute to a relapse.

At some point during the first few sessions, your adolescent and the therapist may collaborate to create a list of short-term and long-term goals. It's a good idea to revisit this list periodically to see whether progress is being made. As with medication, though, it's essential to give psychotherapy enough time to work. If you expect instant results, you're likely to be disappointed. On the other hand, it's reasonable to expect gradual but noticeable progress over time. Your child's therapist may be able to give you some idea of how soon your child is likely to start noticing improvement and how long therapy is expected to last. If the therapy is taking much longer than planned, however, feel free to ask the therapist why that is. If the answer is unsatisfactory, you might consider seeking a second opinion, just as you would for any other illness.

Private Lives

Study after study has shown that by far the most important factor determining success in psychotherapy is the bond between patient and therapist. As the person paying the bills and dragging your child to the sessions, you may reasonably want to participate in the actual process behind the therapist's closed door, or at least be in on some of the secrets being revealed. You may also be desperately worried about your child's safety and anxious to know what you can do to help.

When it comes to adolescents, there are some ways that parents will need to be involved in the therapy. This includes providing information during the initial assessment, after which some therapists will have a first session jointly with the parent and child. During this process, the therapist should establish a plan for how to go forward. Most will make some time for the parent to have updates every several weeks or so. The manuals for CBT and IPT include parent sessions as part of the treatment plan. But other than that, bear in mind that your child may not get the best results if he or she suspects the therapist is routinely spilling secrets to you. You may help your child most by respecting this important new relationship.

An exception to this rule is if your child is in danger of harm or harming others—from being abused to experimenting with dangerous drugs. In that case, the provider is obliged to act, which may include letting you know or even calling the police.

Here's something else to keep in mind as your child begins treatment. The 21st Century Cures Act, signed into law in 2016, requires providers to make their medical notes accessible to their patients. Most adolescents starting at the age of 12 (the age varies depending on the state) will therefore be able to read their medical records, including the therapist's notes, online, and have the option to let their parents read it as well. Some research suggests that this transparency improves communication and satisfaction with treatment. Yet it can also raise some problems, including reactions to the shared information. It's one thing to talk about issues in the privacy of an appointment, but another thing to see them described on a page (or screen). You and your adolescent should talk to your provider to understand their approach to documenting sensitive information.

As your son or daughter's therapy progresses, pay special attention to the quality of the relationship between your child and the therapist, as that will make all the difference as to whether it succeeds. Does your child resist attending sessions? Do you find the therapist's manner abrasive? You may have a few false starts before you find someone truly effective.

Can Nutritional Supplements Help?

As a general rule, supplements should never be considered substitutes for medication in treating bipolar disorder, and they should be used with great caution, if at all. Researchers have found some evidence that some may help, but the studies are limited to date. That said, plenty of nutritional supplements are *advertised* as being able to improve mood. Yet you should keep in mind that if supplements did everything their manufacturers claimed, the world would be full of slim, happy, smart, creative people, albeit all with a lot less disposable income.

Supplements can be sold online and over the counter—that is, without a prescription—and because they aren't regulated by the Food and Drug Administration, sellers are free to claim whatever they wish. Be sure to check with your child's doctor or at least a pharmacist. Even though they're called "supplements," some don't truly supplement but rather interfere with other drugs. Beware in particular of "megavitamin dosing." Not only is there no evidence that it works; giving children large doses of vitamins can be fatal.

That said, researchers have found that the following two supplements, which you may have already heard about, *may* have some promise for treating mood disorders, although at this writing, the evidence is not convincing. They are *St. John's wort (Hypericum perforatum)* and *omega-3 polyunsaturated fatty acids.*

St. John's wort has been used for centuries to treat mental disorders and nerve pain, and in Europe it is sold by prescription for depression. In the United States, it's available over the counter, and it is one of the top-selling herbal products. The most common side-effects include dry mouth, dizziness, diarrhea, nausea, fatigue, and increased sensitivity to sunlight. Beware if your child is taking selective serotonin reuptake inhibitors (SSRIs) or oral contraceptives, as this herb can decrease their effectiveness.

Omega-3s are found in foods including cold-water fish, such as salmon and tuna, flaxseed, walnuts, and pecans. They have anti-inflammatory properties, which may help explain why some studies have shown positive results for adolescents with bipolar disorder. A few small studies have found modest improvements in both manic and depressive symptoms, and research is ongoing. But at this point no large, well-controlled studies have shown omega-3s to be effective.

You may also have heard of a supplement known as SAMe, *S*-adenosyl-L-methionine, since some high-quality studies have found it may help symptoms of mild depression. Occurring naturally in the body, SAMe is known to play an important role in regulating serotonin and dopamine. Common side-effects include nausea and constipation. SAMe may not be a good idea for kids with bipolar disorder, since, just like the SSRIs, there's a risk of triggering mania. Be sure to talk to your child's doctor if you're thinking of trying SAMe or any other supplement. Just because you can buy them over the counter doesn't mean they're safe.

What About Just Sitting There?

Can you argue with 35 million fellow Americans? That's how many have tried meditation at last count, according to the Centers for Disease Control and Prevention, and the numbers are growing all the time. If you stop reading right now and breathe calmly, accepting thoughts as they come and go, even for just five minutes, you may get a sense of why meditation—or "mindfulness"—has become so popular in our turbulent times. An increasing amount of research, mostly involving adults, points to myriad benefits, including relief from depression and anxiety and even a lengthening of the telomeres, the little caps on the ends of your cells, that are associated with lower mortality. Although mindfulness has deep roots in Buddhist spirituality, nondenominational meditation can be good for everyone, especially family members in homes where someone is depressed. The trick—and it's a big one—is that it's much too easy to feel like there isn't time, especially when you're coping with a family crisis. Try starting for just those five minutes.

> "When my son was in middle school, I took him to a middle-schoolers' meditation class at a Buddhist retreat center near our home," says Beth. "The teachers would have the kids run around the room to get their ya-yas out before settling down to meditate for just 15 minutes. For the rest of that evening, my son would be amazingly at peace and organized in his mind. It was one of the best things we ever tried."

Beware of False Hopes (and False Advertising)

If you believe in any supplements and techniques strongly enough, they may work better than placebos. But when dealing with bipolar disorder, it's truly best to stick with conventional, time-tested methods, and by all means not discontinue them to try special diets, chiropractic adjustments, or the many other touted "cures" advertised to desperate parents.

Your guiding rule should be caveat emptor—buyer beware. You have only so much time—and money—and if your child is truly suffering a serious illness, your best bet is to stick with the best-studied conventional treatments. In Chapter 4 we'll help you figure out how to get them.

Chapter Four

Finding a Provider

Now that you understand the available treatments, how can you find the best clinician to deliver them? Even many parents with abundant financial resources and know-how become frustrated in trying to track down—and afford—competent mental health care for their children.

> "We needed help from someone. But when we tried to find it, it wasn't there," writes the journalist Paul Raeburn. "We took the children to a series of psychiatrists who repeatedly misdiagnosed them and treated them incorrectly, sometimes making them worse. We talked to therapists who threw us off course again and again with faulty assessments. We took the children to hospitals that did not keep them long enough to help them, because our insurance company wouldn't pay for the care. . . . We spent tens of thousands of dollars, some of the money wasted on inappropriate care, to try to fill the vast gaps in our insurance plan."

One in five Americans has a mental health problem in any given year. Yet mental health care is shockingly underutilized—and also often unhelpful. The problems include lack of awareness about affordable treatments, insufficient coverage by insurance firms, and unavailability of suitable providers. You're going to have to navigate a daunting, complex system. So even if you're in crisis, try giving yourself a calm window of time to move ahead. You'll need to use whatever research skills and social networks you possess to find the best, most affordable care. Along the way, you'll also need to learn about insurance plans and mental health benefits.

Why This Is Harder Than Ever

As you may already know, throughout the United States there's a serious scarcity of mental health experts—particularly psychiatrists—trained and qualified to treat adolescents. For several reasons, psychiatry has struggled to attract clinicians trained to work with youth. Many new doctors can't afford the five required years of post–medical school training. Others may be deterred by continuing stigma surrounding mental illness, as well as insurance firms' stingy reimbursements for psychotherapy.

At last count, there were only 9.75 US child psychiatrists for every 100,000 children under age 19. The American Academy of Child and Adolescent Psychiatry (AACAP) says we need more than four times that many. Specialists are often swamped by the demand, and the average person seeking help for a mental illness waits several weeks for a first appointment. Many overwhelmed psychiatrists and psychologists have closed their practices to new patients, no longer accept payments through insurance, or are no longer able to deliver high-quality care.

"Our psychiatrist at our HMO disappeared for seven days after Ellen was hospitalized," says Charlene. "He apologized afterward but said he had like 1,000 kids to manage. I'm sure the situation was exacerbated by the pandemic."

You may have a particularly hard search if you live far from a big city, where psychiatrists and psychologists tend to congregate. More than two-thirds of US counties lack even a single adolescent psychiatrist, meaning at best, parents will face long drives and long waits to get their children care.

Many families simply can't afford psychiatric services, lack the time to ferry their kids to appointments, or are frustrated by the complexities of our mental health system. The sad result of these obstacles is that the average delay between the onset of symptoms and treatments for someone with a mental health problem in the United States is *11 years*. And only 2 out of 10 children with mental, emotional, or behavioral disorders *ever* receive care from a specialized mental health care provider. This is especially worrying news, particularly given that mental illnesses may worsen without treatment.

Unequal Care

We have lots of advice to help you beat these odds. But first, here's one more word of warning. The hardships we've described disproportionately affect people of color and families with low incomes, not only because it's often harder for them to find and afford the care, but due to lingering stigma both within their own communities and within the medical system. African Americans, for example, are on average less likely to seek treatment for psychological symptoms. If they do, their medical providers may not be culturally competent, failing to recognize varying mood symptoms in racial groups other than their own. Researchers have found several common biases among clinicians, including the misconception that people of color are more immune to mental or physical pain, due to the challenges they're accustomed to facing on a regular basis. The resulting mutual distrust can complicate all kinds of medical care.

"I can't tell you how many times I've had my children racially profiled," says Wanda, whose two daughters have been diagnosed with severe depression. "My older daughter was in a car accident, but when she got to the hospital, the nurses wouldn't give her pain medication. They assume we're addicts."

These problems help explain why people of color are more likely to be inadequately treated or remain untreated, ending up more debilitated by chronic mental illness. The unfortunate truth is that you may need to work even harder to find your child good care. The work may include overcoming both your own biases and those of your community.

Chamique Holdsclaw, a former women's professional basketball player, wasn't correctly diagnosed with bipolar disorder until age 33. Until age 11, she had lived with a father with untreated mental illness and a mother with untreated alcoholism. It wasn't until her grandmother adopted her that she first got help for her own depression. "In our community, there's a strong feeling that you don't talk about these things, and that if anything you pray them away," she says. "But my grandmother was ahead of her time."

That's all the bad news for now. We've come to our promised suggestions for finding care for your child. Note: The following tips assume you're not in a crisis and have some time to research your options. For tips about coping with emergencies, see Chapter 9.

1. Rule Out Other Explanations

Before you seek care for bipolar disorder, make sure that's what your child needs. Rule out any physical problems, such as sleep disorders, brain injuries, or infections.

2. Aim for the Gold Standard

If you're ready for a formal diagnosis, find a psychiatrist who treats adolescents and specializes in bipolar disorder. Pediatricians should never be first-line providers, since this illness can challenge even specialists. If you can't find a psychiatrist who specializes in adolescents, be open to seeing one who treats adults. All psychiatrists must at least have some training with minors.

> "We didn't know Ruth had bipolar disorder until her second year in college, when I got a call from her friends saying she was on her way to the hospital in an ambulance after taking a bunch of pills," says Ruth's mother, Rhonda. "I saw my husband age 10 years that night." Ruth had

been misdiagnosed with attention-deficit/hyperactivity disorder (ADHD) and depression in high school, but after her crisis, "We found a great psychiatrist—outside our health plan of course—who has really helped her," Rhonda says. "I'm still having a hard time forgiving myself for not getting this right years ago."

3. Enlist Your Child's Pediatrician in Your Search

Pediatricians can often help find the right specialist. They know the local professional landscape as well as anyone and are likely invested in helping your child. Then, once your child has been on the same medication for some time—at least several months—and appears to be stable, you might shift the care back to the regular doctor. Many pediatricians will be willing to renew prescriptions, possibly in consultation with the mental health provider, cutting down your costs. One more suggestion: If your daughter's mood is plunging on schedule each month, consider asking her doctor for birth-control pills that can combat premenstrual blues.

4. Check Out These National Referral Services

These organizations and others we list in the Resources section can help with your search for affordable mental health care:

The National Alliance on Mental Illness (NAMI) has a helpline for free assistance Monday through Friday, 10 a.m. to 10 p.m. EST. You can reach the helpline at 1-800-950-6264. NAMI also offers a free, 24/7 crisis text: just text 988.

The Substance Abuse and Mental Health Services Administration (SAMHSA), a government agency, provides a treatment locator for low-cost facilities.

The National Association of Free & Charitable Clinics, Mental Health America, and the Open Path Psychotherapy Collective also provide online tools to find affordable mental health services.

5. Be a Smart Health Care Consumer

If you're like most modern parents, you'll start your search for help on the internet. Maybe you'll also try to educate yourself about bipolar disorder online. On balance, the internet has been a boon for consumers seeking to educate themselves and compare products and services. But beware: It's also a haven for hucksters who prey on the panicked and vulnerable. Aim for information from websites ending in .edu, for "educational." The .com suffix means "commercial," and you'll see it on sites offering services for pay. Don't believe everything you read on .com sites and make sure that any provider you engage has genuine credentials and isn't trying to sell a fringe therapy.

Check out potential providers online on your state's medical board website, where you can confirm they have a license and see if they've had any complaints against them. You may also want to look at review sites, like Yelp, Healthgrades, RateMDs.com, and Vitals.com, but don't take them at their word. Satisfied clients of psychiatrists and therapists rarely want to violate their own privacy, but cranks tend not to worry about that, so these reviews may be misrepresentative and misleading.

6. Trust Your Gut

If you don't think your child's doctor is seeing what you're seeing, keep asking questions—or change doctors.

"During Ruth's evaluation in high school, I asked more than once if her psychiatrist was sure she wasn't bipolar, because I had seen signs of subtle manic behavior," laments her mother, Rhonda.

Being wealthy and well-connected is no guarantee against inadequate mental health care. Danielle Steel suspected her son Nick had a serious illness, but he wasn't correctly diagnosed until he was 16, long after he had become suicidal. Three years later, he fatally overdosed on lithium.

In the years leading up to that tragedy, Steel switched doctors several times and kept pleading for more to be done. "I am a capable, reasonable, rational, intelligent, fairly strong-willed, competent person, with ample funds at my disposal, terrific resources, and an ability to get things on track quickly," she has written. "If I couldn't make things happen for Nick, and get help for him, I shudder to think at what happens to people who are too shy or too frightened to speak up."

7. When Choosing Psychotherapists, Keep an Eye on the Relationship

As we've mentioned, your child will likely need a therapist to talk to, perhaps in addition to medication. Beyond making sure that the professional is licensed and has a good reputation, you don't need to worry too much if the therapy is called "psychodynamic" or cognitive-behavioral or interpersonal, if your child willingly shows up for appointments and seems to trust the process. The "therapeutic bond" is essential for progress.

While not intervening too much, you should certainly be aware if your child isn't bonding with the therapist, since that would doom the process. You may have a few false starts before you find someone truly effective.

Professional Help: Who Does What?

Several different kinds of professionals provide mental health services. We rank these below according to years of training, noting who can prescribe medication or provide psychotherapy.

Type of Professional	May Prescribe Medication?	May Provide Psychotherapy?
Psychiatrists	Yes	Yes
Primary care physicians	Yes	No
Psychiatric nurses	Yes, with advanced training	Yes
Clinical psychologists	No*	Yes
Clinical social workers	No	Yes
Mental health counselors	No	Yes
Marriage and family therapists	No	Yes

* Psychologists aren't physicians, which limits them when dealing with medication. Yet they can legally prescribe medications in five states: Louisiana, New Mexico, Illinois, Iowa, and Idaho. They may also prescribe medications anywhere in the US military and the Indian Health Service if they are credentialed in Louisiana or New Mexico.

When Should You Enlist a Neuropsychologist?

Your child's primary doctor or mental health professional or perhaps even teacher may suggest an appointment with a neuropsychologist, if they suspect there is a problem with cognition, concentration, or memory which may affect learning. You have every right to ask why the referral is needed. Perhaps your child has a brain injury, illness, or developmental problem that's contributing to the mood disorder. A neuropsychologist may be particularly helpful if you're seeking accommodations at school and need to establish a diagnosis of a specific disorder, as we'll later explain more in depth. A thorough evaluation, which could include several cognitive tests, can be expensive. (In rare cases, public schools will pay, although it may require a lawyer's intervention.) The advantage is that you'll learn a great deal about the way your child's brain works, from processing speed to memory to impulsivity. This can help you clarify the diagnosis and figure out what to do next.

> "I had no idea why Charlie was getting so frustrated so much of the time until we found out how slowly he processes what's said to him," says Carmen, who paid for a full day of neuropsychological tests. "He's a smart kid, so he has been able to cover up for this deficit for years, and we might never have known."

How Do You Build Rapport With Your Provider?

Once you've chosen a treatment provider, it's essential that your child feels comfortable with the relationship. You can contribute by working on your own bond with the therapist.

Let the provider know you have faith in the process and are available to answer any questions. Pay your bills on time and respect the provider's limited time, knowing he or she is probably swamped all day with calls and emails. Make contact only when it's really needed; use cell phone numbers, if offered, only in emergencies, and if you have time-consuming concerns, consider scheduling a paid appointment to discuss them. Most therapists will be willing to schedule a separate session for a parent to help with common dilemmas such as whether it's advisable to let a kid stay home from school occasionally for a mental health day.

> "I had a really hard time figuring out which small stuff, if any, to sweat," says Jeanne. "It has helped me beyond words to be able to run this stuff by someone with experience."

Make a point of telling your doctor about your child's strengths as well as the problems. Try not to be defensive, but also don't be afraid to switch if the relationship isn't working out.

How Should You Prepare for Appointments?

When meeting for the first time with your child's mental health care provider, come prepared to answer questions about behaviors that concern you. You may be asked when they started, how often they occur, how long they last, and how severe they seem. Don't neglect to fill out questionnaires that many clinicians now provide before a first appointment, so that they can spend more time with you and your child. The provider may also wish to communicate by phone or email with teachers, social services workers, and the primary care doctor. He or she will want to know if there have been any major new stresses or changes in the patient's life, and if any first- or second-degree blood relatives (the latter including aunts and uncles, grandparents, and nephews and nieces) have suffered from bipolar disorder.

Before the appointment, it will help for you to write down some of the answers to these questions, and also make a list of all medications, vitamins, herbs, or other supplements being taken, and in what doses.

You're likely to be nervous during the appointment, so it will save time and avoid errors to do this in advance. You may want to make a written timeline to illustrate when your child's problems first appeared, including any events that may have triggered them.

Digital Care and Telepsychiatry

The COVID-19 pandemic gave a big boost to a trend, already underway, toward internet options for health care, including psychotherapy. Seemingly overnight, mental health providers got used to scheduling meetings with patients on Zoom or other platforms.

The pandemic also fueled rapid growth in services allowing patients to text with their therapists. Online counseling services such as Talkspace, which is covered by many major insurers, and BetterHelp are much cheaper than traditional in-person therapy. Still, the results of this trend have been mixed. On one hand, the advent of "telehealth" has helped address the shortage of providers by eliminating the need for patients to commute and giving them a much broader geographical choice. Some adolescents also feel less wary of meetings with therapists online, at least at the start.

Still, many mental health providers worry that the move to two-dimensional settings, and in particular to therapy by text, diminishes therapeutic relationships that would otherwise benefit from all the subtle nonverbal communication that goes on within the walls of an office. As a practical matter, therapists don't get a full view of their patients online, meaning they may easily miss visual clues to self-harm or abuse. What's more, many low-income families are up against the "digital divide," lacking adequate systems of WiFi and computers, or even a private, quiet room for a therapy session.

Despite these limitations, however, this trend isn't going away—just the opposite. So do some experimenting to see what suits you and your child the best. The best option may be a hybrid model, allowing your child to participate in person for the most important meetings. For psychotherapy, however, we recommend you opt for the in-person, personal relationship if possible.

"I had Megan meet with multiple therapists and make the decision herself," says Jeanne. "I let her pick who she felt she could connect with best, and of course it was a therapist who incorporates animal therapy with her therapy dog."

What Other Mental Health Services Are Available?

A variety of options for treatment fall along the continuum between occasional visits to a therapist or physician and crisis response, such as emergency hospitalization. The following are for those with at least some time to choose:

- *Residential treatment centers*—Facilities that provide round-the-clock supervision and care in a locked, dormlike setting. The treatment is less specialized and intensive than in a hospital, but the length of stay is often considerably longer.

- *Partial hospitalization or day treatment*—Outpatient services such as individual and group therapy, vocational training, parent counseling, and therapeutic recreational activities that are provided for at least four hours per day. The adolescent receives intensive services during the day but may go home at night. Some websites refer to these programs by their initials—IOP for intensive outpatient program, or PHP for partial hospitalization program. The difference in the two is mainly in the number of hours. An IOP might be three hours three times a week, often after school, for instance, while a PHP would be a full-time program, say from 9 a.m. to 3 p.m. If your child has a combination of problems, you may want to seek a "dual diagnosis program," which might, for example, simultaneously treat bipolar disorder and substance use disorder.

- *Home-based services*—Treatment is provided in the adolescent's home; for example, help with implementing a behavior therapy plan, medication management, or training for parents and adolescents on how to keep the illness from becoming a crisis. Providers include some state-funded programs and university health systems. The goal is to improve family coping skills and avert the need for more expensive services, such as hospitalization.

- *Respite care*—Child care provided by trained parents or mental health aides for a short period of time. The goal is to give families a much-needed breather from the strain of caring for an ill child, which may include a child with a serious mood disorder who is causing extreme stress in the family. It sounds pretty good, but alas, it is hard to come by. Some families report finding respite support through Medicaid, but the policy varies from state to state and usually comes with strict limits.

- *Mentoring programs*—For several years, a program called Vive, headquartered in Boulder, Colorado, offered a hybrid therapeutic program which would assign a trained mentor to a struggling child and a therapist to coach the parents. The organization has since changed its mission, but the idea was inspired, so if you hear of any copycats, it's worth a try. Simply finding a young adult, perhaps an energetic college student, to spend time with your child can be a great form of respite care! Look for mentoring programs and programs for kids at risk offered by your local community center.

Once again, your child's doctor or your managed care program may be the best source of information about these sorts of services. If that fails, however, try seeking accredited programs on the internet—you might google the name of your county and a phrase like "teen mental health." (In this case, don't be deterred by those .com suffixes, because you are looking for services to buy.) You can also ask other parents, your child's school counselor, your own doctor, a clergyperson, social service agencies, or the mental health division of your local health department.

What Is a "System of Care"?

For adolescents with severe mental illness, it's especially help-ful to combine standard treatment with other types of sup-port. This is known as a "system of care"—a collaborative network of mental health and social services. Since mental ill-ness touches every facet of a young person's life, the best treat-ment may indeed require many kinds of services from a variety of sources, including the child's school.

Ideally, you'll be able to coordinate a team working in and out of school to plan and implement a set of services tailored to your adolescent's emotional, physical, educational, and social needs. Depending on the situation, team members might include the family doctor, a psychiatrist, a school psychologist, vocational counseling, substance-misuse counseling, perhaps a sports coach, and if you're truly unfortunate, a probation officer. But the key word here is "ideally."

Regrettably such teamwork is the happy exception rather than the rule. More likely you'll be enlisting helpers one by one.

After Sandy's daughter Claire was hospitalized for bipo-lar disorder, Sandy organized a system of care that was waiting for her daughter on her release. "She attends individual therapy two times a week and we have fam-ily therapy once a week," Sandy says. "She also attends the partial hospitalization program from the facility she was in patient with and will probably end up doing their intensive outpatient program (IOP) as well. I'm looking into longer-term group therapy for teens after her IOP is finished because I feel like she needs the support of peers who can relate. She even attended her first yoga class in a real studio last week and loved it."

What Is Collaborative Care?

A growing use of collaborative, or "integrated," practices throughout the United States aims to compensate for the shortage of child and adolescent psychiatrists and to ensure that adolescents receive care as early as possible in the course of their illness. This model allows psychiatrists to leverage their time by consulting with others with less specialized experience. (In some cases, psychotherapists will work in the same offices as primary care doctors.) The psychiatrists, who may have offices far from the patients' homes, work mainly as consultants with specially trained nurse practitioners, seeing patients directly only when absolutely needed.

Mental Health Care Isn't Cheap

- Approximate cost of a single outpatient therapy session, in most parts of the United States: $100–$200
- Average cost of inpatient care for youths who need psychiatric hospitalization: $7,593 for 9.4 days for bipolar disorder
- Approximate cost of 1 year at a wilderness program: $513/day, with an average cost of $250,000
- Percentage of US health plans in 2013 that included coverage for mental health treatment: 61

What Should You Know About Health Insurance?

For many parents, one of the greatest challenges in helping a struggling child will be figuring out how to pay for it. Millions of Americans lack any insurance coverage, much less for mental health services. Many of those who do often find out sooner or later that their coverage is inadequate.

"Mental health services and medication just aren't financially accessible for majority of people," says Sandy. "We pay cash for the therapist and I submit the claim to my insurance company and they say thank you and then I never hear anything more. We all need to be talking about this more so we as a society can deal with it."

The great majority of Americans who have insurance at this writing receive it through a managed care plan, such as those run by Kaiser Permanente, the largest US operation, or Blue Cross or Anthem. We describe how this works in more detail below, but the key point is that most of these firms seek to lower costs by having patients get care from doctors with whom they contract to belong to their "networks." They also impose restrictions on mental health benefits, such as limiting the number of outpatient sessions or inpatient days that are covered. In addition, private insurance rarely if ever covers the full spectrum of community- and home-based services that adolescents with bipolar disorder may need to continue living at home. Not to mention a concerning assortment of ancillary costs.

Paula, whose Eagle Scout son landed in jail after a manic shoplifting spree, calculates she spent more than $12,000 that year, beginning with two emergency-department visits after she found him cutting himself and ending with $7,500 in lawyer's fees. "That doesn't include the four lost vacation days I had to use to take care of him, and we haven't yet started to pay for an outpatient hospitalization program," she says.

There have been at least some improvements in mental health care affordability since 2010, with the enactment of the Affordable Care Act (aka the ACA, or "Obamacare"). The ACA made health insurance available to more than 18 million Americans who didn't previously have it. It also expanded many states' Medicaid budgets—although some states refused to take the money—and provided families with incomes below 400% of the federal poverty level with tax credits to reduce their health costs. The ACA has also required insurance plans to cover people with preexisting health conditions and allowed young adults to stay on their parents' plans until age 26.

If you don't already have insurance, or aren't covered through Medicare, Medicaid, or the Children's Health Insurance Program (CHIP), which we'll describe in more detail below, you can sign up for a plan during a period of time once a year—usually starting in November—at www.healthcare.gov. There, you may choose among a "marketplace" of health insurance options, which will vary according to your state's policies. What you pay for insurance through the marketplace will depend on your income. You can reach on-call, free advisors with questions about health insurance at https://www.healthsherpa.com/.

What Is Parity?

A major goal of the ACA is to ensure "parity" for mental health services. Health advocates and lawmakers have sought this for many years. Parity means that mental health and substance-misuse benefits can't be more restrictive than for other medical conditions. In other words, deductibles, copayments, and out-of-pocket limits for mental health care *should* be equal to those pertaining to other types of care. This provision, plus prior guarantees in the 2008 Mental Health Parity and Addiction Equity Act, has indeed led to many more people getting mental health care at reduced costs. But they certainly haven't solved the problem. A big problem is that the law is complex, and many patients don't know how to defend themselves against violations (see below).

Researchers have found that disparities between the two types of care have continued in recent years and even widened in some cases, in part due to noncompliance by some insurance plans. Another glaring issue is that with so many mental health professionals not accepting insurance, patients are often more likely to have to go outside their managed care network and pay more.

Call Their Bluffs

Here are some signs that your health insurance plan may be trying to cut costs at the expense of your family's mental health:

- *"Fail-first" policies.* A health plan may use a "fail-first" policy, denying behavioral health treatment, such as hospital care, because the health plan member hasn't tried and failed at a lower level of care (e.g., outpatient care). This may be illegal if it doesn't have a similar policy for medical care.
- *Limits on the quantity or frequency of outpatient treatment.* Some health plans cap the number of outpatient behavioral health visits allowed each year, without similarly limiting outpatient medical visits. The plan may also limit behavioral health visits to once a week or every other week without similar provisions for medical visits.

- *More restrictive prior authorization policies for behavioral health.* Many health plans require prior authorization for nonemergency inpatient hospital services, both medical and behavioral health. Yet they may have different lengths of time allowed, for instance just one day for behavioral health versus a week for medical care.

(Excerpted from a handout prepared by Health Law Advocates, a national nonprofit organization)

You can read the full handout, including advice for how to help enforce the laws, in the Resources section. Patients who suspect violations should contact their state's insurance commissioner's office. If the plan is through a large employer, you can submit a complaint directly to the federal Employee Benefit Security Administration (EBSA), reachable online at www.askebsa.dol.gov. If the plan is a Medicaid Managed Care plan, your state Office of Medicaid is responsible for enforcing the parity laws.

Remember, you have the right to appeal any denied claim. Ask your doctor for support with this if necessary.

Watch Out for "Carve-Outs"!

Make sure when you choose a health insurance plan to ask about mental health "carve-outs." This is a sneaky way that some insurance companies have used to try to cut expenses. You may assume, for instance, that if you sign up for Blue Shield, you will have access to Blue Shield mental health services, only to find out, after you submit your claim, that you don't! As of 2012, Blue Shield carved out mental health services to another company, Magellan, which paid less to providers. As a consumer, you will need to ask lots of questions each time you pick a mental health provider to make sure they are covered by your network.

Health insurance is complicated. You can find out more information and ask questions of on-call advisers on a federal government site, https://www.healthsherpa.com/. Meanwhile, keep three rules in mind. First: Don't risk going without insurance, because you could be in for some sky-high expenses. Second: Be aware that you can now keep your child covered through early adulthood. Third: If you have a choice, compare available plans, looking closely at coverage for mental health services.

How Should You Choose a Managed Care Plan?

Managed care was designed to control health care costs, through a system in which insurers sign contracts with groups of providers who agree in advance to certain prices for diverse procedures. You can compare your options for a plan by typing your zip code on the HealthSherpa site noted above. (You can also call: 872-228-2549.) The tool will also let you know if you are eligible for subsidies. Some states offer Medicaid Managed Care plans.

There are several different types of plans, including the following:

- *Health maintenance organizations* (HMOs)—requiring you to sign up with a primary care doctor and use other health care providers who work for the HMO's network. You will usually need a referral from your primary doctor for mental health services.
- *Preferred provider organizations* (PPOs)—allowing you to choose from a network of providers who have contracts

with the PPO but also providing some benefits if you choose an outside provider. With this plan, you're less likely to need a referral from your primary care doctor to get access to a mental health care provider. If you go outside the network, you'll have to pay more. This plan also has higher monthly premiums.

- *Exclusive provider organizations* (EPOs)—requiring you to receive all your nonemergency services (if you want them covered) with doctors, specialists, or hospitals in the plan's network. This is the most restrictive but least expensive plan, with the least coverage of out-of-network providers.
- *Point of service (POS) plans*—allowing a choice of providers outside the HMO organization or PPO network. Higher copayments and deductibles are the downside.

If you have a choice among several managed care plans, be sure to compare the benefit packages. Check for clauses that restrict covered services, such as caps on the number of outpatient visits allowed per year or exclusions of certain medications from the approved drug list. If you already have a favorite doctor or therapist, check whether that person is in the provider network. Otherwise, look for the most comprehensive network, including some providers located near your home. Finally, consider the copayments and deductibles you'll have to pay. And try to get a feel for the administrative hassles you'll face once you try to access care. Note: You can cancel and change your managed care plan at any time.

"Two years into our crisis, I realized I didn't have the right insurance," says Sandy. "I needed the most expensive premium because the deductible was then much lower." Sandy had been using Kaiser Permanente and paying out of pocket for a therapist outside of that network. "I knew I had to change once it was clear this wasn't something short-term," she says. "I switched to Cigna and was able to work with a mental health care coordinator from a local hospital who found providers who took my insurance and were right for my daughter."

Ghosted

Many a beleaguered parent has been haunted by "ghost networks." That's when an insurance company offers you a list of supposedly living and breathing psychiatrists who either don't return your calls or are no longer taking new patients or have stopped taking insurance. If this is the case, and you've made a reasonable effort to try their list, you can often apply for a "single-case agreement," in which your insurance plan covers an out-of-network provider for the same cost to you as if it were in-network. If your child is a new patient, you can make a case for a single-case agreement if you can't find an in-network provider near your home, if the treatment provided will reduce the cost of medications or keep your child out of the hospital, or if your child needs a certain type of therapy not offered by the network providers. Just make sure you apply for this *before* starting treatment. One more tip: If you find the claim process overwhelming, there's help online. Check out sites like Reimbursify, which can help with the process, sometimes for a small fee.

Key Takeaways for Managed Care

- Familiarize yourself with the plan's provisions—in particular the cost of premiums, deductibles, and copays.

- Get to know your primary care provider as soon as possible.
- Work out a plan for services for your child.
- Figure out in advance whom to call and where to go in an emergency.
- Get any required preauthorization for nonemergency services.
- Learn about the procedure for appealing a treatment denial.
- Be sure to provide positive feedback when things go smoothly.

How Can You Influence Managed Care Decisions?

One of the main cost-cutting tools used by managed care plans is the "utilization review," a formal review of health care services to determine whether payment for them should be authorized or denied. In making this determination, the managed care company considers two factors: whether the services are covered under your health insurance plan and whether the services meet the standard for "medical necessity." Most treatment denials are based on the medical necessity provision. This is a situation in which your health insurance plan covers the services a doctor or therapist recommends, but the managed care company decides not to pay for them because they aren't deemed medically necessary.

Sue's health plan initially authorized an emergency hospitalization for her son at the closest available facility, even though it wasn't in the plan's care network. The next morning, however, "they wanted us to move him, despite his fragile state," Sue recalls. "He was catatonic. I fought with the insurance company, and I was finally told he could stay." A few weeks later, though, Sue was surprised to receive a large bill. Despite what the representative had told her on the phone, the health plan had denied coverage for part of her son's hospitalization, claiming it wasn't medically necessary for him to remain in that facility.

Managed care companies that use a utilization review are required to let customers appeal a denial of service. If you file an appeal, enlist the help of the health care provider who recommended the treatment. If you're seeking preapproval for emergency services, an expedited appeals process should be available. But if it's after the fact or the situation isn't an emergency, getting a decision may take some time. It took Sue more than three months to appeal her health plan's decision, but she ultimately won coverage of her son's entire hospital stay.

If your first appeal is denied, ask your plan to provide written notification of the reasons and to tell you what information is needed for the treatment to be approved. You can always appeal again. Most managed care companies have three or four levels of appeal, each involving a different set of people.

Help is available if you encounter problems at any point in the appeals process. If you're getting your insurance through work, your company's human resources department may be able to assist. For Medicaid issues, your state may have an ombudsman, whose job it is to try to resolve consumer complaints. Local mental health organizations may also provide helpful advice. If you exhaust your appeals without success, the managed care company and your provider should agree on an acceptable alternative to the treatment originally requested.

Although it may seem daunting, many parents learn to become effective in battling bureaucracies on behalf of their children.

"You have to become a pit bull to advocate for your child," is how Sandy sums it up. What that means, she says, is "understanding that when a roadblock is put up, you have to figure out a way around it or through it to get what your kid needs. It means not taking the first answer thrown your way as it often comes from people who don't know and understand your kiddo and the challenges. It means not allowing people to shame you or blame you."

Some parents, started out just as lost and discouraged as you may now be feeling, yet eventually found their way through the managed care maze:

"You'd be surprised what they'll cover if you really push," says Bob. "Right now, I'm in a battle with the insurance company about one of the meds our psychiatrist prescribed that they don't want to cover. That's when I get busy. I go out and research it. Sometimes, I write the letters that my doctor signs."

What Financial Help Is Available?

Many parents are unaware that *public schools* will sometimes foot the bill for some services for children in need, as part of an individualized education program (IEP), something we'll explain in depth in Chapter 7. Typically the services are limited to diagnosis and evaluation, but sometimes go beyond that to include counseling and other interventions.

This could be one of those cases where if you don't ask, you don't get, so make sure to ask. You may be in for a nice surprise.

Many *clinicians*, when paid out of pocket, may cut you some slack. Ask if they have sliding scales.

Federally qualified health centers are community-based providers that receive federal funds to provide care to underserved groups, such as migrants, homeless, and public-housing residents. They aren't allowed to turn anyone away, and you don't have to have insurance. You can find these clinics in your area by looking online.

Medicaid, paid for by a combination of federal and state funds, is by far the biggest US payer for community- and home-based health services of all kinds. Medicaid provides care to more than 72 million Americans who live in poverty. It is supplemented by CHIP, which delivers coverage for children whose families have a slightly higher income level. CHIP will pay for routine checkups, immunizations, doctor visits, prescriptions, dental and vision care, emergency services, X-rays, and more. (Each state has its own rules about who qualifies, but in most states, children in a family of four earning up to $50,000 a year will be eligible.) If you apply for Medicaid coverage in your state, you'll find out if your children qualify for CHIP. You can apply for and enroll in Medicaid and CHIP at any time of the year. Most of the care is free, but there may be some copayments or monthly premiums for coverage. This also varies in each state, but by law can't be more than 5% of your family's income.

If you have private insurance and your child has a chronic condition, you may be able to have Medicaid as a secondary insurance—potentially a huge advantage. In this case, your primary policy will pick up normal costs while the Medicaid plan covers copays, and sometimes also the deductible, minimizing your out-of-pocket costs.

Some Medicaid recipients say the system has had the advantage of protecting them from the scarcity of private adolescent psychiatrists.

"I've found it a lot easier to glean services through public assistance as the doctors are already in place at public family service organizations," says Mary, a mother and graduate student in San Jose. "It's true they're not always top-notch. We had problems with two who prescribed drugs that were totally wrong for my son. But I have to admit I feel a little better about it all after hearing all the stories of how other parents struggle with trying to find a psychiatrist within their private health plans."

Unfortunately, many middle-class families aren't eligible for Medicaid and CHIP. These families find themselves in a classic double bind: They don't make enough money to pay for costly mental health services out of pocket, but they make too much to qualify for government programs.

The "Katie Beckett" option offers one small ray of hope for such parents. The law, adopted in some form by 24 states and the District of Columbia, is part of the Tax Equity and Fiscal Responsibility Act of 1982 (TEFRA) and named after a woman in Iowa who as a child suffered major respiratory issues. (Beckett died in 2012 at the age of 34.) It requires adopting states to pay for extensive care for children under the age of 19 who have complex medical needs or long-term disabilities, who are living at home, and might otherwise have to be institutionalized. Eligibility is based on the child's income and assets, with no regard for the parents' status, and states cannot limit the number of participants. The downside is that the laws are confusing and vary according to state, so if this is of interest, it might be worth consulting with an attorney.

Other encouraging news comes from Colorado, where state legislators recently decided to improve adolescent mental health care after a slew of school shootings. Colorado had ranked 48th among US states in terms of high prevalence of mental illness but low access to care in a major national report. But in 2018, a new law doubled the state's youth mental health budget. Proponents of the law said it would help families stay together, with children receiving services at home instead of institutions.

> "It's called the Colorado Youth Mental Health Treatment Act, and I thank heaven for it," says the mother of a suicidal teenager in the Denver area who was able to have a family therapist come to their home in the wake of a crisis. "It pays for more services that my insurance ever would have done."

If you've got a job, look into whether your company offers discounted or free mental health benefits via an employee assistance program. Also take advantage of any family leave your workplace offers for family medical issues. The federal Family and Medical Leave Act guarantees that eligible employees are covered for up to 12 weeks of unpaid leave in a 12-month period (during which the employer must keep the job open) for several reasons, including to care for a spouse, child, or parent with a serious health condition. All government workers and grade-school teachers are covered by this law, as are most private employers with at least 50 employees. Those who've accumulated a bank of sick leave days can often use those, with no loss of income.

If finding treatment for your child sounds hit or miss, it is. Some savvy parents learn to work the system. But it takes time, energy, and a high tolerance for frustration. Not surprisingly, many parents say that financial concerns are among the most stressful aspects of raising an adolescent with bipolar disorder. It's not just the bills. Some parents find they can't keep their jobs due to all the time they're spending, supervising and finding treatment for a child at risk. Some intentionally let their careers slide so that they can qualify for low-income programs. Still others with good jobs and above-average benefits nevertheless find themselves in an exhausting, never-ending struggle to make ends meet.

As one mother, whose husband is a successful consulting engineer, says: "It doesn't matter how hard he works or how much money he makes. There's never enough. We haven't gone on a real vacation in four years. We don't have money to go out or fix up our house. Every penny goes to taking care of the kids, and it's still not enough."

Amid all the alarms about our mental illness epidemic, the federal government and many state agencies are trying to find better options. We'll tell you about some of them in the Conclusion. For now, however, you may need to keep fighting with your insurance plan and managed care system to pay for the treatments your child needs, without letting all that stress interfere with life at home.

Chapter Five

Helping at Home

"Sally's mania was not only an assault on her but on the entire household," recalls her father, Michael Greenberg. "It was a struggle. There was no magic bullet. We structured our lives around her illness."

B y now you may have found your son or daughter medical treatment and psychotherapy. Bravo! These are major, important achievements. To give your child the best hope of continued mental health, there's a lot more that you can do right at home, every day.

You may be wondering how much difference you can make, given that some experts insist that genes and peers will always trump a parent's power. And indeed, you can't do much about the biology and twists of fate affecting your child's mental health. Yet you can still have enormous influence. You do so with the behavior you model, the warmth of your relationship, where you live—if you can choose—and the serenity and structure you provide in your home.

Threats and Defenses

Researchers have found several potential contributors to the course of bipolar disorder and several factors that may help defend against it. These are also known as "risk factors" and "protective factors." Genes are the single *certain* risk factor for this illness, and they're not something you can change. Yet an otherwise healthy balance of risk to protective factors may help reduce the number and severity of manic and depressive episodes. The chart below lists a few among many of these threats and defenses. Notice which ones you can and can't influence.

Risk Factors

- Genes: a family history of bipolar disorder
- Trauma: such as a death, accident, or loss; or physical, sexual, or emotional misuse, including being bullied
- Conflict: turmoil with family or friends
- Poverty
- Harmful use of drugs or alcohol by the parents or child
- Stressful life events, including transitions such as moving or graduating
- Other problems, including medical disorders, sleep issues, anxiety, attention-deficit/hyperactivity disorder (ADHD), and/or learning differences

Protective Factors

- Supportive family relationships
- A sense of physical and emotional safety
- Predictable home life with structure and rules
- Parental warmth and strong attachment
- Healthy habits, including sleep, diet, and exercise

- Connections to community, including supportive adults outside the family
- Optimism
- Success at school

Development of Skills

The bottom line is that while medication and psychotherapy can often help a lot, there is much more you can do to support your child at home. You might think of these measures as a toolkit that you help assemble, with four main priorities for the kinds of tools you'll need. To make them memorable, we're using the acronym PSPS for a note you can write to yourself. It stands for Peace, Sleep (and nutrition), Predictability, and Strength. Making progress on these four fronts can do a lot to get your child and your family on the right track.

Peace

"I screamed at Alex and ran into the bathroom," writes Paul Raeburn, in his memoir. "Desperately fighting the urge to hit him, I grabbed him by the shoulders, pushed him back toward the toilet, and shoved him down onto the seat. The toilet bowl cracked, and a jet of water shot across the bathroom floor."

Berating himself as a "failed, inept parent," Raeburn describes in excruciating detail his shouting matches with his wife, whom he later divorced, his long absences from home, and how the couple failed to find the right help for their kids. None of that chaos caused his children's mood disorders. Yet some evidence suggests it made them worse. Chronic stress, as we've explained, can harm the brain, contributing to depression. It can also cause trauma that prevents children from forming trustworthy relationships.

That's why you may need to work to keep things calm at home. We realize this is no small task. Living with someone in the grips of bipolar disorder can challenge anyone's peace of mind. Families can get trapped in a vicious cycle, in which an irritable, demanding, uncooperative child provokes conflict, which in turn aggravates the child's bad behavior. Many parents say they've come to feel like hostages in their own homes.

Getting appropriate treatment for the child's bipolar disorder can help break the cycle of conflict but may not suffice. Given the strong hereditary nature of this illness, sometimes other family members or even the whole family will need therapy. What's more, if you are locked in irrevocable marital conflict, if your spouse is abusive to any of your kids, or if a sibling is posing a clear and present danger to others, you've got some hard choices to make. Don't hesitate to get the help you need, even if you must lean on relatives or friends or even call in the authorities. Plenty of families have had to take these steps, and it's obviously better to weather some shame than to have anyone injured, emotionally or physically.

We especially urge you to avoid the temptation to physically punish your child, no matter how frustrated or scared you may be. Maybe your own parents spanked you, or their parents spanked them, but in the past few decades, overwhelming evidence has shown that corporal punishment causes more problems than it cures. Not only will physically hurting your child fail to teach good behavior, you can all but guarantee that the behavior will worsen over time. Many parents have found that getting therapy or coaching can help them find alternatives.

Do's and Don'ts of Coping With Conflict

Do . . .

- Wait until you've both cooled off to talk it over. State the problem and explain your perspective calmly.
- Ask your child to share his or her thoughts and give them careful consideration.
- Use humor to defuse a tense situation, if possible. Just make sure it isn't an angry or sarcastic remark disguised as a "joke."
- Seek a compromise, if possible. When you need to assert your authority, be calm but firm.
- Apologize when you know you were wrong.
- Use "I" statements to avoid placing all of the blame on the adolescent, since that can lead to standoffs. Rather than say: "You always come home late," try: "I noticed that you came home later that we agreed on, and I get very upset when that happens."

Don't . . .

- Let your child hijack your emotions. If you find yourself getting angry, take some deep breaths; count to 10 or excuse yourself for a couple of minutes to calm down. You might also call a friend, divide and conquer with your partner, or seek help from family and friends.
- Take things personally or expect an adolescent in the grips of mania to be receptive to reasoning. Your child is flooded with emotions that will likely prevent a rational response in that moment.
- Hold a grudge or let angry outbursts become a habit in your family. If conflict has become a frequent or severe problem, consider family therapy.

Choose Your Battles

Young people with bipolar disorder can fly into rages that can last for hours and seem like—and feel like—life-or-death struggles. Adrenaline surges; the fight-or-flight instincts kick in, and the mood can be contagious.

Trying to reason at a time like this will be useless. Even more useless will be trying to fight back. Your child doesn't care if he or she is making sense, and the fury will only escalate.

> "What I think of when I imagine ever going through this again is that I wish I'd come up with a 'safe word,'" says Charlotte Stevenson, a teacher with bipolar disorder whose son has the same diagnosis. "There are times when you as a parent start to feel unsafe. Like this or that behavior might erupt into violence or cruelty or total disrespect. But the child should also be able to use the word, if he or she feels like you're berating them."

Choose your battles. You should certainly have some hard-and-fast rules, such as no hitting a sibling. But this is not time to sweat the small stuff. Minor transgressions, such as sneaking in an extra half-hour of video games, are often best ignored.

Explanation or Excuse?

Is your child truly capable of better, less vexing behavior? Is he or she manipulating you, or is the illness getting in the way? These are some of the most challenging questions for parents of kids with bipolar disorder. No one wants to overindulge their child, or to be overly permissive, but nor should you punish disobedience that's unintentional.

There are no easy answers, but it's worth considering that your child's brain chemistry may be driving the behavior. Recall that some of the most effective medications to treat this illness are also used to control epileptic seizures, raising the question of whether bipolar rage is a related phenomenon.

It may also help to imagine what your child's day was like, perhaps including teasing, rejection, and failure at school. Sometimes a parent's tough talk is needed; at other times it just makes things worse.

The Buddhist teacher and clinical psychologist Tara Brach has coined an acronym that may be helpful for you in dealing with all the difficult emotions your child may evoke. It's called "RAIN," for:

Recognize what is happening;
Allow the experience to be there, just as it is;
Investigate with interest and care;
Nurture with self-compassion.

Give yourself the calm mental space to be curious about the motives for your child's behavior before you react.

Sleep and Diet

Key to preserving the peace in your home will be to help your child get sufficient sleep. Studies of adults and adolescents with bipolar disorder show that regularizing daily routines and sleep schedules can help keep moods on an even keel.

Sleep is paramount for anyone's physical and mental health yet is often undermined by mental illness. Kids with bipolar disorder may stay up all night on a manic high that lasts for days, seemingly without need of rest. (About 40% of children with bipolar disorder experience this symptom of mania.) Perversely, sleep deprivation can *trigger* mania.

We understand that your child's problems with sleep have probably already interfered with *your* sleep, especially as late-night emotional crises find their way past your bedroom door. (Think Bradley Cooper, as Pat in *Silver Linings Playbook*, storming into his parents' bedroom at 4 a.m. to complain about the ending of a book by Ernest Hemingway.)

> "I barely slept for a year while standing vigil over Sally, listening for any movement from her bed, when she would get up to smoke a cigarette, sit by a window wide awake, try to leave the apartment and walk about the city in the middle of the night," recalls Greenberg. "Pat and I were on constant trigger alert. It was a kind of hell."

Helping a child with depression sleep soundly through the night is easier said than done. Many parents never master it. Complicating everything is the biological changes that begin in puberty, when kids start falling asleep about two hours later and then naturally wanting to sleep later in the morning. This sets them—and you—up for a major predicament.

The American Academy of Sleep Medicine recommends that children ages 6 to 12 should sleep from 9 to 12 hours per day and that teenagers 13 to 18 sleep 8 to 10 hours. Yet a 2013 Centers for Disease Control and Prevention (CDC) study found that 68% of US high school students reported getting less than 8 hours of sleep on school nights. Your kid isn't just being stubborn. Part of the issue is that most adolescents' sleep patterns aren't in sync with their school schedules.

Both the American Academy of Pediatrics and the CDC recommend that middle and high schools start no earlier than 8:30 a.m. Unfortunately, at last count, more than 90% of US high schools and 83% of middle schools were ignoring that guidance.

Schools' unsupportive schedules lead to ongoing arguments between parents and kids—especially kids whose illness already makes them irritable. You may find yourself cajoling your wide-awake child to go to bed early and then, the next morning, urging your drowsy child to get out of bed for school.

If your child has a diagnosis, you may be able to arrange a later schedule at school as part of the accommodations we'll explain in Chapter 7. Short of that, we suggest you help your child understand the link between sleep and emotional well-being, emphasizing that getting good sleep is a personal responsibility over a lifetime. Try to keep daily charts of sleep habits and moods, preferably as a collaborative project. If you don't have time or energy for charts, consider keeping notes on your phone.

> "I wish I'd been more consistent about tracking my daughter's moods and symptoms early on," writes Dorothy O'Donnell. "Over the years, I've learned that recording things like sleep problems, changes in her energy level, and any new or unusual behavior provides valuable information for me, her treatment team, and school staff. Having a record of Sadie's moods also makes it easier for her psychiatrist to determine if a medication adjustment is necessary."

Goodnight, Mood

America is suffering a national epidemic of poor sleep, and adolescents are among the worst casualties. This goes double for adolescents with mood disorders.

"Multilevel interventions are needed," says Wendy Troxel, a senior scientist and sleep expert at the RAND Corp. Families, schools, and state and local governments should contribute to finding solutions.

Until our society gets smarter, here are some suggestions for how to improve your kids' sleep:

- Make sure first to get your child evaluated to see if any physical issue is interfering.
- Keep their bedrooms dark, cool, and quiet, with no computers or TVs. Insist that phones and laptops be used only in one central place in the home.
- Phones should be turned off and ideally handed to you one to two hours before bedtime.
- Buy a few old-fashioned alarm clocks rather than letting your kids use their phones.
- No alcohol before bedtime (and not before the legal drinking age of 21—they're adolescents!). Also, no caffeine or exercise within four hours of going to bed.
- Keep weekend bedtime hours within reasonable limits to avoid the "social jet lag" from waking early Monday after sleeping in on Sunday.
- Encourage your child to get plenty of exposure to natural light, ideally in the morning. Light cues the brain to kick-start our circadian rhythm. If that's not possible, try a sunlight lamp designed for people who suffer mood changes in the winter.
- For insomnia, try two of your grandmother's remedies: a hot bath 90 minutes before bed and a cup of cold or warm milk, which is rich in tryptophan, a sleep-inducing amino acid.
- Keep an eye on sleeplessness, which needs to be addressed right away. Good-quality sleep is essential to improving

your child's mood—so important that your child's doctor may recommend temporary sleep aids such as Benadryl, melatonin, or low-dose trazodone, which are milder than other sleep medications and are not addictive. Be wary of using other medications for your child's sleep, because many can be habit-forming, and be sure to keep your own medications safely secured.

Nutrition

There is growing evidence that the way we eat can support or subvert our mental health. In fact, dietary guidelines from the US Department of Agriculture and the US Department of Health and Human Services now recommend healthy diets to prevent depression. A 2020 review of research suggests that the so-called Mediterranean diet, as well as similar regimes that include lots of fruit, vegetables, whole grains, fish, olive oil, and low-fat dairy products, may indeed prevent depression, or at least slow its progression and help in its management. Other evidence suggests that omega-3 fatty acids, contained in fish and some plants, have positive effects on clinical depression, including in people with bipolar disorder, although they don't seem to help with mania. (See our suggestions on supplements in Chapter 3.) Further study is needed to determine the benefits for children and adolescents.

In contrast, the typical American diet, involving lots of red meat, processed food, sugar, potatoes, and high-fat butter and milk, has been associated with an increased *risk* of depression. A plausible explanation is that bad nutrition can cause chronic inflammation, a potential contributor to mood disorders. Not incidentally, the typical American diet also contributes to obesity, which itself is linked to depression.

Alas, still other research has found that adolescents with symptoms of bipolar disorder and depression are generally less eager to engage in healthy behavior, such as following a healthy diet. But that's where you come in. Throw out the junk food: Make sure to the extent you can that you have fresh fruit and other healthy foods around the house. If need be, pack lunches.

Weight Management

Obesity has become epidemic in the United States in recent decades, and the numbers continue to rise, including among youth. Since the 1970s, the percentage of children and adolescents affected by obesity has more than tripled. In 2017–2018, on average, an estimated 19.3% of US children and adolescents aged 2 to 19 years were obese. The numbers were alarmingly higher for racial minorities: more than 24% for Black children and nearly 26% for Latinos.

This is bad news for kids, both physically and mentally. Being overweight can lead to physical illnesses such as diabetes, sap self-esteem, and make kids targets for bullies. Obesity is also closely linked with major mental illness, including bipolar disorder. A 2021 longitudinal study following nearly 15,000 children found that children with a significant increase in body mass index (BMI) around puberty were four times more likely to become depressed by age 24.

There appears to be a chicken-and-egg relationship between being overweight and being depressed. One 2010 study found that obese people were at a 55% greater risk than others to become depressed during their lifetimes. At the same time, many depressed folk gain weight for reasons that can include low motivation to exercise and the side-effects of many medications, particularly those often used for bipolar disorder.

If this is a problem for your child, consider these suggestions:

- Ask your pediatrician whether your child's BMI is within the healthy range. Also ask for a check of your child's fasting insulin level, especially if you have a family history of diabetes. If either the BMI or insulin level is high, you need to strongly intervene.
- Be a good role model with what you eat and when. Many studies show that kids are influenced by their parents' behavior around food.
- Have lots of fresh produce and other healthy foods around, while limiting purchases of ice cream, soft drinks, candy, and processed snacks.
- Be careful how you talk about weight. Obviously avoid fat-shaming, nagging about diets, or ordering kids to eat every morsel on their plates.

Predictability

To best support your child's mental health, you'll want to make your home more safe, stable, warm, and emotionally supportive of all its members. We have several ideas for how to do this.

Safety First

You want your child to be happy, healthy, and successful in life. But in the short term you may feel you're doing all you can just to make sure that he or she survives another day. An adolescent brain develops rapidly, and within a few more years your child is almost sure to be less impulsive and more risk-averse. For now, however, you need to take precautions, especially considering that bipolar disorder can make young people extra reckless.

This is crucial: All parents, but especially parents of children with mood disorders, should keep any firearms in the home unloaded and under lock and key.

The American Foundation for Suicide Prevention (AFSP) recommends that the best way to help protect someone in distress is to "temporarily remove all lethal means, including firearms, from the home until the person is no longer in a state of crisis." It's illegal to store firearms in self-storage units, yet it's often possible to find local businesses and law enforcement agencies willing to take them temporarily. Students at Johns Hopkins University recently developed an online map of safe gun-storage facilities in Maryland. Options for storage vary by community and state, but they can be easily found by calling your local police department.

The odds of a young person dying by suicide are many times higher in homes where guns are present than in homes without guns. Of the nearly 2,400 children and adolescents aged 5 to 18 who died by suicide in the United States in 2018, 40% used a firearm. What's more, youth who use firearms for suicide tend to provide fewer warning signs leading up to their deaths than those who use other methods, implying that suicide by gunshot may often depend simply on access to a gun.

We assume that if you're reading this book you are an exceptionally responsible parent, so please forgive what may seem like a no-brainer reminder: Kids suffering from bipolar disorder should not have access to firearms—including for hunting or whatever other hobby may involve them. Later, maybe, but this isn't the right time.

Authoritarian Versus Authoritative

Abundant research confirms that the most effective parenting style to support mental health is neither the once-popular "authoritarian" (or dictatorial) method nor the recently appealing "permissive" (laissez-faire) one, but rather, a more nuanced, "authoritative" style, that is nurturing, warm, and flexible, but doesn't back down. (One of the best arguments for a warm parental style is research showing that children who grow up in poverty are two to three times more likely than others to develop mental health problems, but that a mother's emotional support can reduce those odds. The research did not look at fathers' support, but we assume it is also helpful.)

Authoritative parents set clear limits on behavior. They may listen to a child's viewpoint, but don't always accept it. Say a daughter is caught having shoplifted mascara. An authoritarian parent may yell or spank, while a "permissive" parent may accept the daughter's excuses. The authoritative parent will take time to explain why stealing is wrong and find a punishment that conveys a lesson, such as taking the girl to return the mascara and apologize to the store owner.

In the best-case scenario, you began setting clear rules and even assigning chores for your children long before they started questioning everything you say. The younger kids are when they first understand your expectations, the more likely they will rise to them. Still, firm limits are well worth setting and maintaining even with feisty adolescents.

Chamique Holdsclaw remembers the shock of moving from her parents' middle-class apartment in Queens to her grandmother's public-housing apartment—in the same borough, but a world away. "I had so much freedom when I was living with my parents that I'm glad nothing bad happened to me," she recalls, laughing. "At just 9 or 10 my friends and I knew the subway system like the back of our hands. But my grandmother's discipline and structure really hit hard. She never let me hang around outside, unless it was church or volunteer work. Although she did let me play on a basketball court that was right outside her window, so she could watch me." Holdsclaw soon learned how good it felt to get exercise, develop a skill, and join a team. The rest, of course, is history.

Many parents find it helps to write down the most important family rules and post them in a prominent place, such as taped on the refrigerator. Among other things, this holds you accountable for enforcing them. You may also want to draw up a behavior contract for your children to sign. This would specify both rules—such as evening curfew times and limits on screen time—and consequences for breaking them. Don't have too many rules, however—the more you have, the greater the risk they'll be broken—and try to focus more on positive reinforcement than punishment. Catching your child being good is a powerful motivator. The great psychologist William James said, "The deepest principle in human nature is the craving to be appreciated." Make the effort to find and remark on something your child is doing right—even little things like getting up on time or being nice to a sibling.

If you must dole out a punishment, make it fit the crime. If your child has found something he or she truly loves, such as going to the gym or spending time with a friend, you may be tempted to take that away in response to bad behavior. Find an alternative. If, as we assume, your overriding goal is helping your kid stay sane, the last thing you want to do is take away what may be his or her few sources of joy.

Communication 101

As a parent, what you say and how you say it can have a powerful effect. You have the opportunity not only to express your expectations for the family but also, ideally, to provide alternatives for the hostile language in your child's head.

The psychologist John Duffy, who writes advice books for raising teens, says parents should maintain an "emotional bank account": the savings of trust and warmth and happy memories that help you get through the most challenging times. If you're reading this book, we assume you already value your relationship with your child. Remember that your routine communication is the hard currency of that relationship. Pay attention to the ratio of positive to negative feedback you're delivering.

A Denial-Free Zone

While considering how you talk with your child, think also about how you talk to *yourself*. Many parents reasonably wish their children weren't suffering and that life could return to normal, ASAP. Supporting these hopes is the often-intermittent nature of the child's depression, with sometimes long periods when everything seems fine. But then comes the next emergency, leaving everyone surprised and unprepared, without a safety net. Far better to avoid wishful thinking and make a plan that you'll follow faithfully from the first evidence that there's a serious problem.

Once your child is diagnosed, be a model of forthrightness. Talk calmly but frankly about emotions, acknowledging them without nagging. One mother says that every few days she'll ask her 13-year-old son, "How's your mood?" It's been a helpful invitation not only for her child to talk about anything bothering him but to consider how moods are always changing and are separate from his permanent identity.

One of the best things a parent can do for a depressed child is to be open about his or her own emotional struggles. In the early 1980s, Harvard psychiatrist William Beardslee developed an intervention called "Family Talk," based on the understanding that a parent's depression is a major risk factor for depression in a child—particularly when it's kept a secret. In the formal program, a clinician meets with the family over several sessions to help improve the way the family communicates. But families can also try the approach informally by meeting together and talking frankly about depression as a biological illness that can be managed with insight and care. Small studies suggest "Family Talk" has long-lasting benefits for children.

Such honest conversations are not always easy. It's important to avoid oversharing. Some kids may be made more depressed by parents who suggest the kids should be taking care of *them*. It's especially risky if you're fighting with your partner and one or both of you craves support from the children. No matter what your situation is, you need to set clear boundaries, with no ambivalence about who is the child in the relationship. If you choose to open up, carefully consider the potential impact on your child. For example, it's best not to talk about any suicidal impulses you've had. A good basic script is: "I know it's hard to ask for help. There was a point in my life when I also needed help, but once I got it, it worked. As your mom (or dad), I want the same for you, and it's my job to help you get it."

Try not to let on how anxious you may be about your child's struggles, but don't hide or downplay the truth. Your adolescent already knows something is wrong, and if kept in the dark, he or she may decide the situation is bleaker than it is. By comparison, the truth can be reassuring. There's an illness, but it's eminently treatable.

A child's "taking ownership" of his or her own mental health and care is critically important as time goes on, although sometimes a parent needs help with the passing of the baton.

Sandy felt overwhelmed by guilt after discovering that her daughter Claire had been sexually assaulted by a relative several years earlier, a crime that Sandy had been helpless to prevent. Getting coaching in individual sessions with Claire's therapist helped her put the guilt aside so she could focus on helping her daughter get better. At one point, when she felt Claire was ready to hear it, she says she told her she wanted to see her participate more in her own therapy. "I can't do this for you, as much as I wish I could," she said.

The Art of Being Available

Most adolescents are starting to separate from their parents, sharing less of themselves and their feelings. For a child with bipolar disorder, shame and despair may increase that reluctance to confide. There's an art to letting them know, without hovering, that you'll be there when they need to talk, that you'll respect their privacy, take them seriously, and avoid judging them. Try not to give your anxiety the upper hand. Listen more than you talk, and don't always try to "fix" things. Three powerful words to remember are "Tell me more!"—but only when the time is right.

"My daughter's therapist told me there are times when it doesn't help to try to talk with her, when she and her depression are like this," says Sandy, putting one hand over another to illustrate inseparability. She then held both hands out, separately, adding, "You have to wait until it gets like *this*, when she has room to have more perspective."

Many parents say it's easiest to talk while driving somewhere together, since it doesn't entail eye contact. Put away the cellphone and turn down the music. For your ice breaker, avoid pat questions like "How was your day?" which may elicit little more than a grunt. Be strategic about mining positive emotions. If your kid likes working on computers, ask for technological advice. If he's merely watching TV or reading, ask what he likes about a favorite show or book.

A car in motion is often the best setting for sensitive topics such as drugs and alcohol, sex, or depression itself. You might broach the topic by asking what *other* kids at school are doing. If your child shares a mistake, make it clear that your love won't disappear even if you dislike the behavior.

To add to your family's emotional bank account, find pleasurable ways to spend time together, away from screens. Repeated studies have found that sharing family meals can reduce the risk of depression, particularly for girls. To be sure, it's not easy to maintain rituals when family members keep different schedules, and especially when a child with a mood disorder threatens to make each meal a disaster. Often you may feel you're plugging away without any sign of progress. But plug away you must; it's your best investment in a healthier future.

Being There When Your Child Is LGBTQ+

Times have changed—a lot. Not so long ago, kids of differing sexual identities stayed in the closet until long after they left home. Today, largely thanks to social media, they can find resources at a very young age to help them understand themselves and take courage in opening up to others. This is a change that could not have come too soon.

In 2018, a British study based on interviews with 4,800 youths found that lesbian, gay, and bisexual youth between the ages of 16 and 21 were four times more likely to have felt depressed, harmed themselves, and thought about suicide. The causes included bullying and stigma related to their sexuality.

"Both gender and sexuality have been constant points of confusion for me for at least two years now," says Andy. "I wear makeup nearly every day, wore a long flowing dress to homecoming, and paint my nails—all generally feminine things."

Other research has pointed out the obvious: Families' attitudes can have a huge impact on their LGBTQ+ or otherwise sexually nonconforming children's mental and physical health. LGBTQ+ youth from highly rejecting families are more than eight times more likely to try to take their lives as young adults. They are also nearly six times as likely to report being depressed and roughly three times as likely to take illegal drugs. You may feel uncomfortable and even disappointed to learn that your child is not cisgender. We strongly advise you to consider these statistics before you react. Even encouraging your child to keep his or her sexual identity a secret can be harmful. It may take some emotional work for you to accept this unexpected development, but think of it as an investment in your child's safety. Show them you still love them; advocate for them if they are mistreated and require other family members to show respect. Ideally, you'll also find a way to connect your child with an LGBTQ+ role model.

"I don't have any gripe with how either of them handles my being nonbinary, even though I know it's confusing for them," Andy says of his parents. "They'll probably always call me by the name they gave me and they'll always use he/him for me, but if I asked them I think they'd make a valid effort to change how they see me. My parents are both fairly progressive and accepting of changing social norms, and I love that about them."

"Break It Down"

The mood swings involved in bipolar disorder can sometimes cause problems with thinking and understanding. Emotional stress may make it hard for your son or daughter to process what you're saying. Pay attention to your expectations, which may be unrealistic.

> "When my daughter comes to me and I can see that she's spinning, overwhelmed, I always say 'Break it down,' or 'Just tell me one thing at a time,'" says Julie. "And when I talk to her, I have to remind *myself* to keep it simple. I've trained myself never to give compound instructions, like go to your room, get your binder, get back here, and start your history homework. Or at least not to get frustrated when she can't manage that."

Your child may be able to speak four languages and solve advanced calculus problems in his or her head, but until the symptoms subside, don't expect mature or even coherent reactions. Maybe getting tonight's homework done shouldn't be the priority. Maybe you'll need to muster extra patience with what might seem like the simplest of transitions, like getting ready for school.

> "Eventually, I let go of worrying about her grades and whether she'll get into a good college," writes Dorothy O'Donnell, about her daughter Sadie. "I try to focus on nurturing her many strengths instead, especially her abundant creativity. The more she taps into it, the better her odds of finding her own path to happiness and success. I catch glimpses of this happening when she sings in chorus; writes a compelling—if poorly punctuated— story about her imaginary adventures on Rat Rock Island,

or draws one of her trademark, vividly colored, saucer-eyed fairies; and increasingly, as she experiments with expressing herself through clothing. There's no doubt the compliments she receives for her stylish getups have boosted her self-esteem. She may never look forward to school, but entering her classroom with a head-turning outfit each morning makes it a little easier."

Problem-Solving

Short of trying to be your child's therapist, you can step in occasionally as a cognitive coach. Help your son or daughter understand that the first step toward solving a problem is to define it. Subsequently, you can brainstorm together about possible solutions, considering the pros and cons of each option, until your child is ready to choose.

Jane Gillham, a clinical psychologist at Swarthmore College, says parents can help their kids by expressing the way their own moods might influence their thinking, and even whether they sometimes "catastrophize." "When you catch yourself jumping to a conclusion, point it out," she suggests. "Then talk through the process of evaluating not only the worst-case scenario but also the best case and most likely case. Children often learn by imitating those they admire. By modeling the process of evaluating your own thinking, weighing the evidence, and correcting the inaccuracies, you can help them learn these essential skills."

If your son or daughter shares a thought that seems unrealistically pessimistic, you can gently make that clear. Let's say your child is talking about a temporary problem as if it will never end. You might say something like: "I know this is really hard right now, but let's think about how you've gotten through similar situations."

Talking—Or Not—to Others

If your child confides in you, be sensitive about how you use the information. There will be times when you need to reach out to others, including other parents, for advice or support, and there are also people, such as teachers, who have a legitimate reason to know what's going on in your child's life. But try to preserve trust. As with everything else, it's best to talk about this honestly. If your child strongly prefers that you not discuss the problems with a certain person—such as a family friend, a favorite aunt, or another sibling—ask yourself whether this other party really needs to be informed. If you do go ahead, do your best to make sure the person will keep the information confidential, and as a rule don't include any sensitive information in emails or texts that can be forwarded.

It Takes a Family

A big part of your work in creating a safe and predictable home is getting every member on board with that plan. Clearly, if your partner isn't in agreement about treatment plans and home rules, predictability flies out the window.

To stay on the same page, the two of you may need to do some work on your own relationship. Coping with the physical, emotional, and financial demands of raising a mentally ill adolescent could stress any couple. Although some relationships don't survive, others find that the challenge brings them closer, providing a sense of shared purpose. Couples who've endured credit their success to simple, familiar rules applicable to any well-functioning family. They say they prioritize their marriage, putting each other first and not allowing their children to play them off against each other. They are open about their differences but find ways to cooperate. They are self-aware enough to notice how they react to each other when reacting to their kids. And if needed—which it usually is when raising children with issues—they get couples' therapy.

"I started to see how the less emotional he got, the more I got," says Charlene, about her husband, Ted. "So pretty soon I became this huge ball of emotions."

Parenting without a partner involves a different set of issues. You may need to accept you need more help than you're getting. Don't be shy about leaning on extended family and close friends for emotional support and practical help. If they aren't available, you may want to try to find a mentor who can develop a lasting relationship with your child and give you a few free hours a day. Look into Big Brothers Big Sisters, the largest US mentoring nonprofit, or see if you can hire a local college student—perhaps someone studying psychology.

Siblings: The Good, Bad, and Ugly

The film *Silver Linings Playbook* includes a scene that unfortunately says it all about many sibling relationships. Pat has just returned from the hospital and is trying to improve his life, back home with his parents. His brother Jake stops by, and after apologizing for not having visited him, says:

"I don't even know what to say to you anymore. You lost your wife; I'm getting engaged, and I want to be able to talk to you about those kinds of things. You lost your house; I'm getting a new house. You lost your job; things are going great for me at the firm."

In the best of families, siblings compete for the limited resource of their parents' attention. They can genuinely love each other and still tally points. This is one of the most basic evolutionary instincts, a force much larger than any of our best intentions. But it will add an extra burden if one or more of your children is coping with bipolar disorder.

Brothers and sisters may bear the brunt of a sibling's angry and even violent behavior. They may mourn the loss of the close connection they once shared with that sibling and long for a more "normal" family life. Often they get lost in the commotion as parents labor through consecutive crises.

Once again, communication is key. As soon as younger children can understand you, explain in simple terms what your child with bipolar disorder is going through. Often a sibling will wrongly assume that his or her brother or sister can control the behavior.

"I've had many talks with my younger son about how he'd be a lot more empathetic if his brother was in a wheel-chair," says Beth. "To be honest, I don't think they've helped. My only hope is that years from now it may make sense, and maybe then they can have a relationship."

Everyone reacts differently. Some brothers and sisters of a sibling with bipolar disorder withdraw from family life. Some may throw themselves into schoolwork and extracur-ricular pursuits in hopes of staying out of the house as much as possible, or of simply establishing themselves as "normal." Some may develop their own emotional problems in a bid for attention.

Be alert to subtle provocative behavior by the better-behaving sibling toward the child with the mood disorder. This may influence your other child's way of getting your attention.

"My younger son would whisper insults like 'loser!' which at first I didn't hear, but which would always cause my older son to explode," says Beth. "This was his way of making sure that he could always look like the angel when his brother was the devil. Pretty soon I realized what was going on, and started handing out consequences when he did that."

Some siblings feel embarrassed by the behavior of an ill brother or sister. That was the case for one family in which a teenage brother and sister went to the same high school. The girl, who had bipolar disorder, became unruly during manic episodes.

"There were times when they had to restrain her at school," their mother recalls, "and the other kids would be saying, 'Look at your crazy sister.'" While her son was chagrinned, she says, he also felt protective of his sister, with whom he had been close when they were growing up.

When such mixed feelings arise, talk about them honestly. But do your best to resist the impulse to confide in one sibling about your own frustrations with another, as that decision is sure to backfire.

Few parents set out to neglect their children. Yet when you're feeling overburdened and exhausted, it's easy to take the path of least resistance. Unfortunately, allowing yourself to be swept along by events means you'll be pulled more toward the child with the problem and away from those who aren't as obviously demanding. It takes effort to notice and correct this tendency. Try to set aside some daily one-on-one time with each child. And avoid as much as possible having different rules for different children.

Strength

The Art of Bouncing Back

If you've read even one recent parenting book or attended a single recent meeting at your child's school, you've undoubtedly heard the modern buzzwords "resilience" and "grit." They're trendy for good reason. Both connote the vital ability to adapt to stressful life events and bounce back from adversity, each of which is key for a child coping with bipolar disorder. Optimism is a major ingredient of grit.

Everything we've already told you in this chapter about communication, problem-solving, and family cohesiveness can help create a more optimistic child. Some research suggests that mindfulness can also help, particularly when it is focused on developing a sense of gratitude. Just as a brain can get increasingly adept at depression, it can also train itself to be more positive. There are many ways to practice this art, from a meditation class to writing a letter of thanks to someone to confiding in a journal, to simply taking time each evening to name three things that went well. Don't wait for Thanksgiving to roll around, in other words. Without trying to force a change of feelings or deny the reality of an illness, find ways to talk about gratitude with your kids.

"I Can Do It!"

"Self-efficacy" is the formal term for people's faith in their ability to perform well in a particular situation. People with high self-efficacy believe they can achieve desired results through their own efforts. The concept is closely linked to optimism, and it has been associated with a decreased risk of depression in young people. There is a lot you can do to help build self-efficacy in adolescents. Get to know their strengths and weaknesses, and what motivates them, whether it's social, creative, academic, athletic, or altruistic. Give them honest (but not overcritical) feedback. Provide as many opportunities as you can for them to explore new pursuits and sharpen skills. (You can often find inexpensive classes at your local community center.) Look for challenges that aren't overwhelmingly hard but that still reward effort. A part-time job can go far in that direction, with rewards in the monthly paycheck.

This may involve a little pushing and cajoling, at least at first. There's nothing like depression to sap motivation to try new things. Yet that first step out can often be enough of a reward to keep going. That's why what's known as "behavioral activation"—getting someone to take that first hard step—is considered a therapy all by itself. It may take the entire family to participate, at least initially, to fight the inertia. If during the weekend you notice your family staring at screens, it's time to pull everyone away for a walk, board games, or simply a good conversation.

Kelly Lambert, a neuroscientist at the University of Richmond in Virginia, studies the rodent equivalent of optimism. In one of her experiments, she observed two groups of rats: one that had to dig in the dirt to find tasty Froot Loops ("worker rats") and another that was simply given them ("trust-fund rats"). Subsequently, Lambert presented both groups with a problem-solving challenge: a little ball with a Froot Loop inside it. The worker rats worked harder and longer to get at the Froot Loop, a result Lambert calls "learned persistence."

Lambert is such an advocate of this approach to combat depression that she has coined the term "behaviorceuticals" to convey the idea that some behaviors may be as powerful as pharmaceuticals. "Physical exercise is great but seeing a direct result of our effort when we engage in certain tasks or hobbies can build both emotional resilience and self-efficacy," she says, adding: "The worker rats have healthier stress hormone profiles, a characteristic that protects against the emergence of depressive symptoms. These effort-based rewards likely served as our ancestors' 'prehistoric Prozac'—keeping them foraging and hunting for that next dose of mood-boosting neurochemicals."

Of course, there are all kinds of differences between humans and rodents! But the basic structures and chemical workings of our brains are surprisingly similar, which is why scientists so often pick rats and mice as stand-ins.

Think Bigger

Another potential countervailing force to depression that your own mother may have mentioned is to think more about other people. This isn't something we'd encourage you to suggest in the middle of an episode of mania or depression. But it's certainly worth cultivating. Researchers have found strong links between altruistic behavior and emotional health. A 2021 study of brain scans of 72 adults who were genetically at high risk for depression suggested altruistic feelings protect against severe depressive symptoms. Maybe your child can begin by caring for a pet dog or cat. It's fine to start small, and many parents have told us that introducing a four-legged friend was one of their best moves. Additionally, churches and synagogues often organize volunteer programs you can participate in as a family.

"I was so lucky that one of my son's high school teachers insisted the kids complete a number of hours in a local volunteer program," says Beth. "The sad truth is I probably wouldn't have been able to convince him myself. But because he needed to pass that class, he got involved in a project that helped teach kids in low-income neighborhoods about nutrition and exercise, and he not only enjoyed helping them, but got more interested in taking care of himself."

Exercise and the Great Outdoors

We're guessing you've already heard about the mood-lifting benefits of simple exercise. The research that supports this is abundant and increasing. Harvard psychiatrist John Ratey, author of *Spark: The Revolutionary New Science of Exercise and the Brain*, compares exercise to a medicine cabinet full of natural stimulants and mood boosters, including the feel-good neurotransmitter serotonin and endorphins, the endogenous opioid hormones that relieve pain and anxiety. That's on top of the other physical benefits of getting moving, such as helping you stay in shape—boosting self-esteem—and improving sleep. For some depressed people, regular exercise works as well as antidepressants, although it's probably not enough for someone whose illness is severe.

> "As someone who knows how important regular exercise is in managing my own anxiety and overall mental health, I always tried to make sure that Sadie got a lot of it," says Dorothy O'Donnell. "And she always knew it was good for her. In fact, when she was hypomanic or having a mixed state episode, she would tell me she had to move because she felt like she was going to jump out of her skin. Either we needed to go for a long walk or hike, go to the park or when she got a bit older, go for a run."

Scientists have found that regular physical exercise even helps improve nerve cell growth in the hippocampus, where depressed people tend to have deficits. Again, your adolescent may resist getting started, but once in a groove may be delighted with how much better he or she starts to feel. Talk up the benefits of an after-school sports program. If you can afford it, buy a monthly gym membership. Or just start taking walks together.

Increasing evidence suggests you'll get extra benefits by getting outside. A 2014 study found that merely living in neighborhoods with higher levels of green space was linked with significantly lower levels of depression, anxiety, and stress. If you don't have the resources to live in such a neighborhood, try to find ways to spend time in parks or on trails.

Don't Forget the Love

It's vitally important to remember that however horribly your adolescent may be behaving amid emotional turmoil, you remain at the center of his or her world.

The author Toni Morrison gives this advice: When your child walks into the room, your eyes should light up. When kids are causing trouble, voluntarily or not, it's so easy to meet their entrance with a weary or frustrated or critical face. But then you're just adding to the harsh soundtrack in their heads. Kids often feel they can "afford" to behave at their worst with their mother or father, yet even amid a tirade may be seeking reassurance and affection.

We're not suggesting this won't take a great deal of emotional energy. Don't forget to eat, sleep, exercise, and find occasional outdoor escapes of your own. In particularly difficult times, you may also need ways to remind yourself of how much you love your child. Keep a baby picture handy. You need to bring your A-game to this limited time when your kids are still young and in your care.

So now you have the script. We hope it will help you deal with the forbidding topics of the next chapter, namely: sex, drugs, alcohol, and social media. These make up the toughest challenges for a parent of any adolescent, but especially one who is coping with a mood disorder.

Chapter Six

Sex, Drugs, and Social Media

Parenting by many measures has become harder than ever. The good news is that this is true because we *know* so much more.

Unlike our parents' parents, for instance, most Americans now understand that "spare the rod, spoil the child" is bad advice. Surveys show Millennials and Gen Z parents are spanking much less than their own folks did. What's more, contemporary moms and dads know that mental illness is real, that children aren't exempt, and that a wide variety of treatments can help make things better.

All of this implies a lot more emotional work for caregivers. But there is also so much more to gain. This includes not only being able to provide better support as our children embark on adulthood, but a greater chance to have more honest and loving relationships. These are ideals you might keep in mind during some of the most labor-intensive times, which may involve dealing with one or more of three vexing challenges: sex, drugs (and alcohol), and social media.

As with most other topics in this book, these are relevant hurdles for almost every parent of an adolescent yet become much more serious when your child has bipolar disorder.

Below, we'll offer some evidence-based tips to cope with each of these dilemmas.

Starting With Sex

Young people today are less sexually active than in previous decades, but quite a few of them are still hooking up. In 2019, more than 38% of high schoolers said they'd had sex, with more than 27% of teens reporting relations in the previous three months, according to the Centers for Disease Control and Prevention (CDC). Twelve percent reported they had not used any method to prevent pregnancy, and less than 10% had ever been tested for HIV.

While sex in a healthy and reasonably mature relationship can be a joy, you have reason to worry that mania, loneliness, and lack of self-esteem may drive your depressed child into dangerous liaisons. Bipolar disorder not only makes sex more likely, and at an earlier age; it also makes it more dangerous. One study found that 71% of diagnosed youth were sexually active, with high rates of sexual assault (11%), pregnancy (36%), and abortion (15%).

Hypersexuality—compulsive, excessive sexual thoughts and behavior—is a surprisingly common feature of mania, occurring in about 4 out of 10 youth, according to one study. It's also extremely vexing for parents. You may worry your child will embarrass you in public by talking about sex or inappropriately touching someone. You may fear raising suspicions among strangers that the odd behavior stems from sexual abuse at home.

By adolescence, you may already have had years of practice saying things such as "Your private parts need to be kept private." Danielle Steel has written that her son Nick, even as a toddler, "was absolutely enamored of women. . . . He groped, he hugged, he caressed."

It can be taxing to try to discourage inappropriate public behavior without making your son or daughter feel ashamed. Yet as your child grows older, it can also be downright frightening to imagine what might happen as he or she ventures out into the world alone.

Getting a diagnosis and appropriate treatment is your best hope of helping your child behave more responsibly. We also hope that by now you've done enough work on your relationship to have open communication about delicate issues. Once those two conditions are met, the following suggestions, most of which are appropriate for most kids, may help you further encourage healthy sexual behavior. You may be surprised to hear that most adolescents say they share their parents' values about sex and benefit from encouragement to delay it.

Think of this process as not one big talk, but a series of gentle check-ins that may go on over years.

Talking With Kids About Sex

- *Emphasize that you are not making moral judgments* but are concerned about your child's health, safety, and self-respect. Don't act like a know-it-all; it's okay to acknowledge this topic can be hard and confusing.
- *Talk about how to say no.* Schools have been doing a better job recently in teaching the basics of "consent," but it won't hurt to have a conversation to make sure it has

sunk in. Help your child understand that you can't give consent when you are drunk or high.

- *Explain the dangers of "sexting,"* the receiving and sending of sexually explicit photos by text. You might be surprised by how many kids do it—more than 27% of those between 12 and 17 years old, according to one large analysis in 2018. Kids need to be reminded that once they send anything into the ether, they've lost control of it forever—and it may well survive on some website for years. The humiliation that follows errant texts could aggravate depression or even trigger a suicide attempt.
- *Meet your child's romantic partner,* and if possible also the partner's parents. And yes, this assumes you've done the work you need to do on your relationship with your child.
- *Even 12 years old is not too early to start talking about birth control.* The risks begin at puberty. Remember, you can't follow your kid around 24/7, so if your daughter says she needs it, as hard as that may be to imagine, it's probably better to help than not.
- *Let your child know that masturbation is healthy,* as long as it's done in private and not to the exclusion of other healthy pursuits.
- *If your child is experiencing mania, consider restricting internet use and even keeping him or her home from school.* At the very least, keep a close watch. If your child is supposed to be taking medication, hypersexuality could be a sign that he or she is skipping it or needs a higher dose or different drug.
- *Enlist your child's doctor* to discuss the risks of sexual activity, and be sure to keep up regular prevention visits so that the doctor can establish an ongoing dialogue.

During Chamique Holdsclaw's high school years, many adults warned her to take care not to get pregnant. But her grandmother made the biggest impression by reminding her of her own worth. "She would tell me, 'It's not where you're from. It's where you're going,'" Holdsclaw recalled. "And I never wanted to let her down."

Alcohol, Weed, and Pills

Another challenge for parents that becomes a lot harder when your child has bipolar disorder involves drinking and drugs. In the short term, getting buzzed or high can ward off symptoms of depression and anxiety. Over time, however, it makes them worse.

More than half of US kids will try drugs, with many able to avoid getting hooked. Yet kids with mood disorders of all kinds are at high risk of dangerous drug use, including addiction. Other risks include unwanted pregnancies and sexually transmitted diseases (STDs), school failure, trouble with police, injuries, accidents, and increased risk of suicide. Alcohol and drugs can also sabotage the benefits of medication, preventing it from working or intensifying side-effects.

Booze

Adolescents on average are drinking less than they used to. Yet similarly to trends with sex, there's still a lot of drinking going on.

A 2019 CDC national survey of high school students found that in the previous month, nearly one-third had drunk alcohol, 14% had engaged in binge-drinking, and 17% had been in a car with a driver who had been drinking. And again, the risks are serious: Heavy alcohol use can lead not only to accidents and death but changes in brain development that may have lifelong impact, including future alcoholism.

Cannabis

Unfortunately, even as fewer adolescents are drinking, many more are using marijuana. Roughly 8% of eighth graders in a recent survey said they had "vaped" at least once in the past year. And as you may have heard, this isn't your mother's marijuana. Today's weed is grown in ways that make it more potent, concentrating the active ingredient, tetrahydrocannabinol (THC), by at least three times as much as in years past. Compounding the danger is that marijuana has become much more prevalent and easier to obtain. As of this writing, it's legal for recreational use in 19 states plus Washington, DC, and permitted for medical use in over 35 others. Nowhere is marijuana legal for minors, yet that hasn't slowed down the consumption. A 2021 study of California youth found that teenagers' marijuana use climbed by 23% during the year after the drug was legalized for adults.

Vaping, "edibles," tinctures, and teas have made the drug more convenient to use and to hide from parents. Newish, synthetic marijuana-like drugs with names like "K2," "Fake Weed," "Legal Weed," and "Spice" are easily confused with marijuana but more dangerous to consume. Some cause increased heart rate and blood pressure, anxiety, vomiting, and even hallucinations.

Kids have been encouraged to believe that marijuana is safer than alcohol because it's "natural" and sanctioned for some adult medical problems. In a controversial trend, some doctors have even prescribed cannabis to minors, for complaints ranging from cancer to anxiety to attention-deficit/hyperactivity disorder (ADHD).

The Food and Drug Administration has approved CBD (cannabidiol, the second most active ingredient in marijuana) to treat some forms of epilepsy in children. There are no other approved uses for minors—for good reason.

Experts believe that adolescents' developing brains are more vulnerable to marijuana's active ingredient, THC, which can disrupt attention, memory, and concentration. In the summer of 2021, researchers at the National Institutes of Health announced evidence of an additional danger. A survey of 280,000 young adults—aged 18 to 35—revealed a link between cannabis use and higher levels of suicidal thoughts, plans, and attempts. Moreover, note that even without THC, CBD can interfere with bipolar disorder medications.

While alcohol and marijuana are the most prevalent temptations, other potentially more dangerous drugs, including cocaine, methamphetamines, LSD, and MDMA (Ecstasy), are often disturbingly easy to obtain, even on high school campuses. Another worrying trend is that of youth raiding their parents' medicine cabinets for prescription drugs. In "Skittles parties," guests throw pills such as Ambien and Ativan in a circle and then consume handfuls of them.

Your Vigilance Is Needed

Adolescents' brains are remarkably "plastic"—flexible and growing. An advantage of this is they can learn things, such as new languages, faster than their elders. Unfortunately they also tend to progress more speedily from substance use to addiction and sometimes to death by overdose. In recent years, nearly 100,000 Americans a year have died that way.

Nic Sheff narrowly avoided this fate, says his father, the writer David Sheff. He began smoking marijuana and drinking alcohol as a young teenager, and this quickly escalated.

> "He was smoking every day, drinking to the point of passing out, and systematically tried pretty much every drug you can name," Sheff wrote in an email. "There were a couple overdoses; he was in emergency rooms, and once an ER doctor told me that they were going to have to amputate Nic's arm because it had become infected from shooting heroin and meth. They saved his arm and he did better for a while, but he relapsed and overdosed again. He was about 25 then. This time an ER doctor called and said, 'Mr. Sheff, you'd better get down here. We have your son. We don't know if he's going to make it.'"

The story illustrates both the high risk of addiction for kids with bipolar disorder and the difficulty many parents face in getting an accurate diagnosis of the underlying illness. Over a decade of coping with his son's addiction, Sheff admitted him into half-a-dozen different outpatient and residential treatment programs with many different specialists before a psychiatrist asked to see Nic's psychological testing. Sheff said there hadn't been any. Incredulous, the doctor ordered a battery of tests and further evaluated Nic to determine that he had bipolar disorder. His father believes that diagnosis—and subsequent treatment—saved his life.

"What we now know is that Nic spent more than a decade using and nearly died because he was suffering from these psychiatric disorders that had never been identified, properly diagnosed and treated," Sheff says. "He used drugs to try to escape the pain he was in, but of course they only made his mental problems worse."

Sheff, who went on to write three books about addiction and create a fund to support anti-addiction programs, warns other parents: Don't ever normalize drug use.

Once, after Nic was caught with weed at high school, a counselor said: "Nic's a great kid. He's smart. He has lots of friends. He's a good athlete. Lots of kids use drugs—they're experimenting, partying. Nic will be fine," Sheff says. "Nic wasn't fine. What the counselor should have said is that kids use drugs for reasons. We have to do what we can to find those reasons. If I'd found a psychiatrist or psychologist then who could have diagnosed Nic's mental illnesses, it's conceivable that we could have nipped his use in the bud. He believes and I believe it never would have escalated the way it did. I learned that we—parents, teachers, others who work with kids—can't accept drug use as a norm and harmless. We shouldn't assume it's not that big a deal and there's nothing we can do. There's a lot we can do."

Some parents end up in the frightening position of having to care for a child who is tripping on hallucinogens or has intentionally or unintentionally overdosed. If you're worried that your child is becoming dependent on alcohol or marijuana or trying other drugs, you have every right to crack down on the behavior and use drug testing if possible, while increasing counseling sessions.

The following tips may also be helpful:

• Communicate, communicate, communicate.

Tell your child you want to talk about drug use—not because he or she is in trouble but because it's time. Then make sure to listen carefully; don't interrupt or condescend. It's your choice as to whether to disclose your own past drug use. But if you do, use caution and don't minimize the risks for still-developing brains.

> When Cindy's mother, Julie, talks to her about drugs, she emphasizes the risk of being publicly humiliated: a sure-fire way to get a teenage girl's attention. "Cindy is so rebellious that I know she's going to do what she's going to do," says her mom. "So I've tried to coach her about moderation and caution. I've told her lots of stories about friends of mine who've gotten into trouble. One was photographed vomiting at a party. This was before the internet, but she still had trouble living it down."

- Remember the no-brainers.

Lock up or throw out any unused dangerous substances such as narcotics or stimulants that may have been prescribed for a family member but are no longer needed. Lock up or carefully hide those still in use. Many a parent has learned this lesson the hard way and to lasting regret.

The most responsible way to get rid of such medications is to take them back to the pharmacy or see if your local law enforcement collects them. (You can search online for Drug Enforcement Agency guidelines.) If you must throw them in the trash, make sure the garbage isn't accessible to animals or children.

- Be the best possible role model.

Adolescent drinking appears to rise and fall along with drinking by adults in the same household—and even in the same community. We advise not giving your child alcohol until the legal age of 21. Some parents think if it's in the home, it doesn't count. It does, and it sets a precedent.

- Talk about safety.

Remind your child never to drink anything he or she hasn't opened, or from a cup left out of sight for any amount of time. And obviously, no pills.

- Don't hesitate to set clear rules.

That doesn't mean they won't be broken, but studies show that on average your child will be less likely to get into serious trouble if your expectations are clear. You may also want to press home the possible consequences of getting caught at school, which might include getting suspended, or kicked off a sports team, or even sent to juvenile hall.

- Ask pointed questions.

If your adolescent is going to a party, don't hesitate to ask where it's at and whether there will be adult supervision. Don't be shy about checking with the adults who are supposedly in charge.

- Consider an "amnesty" policy.

A blogger for the Child Mind Institute suggests this idea: If your adolescent gets in trouble, he or she can call you and be honest about what's going on without the normal consequences for breaking rules. For instance, your child can call you from a party, if he or she has been drinking, and ask for a ride or an Uber rather than drive. It doesn't mean you won't have a frank talk the next morning; you're just prioritizing their safety.

- Prepare for emergencies.

If you suspect your child is using opioids, equip yourself with naloxone in case of an overdose. Keep it in your car, purse, or pocket. It's easy to use, as much as we hope you won't ever have to use it.

Yellow Flags

The American Academy of Child and Adolescent Psychiatry provides a list of warning signs that your child might be using marijuana:

- Acting silly and out of character for no reason
- Hanging out with a new group of friends who seem like they might be using
- Using new words such as "420" (slang for cannabis consumption), "dabbing" (a dance move resembling sneezing after smoking weed), and "shatter" (a cannabis extract)
- Being more irritable
- Losing interest in and motivation to do usual activities
- Falling asleep in class or at the dinner table
- Having trouble remembering things that just happened
- Coming home with red eyes and/or urges to eat outside of usual mealtimes
- Stealing money or having money that cannot be accounted for

The Addictive, Inevitable e-Universe

If your son or daughter is like most other youth in the internet age, he or she is spending several hours a day in virtual life: on computers and smartphones, texting or immersed in social media. (In one survey, more than 90% of middle-schoolers had their own smartphone and nearly three-quarters had started using Instagram or Snapchat.)

Maybe you're doing the same. We don't mean to judge, but we do want to alert you to the influence you'll have on everyone around you. This behavior is highly contagious.

And after all, not only is the internet not going away anytime soon, it offers advantages particularly well-suited for adolescents with bipolar disorder. Social media can help withdrawn kids find friends, connecting them to "peeps" who share the same interests but might be shy or live far away. Social media can also nurture budding hobbies and interests; kids have used it to learn to play guitar, follow musicians, or join a group of environmental activists—all without having to drive anywhere. Kids with mood disorders have also been able to educate themselves about their illness, in private, and find online support without stigma. Furthermore, while remote learning was far from ideal, it nonetheless saved millions of students from falling behind more than they would have during COVID-19.

All that said, it's probably no coincidence that the spectacular growth of social media ever since Facebook was founded in 2004 has coincided with the rapid growth in adolescent anxiety, depression, and eating disorders, as well as the suicide rate.

"Young people are bombarded with messages through the media and popular culture that erode their sense of self-worth—telling them they are not good-looking enough, popular enough, smart enough, or rich enough," US Surgeon General Vivek Murthy wrote in his 2021 report on the adolescent mental health crisis.

Many experts believe that time spent with online "friends" does little to establish a sense of connection and in fact increases loneliness that can be a key factor in depression. In fact, levels of happiness in the United States have declined over the years that internet use has increased.

In 2018, the American Psychiatric Association (APA) found a clear link between social media use and adolescent depression. "Negative online exposure can have detrimental effects on the physical and mental health of teenagers," the APA warned, "causing depression, anxiety, increased suicidal thoughts, and even reports of completed teen suicide."

To be sure, there's a lot to unpack in the phrase "negative online exposure." We don't yet know precisely how spending time online might be adding to the rise in depression, but there are many reasonable theories. Adolescents with bipolar disorder are particularly vulnerable to digital dangers that include online predators, cyberbullying, addiction to the exclusion of healthier pursuits, sleep deprivation, online humiliation and/ or legal problems after impulsive oversharing, and exposure to a range of toxic content, including pornography and violence.

In 2021, former Facebook manager Frances Haugen drew global attention to the harm Facebook causes to young people's mental health. Haugen leaked thousands of internal documents to the *Wall Street Journal*, following up with hours of explosive testimony before Congress. In particular, she faulted Facebook for enabling "cyberbullying," which she said was extra-hurtful in that it followed children home after school. All too often, she said, the last thing children absorb before going to sleep is someone being cruel to them. She also described how girls are often led by Facebook's algorithm from content about diets to sites that encourage anorexia, a common coexisting condition of bipolar disorder. "What's super tragic is Facebook's own research says as these young women begin to consume this eating disorder content, they get more and more depressed," she said, even as they're using the app more often.

The *Wall Street Journal's* lengthy exposé even hinted at a link between the rise in adolescent suicides and increasing use of Facebook, citing surveys that showed that among teenagers who reported suicidal thoughts, "13 percent of British users and 6 percent of American users traced the desire to kill themselves to Instagram." (Facebook has responded that "no single study is going to be conclusive.")

Social Media, the Internet, and Suicide

As much as we may love the convenience of smartphones and near-constant connectivity with our social networks, unfortunately the internet can present considerable dangers to vulnerable minds and lives. Websites exist that offer information on how to attempt suicide, and these draw an alarming number of page views per month. Evidence indicates that most people who view these sites are 30 or under and have struggled with mental health issues. Several European nations have managed to restrict access to certain of these sites, but so far the United States has lagged behind.

Challenging as it may be, it is important that you know what your child is doing online. It is important to talk directly and honestly with your teenager about their online use and to explain your concerns for their privacy and safety. For instance, make sure they know not to share their location or personal information. Let them know that you are available to review content with them if they have questions and/or worries. Educate them on trusted sources of health and other medical information. You might also consider, as part of the privilege of "phone ownership," explaining that you expect to be able to use parental controls, or that you may need to review content on your teen's phone (with their involvement). It is also helpful to keep screens and devices in a visible location in your home, where you can monitor what your child is up to, and the amount of time they spend engaged in various activities online.

TMI

There's no question that kids all over the world are feeling depressed by the 24-7 drumbeat of bad news online. In particular, the looming existential threat from climate change has led to shocking rates of pessimism. In a 2022 survey of 10,000 people aged 16 to 25, living in 10 countries, three-quarters said "the future is frightening," and 56% said "humanity is doomed."

"Why Should I Study for a Future I Won't Have?" read a sign carried by high school sophomore Sophie Kaplan, who joined a protest march in 2020. "I don't understand why I should be in school if the world is burning," Kaplan told a reporter. "What's the point of working on my education if we don't deal with this first?"

Such sentiments reverberate on social media (there's even an Instagram site called greenmemesfordepressedteens), while smartphones ping their anxious owners with updates on melting glaciers and burning forests. "Kids tell me they see such little hope," says Brian, a high school teacher in California.

This is a typical internet conundrum. Our increasing, constant online connections make us more informed than ever, which is positive to the extent that we can act on that knowledge but negative to the degree that we feel helpless. Talk to your kids often about how they feel about what they're reading and hearing in the news, and whenever possible, think of things they can do to counter despair. If they'll tolerate your company, you may even want to join with them to register voters or write postcards to Congress. The famous Fred Rogers has recalled his own mother's advice when he was young and would see scary things in the news. "Look for the helpers," she would say. "You will always find people who are helping.'"

Mental Illness FOMO?

Here's a different sort of digital conundrum. As we've noted, social media has helped conquer much of the stigma surrounding mental illness, by disseminating stories of famous, successful people acknowledging their struggles and in general normalizing the topic. (At this writing, the Twitter hashtag #mentalillness had more than 1.7 billion videos.)

We sometimes wonder if this benefit can turn into a problem, making bipolar disorder seem more attractive and even reinforcing symptoms through contagion. (Remember that Kanye West motto: "I hate being bi-polar. It's awesome.") There is no solid evidence that this is happening, but many school faculty and parents think it is a risk.

> "When I look at Instagram these days, I really worry about what's starting to look like a trend of teenagers thinking they all have whatever the latest acronym is, whether it's ADHD, MDD, PTS, or OCD," says Andrea, who has wrestled with serious mood disorders with both of her children. "How much is self-diagnosis, and how much is social media feeding the beast?"

A contributing trend is the "neurodiversity" movement, which often endorses the message that mental conditions commonly seen as disorders, such as ADHD and autism, are normal variations in the human genome, and in fact can be strengths. We applaud positive thinking—as long as it doesn't interfere with taking responsibility for managing a risky mental state.

> "If you've watched somebody you love get very sick, very manic, you would never say, 'Oh, they are benefitting in some way,'" the scientist and author Hope Jahren, who has bipolar disorder, told an interviewer for The New School. She said she disagreed with "this perception that being bipolar gives you some special or creative gift," adding, "I eventually did get well, from a very, very sick place, and that was a medical process."

What's a Parent to Do?

Parents of kids with bipolar disorder need to be extra-vigilant about online dangers. You'll be walking a fine line, to be sure. Kids depend on the internet for schoolwork, socializing, and, increasingly, for establishing their autonomy and identity. You have to give them their space there, especially as they get older. Yet if your child is already emotionally fragile, you can't afford to tune out. At minimum we recommend you get familiar with some of the basics of social media and observe where your kids are spending all that time. You wouldn't let them go to a bar at their age, or invite total strangers into your home, so consider this cautionary tale.

At first glance, a site called Discord couldn't look more innocent. The home page is decorated with bright cartoon animals: a yellow rabbit, a green dog in a hat. The instant-messaging site is a place "where you can belong to a school club, a gaming group, or a worldwide art community," the page declares. "Where just you and a handful of friends can spend time together. A place that makes it easy to talk every day and hang out more often." That cheery welcome made it all the more shocking when Sandy discovered that her 13-year-old daughter was having sexually suggestive conversations there, including sending pictures of herself to male strangers.

"I was horrified," she says. "My daughter had set up false email accounts to chat with these predators, and was lying about her age. When I went to the police they said they see this all the time; it's so easy to do. But I can't believe how out of touch I was. I *work* in the tech industry."

The moral of the story is that you shouldn't wait to talk to your kids about what they're reading online, and also check out the sites yourself. Once again, communication is key. Don't assume your children understand the importance of privacy, and how easily whatever they post can be shared, and make sure they're aware of how different online activities make them feel. With inherently anti-authoritarian teens, sometimes the argument that works best is getting them to notice when and how they're being manipulated by large corporations.

Don't assume you can solve this problem with blanket decrees. One of the most bedeviling things for parents about the internet is that kids are constantly figuring out new ways to get around parental and other controls. For instance, even though a national law, the Children's Online Privacy Protection Act, prohibits companies from collecting online data from children under 13, many kids simply lie about their age.

Anyone with a smartphone understands the temptation to use it for distractions. Social media hook users with interesting news or "likes." A parent can easily feel powerless against such elemental forces, but remember: Silicon Valley moguls like Bill Gates and Steve Jobs have been some of the biggest sticklers in limiting their kids' screen time. Consider following their lead.

1. Be a Good Role Model

You can count on your children to watch what you do more closely than they listen to what you say. Be present with your family, limiting your own screen time. And don't undermine yourself by doing things like texting your children in school after you've told them not to text while at school. Again, consider what the inventors and sellers of these technologies have been doing in their own homes. Some Silicon Valley leaders have reportedly even required their children's child-care providers to sign contracts promising they won't use their phones in front of the kids.

Being a good role model may also mean taking a break from the news and talking about why you're doing so. You might also talk to your kids about how to distinguish fact from fiction.

2. Hold Out for as Long as You Can

Maybe your child shouldn't be the last one in her class to get a phone, but she sure shouldn't be the first. "Children 12 and under should not be on social media," Jean M. Twenge, a professor of psychology at San Diego State University and the author of *iGen*, a book about youth and technology, told the *New York Times*. Bill Gates reportedly didn't give his kids phones until they were 14, and subsequently limited their time with them. The Waldorf School of the Peninsula, based near Google's Mountain View campus, and a popular choice for many Silicon Valley parents, believes that exposing preteens to technology "can hamper their ability to fully develop strong bodies, healthy habits of discipline and self-control, fluency with creative and artistic expression, and flexible and agile minds."

Check out "Wait until Eighth," a savvy movement encouraging parents to join together to wait until eighth grade to give kids a smartphone.

In the meantime, ask your kids' school if they have a digital-citizenship class, and if they don't, why not?

3. Set Limits

You're paying the phone bill, right? There's increasing evidence that establishing limits is one of the healthiest things you can do for your child. Research published in *JAMA Pediatrics* has found that children get more sleep, do better in school, behave better, and are less likely to be obese when parents limit the amount of time spent in front of the TV and computer.

> "My 13-year-old has asked for Snapchat a million times and I've said, 'That's a hard no and you have to stop asking,'" says Grace.

Two worthwhile rules include no phones at the dinner table and no screens in children's bedrooms. You can explain that you're setting limits for their safety and health, and this is not debatable.

If you truly can't get your kids to hand you their phones at night, just turn off the modem at 9 p.m.

4. Collaborate With Teachers and Other Parents

Peer pressure is often irresistible for adolescents, so try to find ways to reduce it. It's reasonable to expect teachers to limit cellphone use at school, and you may be surprised by how many other parents would support other ways to curb online obsessions.

5. Make Sure Your Child Has Plenty of Opportunities for Real-Life Pursuits

Asked how parents should think about their kids' internet use, the neuroscientist Michael Merzenich, a pioneer in brain plasticity, responded: "You just have to consider what they're NOT doing when they are on screens." We've said it before, but it's worth repeating. One of the best ways parents can improve their children's lives is to insist on healthy habits, such as developing skills, getting regular sleep and exercise, and spending time outdoors.

Sometimes kids already understand this and are just waiting for you to confirm it.

> "One day my daughter told me that she had closed off every app," says Maria. "She said: 'It was all toxic. I didn't like the vibe, the comments people were making about each other.' I give her a lot of credit for that."

6. Spend Time Together Online

This may be the ultimate buzzkill for many adolescents. But if you catch them young enough, they may still want to share to the extent that you can get a good view of their online environment. Show you care what they have found interesting or helpful, and also what may have surprised them or made them uncomfortable.

7. As a Last Resort, Use Parental Controls

We say "last resort" because so many of them don't work, are easily evaded, and are rapidly outpaced by new technologies. If you're considering trying them anyway, it suggests you may have lost the battle for your children's trust. All that said, you may want to investigate Apple's Family Sharing settings (Family Link on Android phones), which set time limits on internet use. Common Sense Media is a great resource that regularly reviews apps and blockers. You also might look into new smartphone models such as Pinwheel, which has built-in parental controls.

8. Keep Learning and Paying Attention

Things are changing so fast that we can only help you so much at this writing. See our Resources section for help in keeping up to date. It's time-consuming, we know, but you need to know where your child is going online.

Chapter Seven

Surviving School

G iven your child's diagnosis, you'll need to pay extra-close attention to what's going on in school. It's a critically important environment at a key time in your child's life, with constant and powerful potential impacts on mental health. And apparently many of those impacts may be harmful. When Challenge Success, a nonprofit affiliated with Stanford University, surveyed more than 250,000 adolescent students nationwide, it found:

- 95% said they were sleep-deprived.
- 77% reported stress-related health symptoms.
- 63% said they worried constantly about academics.

Teachers and students say these statistics only begin to describe the problem.

"It's pretty alarming," says Brian, a 24-year veteran teacher at a California public high school. "They're anxious about whether they'll ever get jobs. They're anxious about climate change—many of them say they can't imagine having children of their own. I've known kids who have attempted suicide. It has definitely never been this acute."

These problems were building up before the pandemic raised the stress levels of teachers, students, administration, and parents.

"What's so frustrating for me is that with us wearing masks all day, kids can't see your face, can't read the emotions, so I'm having tons of miscommunication issues," says Brian. "The best way I can connect with kids to support them academically is to get to know them, so I strive to form those relationships, but the pandemic has thrown all that to the wind."

Heightened stress is especially hard on kids with bipolar disorder, for whom any one of several coming-of-age clichés—the nasty teacher, the mean girls, the shattered romance, or even the trigonometry quiz—can trigger a downward spiral.

Fortunately, there's a lot that you can do. This chapter will describe some of the major stumbling blocks in middle school and high school—from other students' cruelty to your child's own academic and behavioral obstacles—and offer some strategies to cope.

Bullies, Isolation, and Boycotts

Common Cruelty

You don't need to reread *Lord of the Flies* to know how cruel kids can be to each other—and especially to those who seem different. Studies show that more than a third of students with behavioral and emotional disorders face high levels of bullying. The numbers are even higher for LGBTQ+ kids—and the impacts should never be minimized.

"It's amazing the number of kids with mental illness who've been bullied and then committed suicide," says Pat Howey, an author and paralegal in the education law division of Connell Michael Kerr, LLP, a law firm in Carmel, Indiana.

Bullying at school is unfortunately widespread. One out of every five students reports that they've been victims. The behavior can range from being teased and/or gossiped about to being excluded or physically attacked: pushed, hit, or spit at. Less than half of bullies' victims ever report it to an adult.

The harassment can occur almost anywhere—in school hallways and stairwells, inside classrooms, in the cafeteria, and on buses—but more and more, it's happening in cyberspace. In one study, one in five tweens (9–12 years old) said they'd been bullied online, bullied others online, or witnessed cyberbullying.

Your child may not tell you he or she is being bullied. Here are some ways that communicate without words:

- Unexplained cuts or bruises
- Sudden requests to stay home from school or reports of missed classes
- New complaints of headaches, stomachaches, or trouble sleeping
- Sudden disinterest in spending time with friends
- "Lost" or damaged clothes or other belongings, or new unexplained requests for more money
- Unexplained loss of appetite

If you have a vulnerable child and are lucky enough to have a choice of schools, make sure to ask if a school you're considering has an anti-bullying program. Not all schools have them, and not all programs are effective, but some research suggests that they can reduce bullying by up to 25%. At very least you want to know that school personnel are aware of the potential problem and doing something about it. Ask how they've handed such incidents in the past, and if they have a "bystander" policy, in which other students are encouraged to befriend bullies' victims and report any bullying they see. Keep in mind that researchers have found that even witnessing bullying can be damaging to students' mental health.

If you suspect your child is being victimized:

- *Check in on a regular basis.* By now we hope you know how important it is to have good communication with your child. Regular chats are your best guarantee of knowing if problems are brewing outside home.
- *Encourage your child to speak up.* Getting adults involved is the only effective way to stop bullying. Urge your child to tell you or report to adults not only if he or she is the victim, but if others are also suffering.
- *Identify one adult ally.* Make sure that before each school year gets underway, you and your child have identified one empathetic adult at the school, whether it's a teacher or counselor, whom you know will be responsive to reports of bullying.
- *Don't DIY.* Tempting as it may be, don't try to fix things by contacting the bully or the bully's family. Deal with the school. Similarly, don't put the burden of fixing the problem on your kid. Studies show that fighting back or even walking away rarely works and often makes things worse.

Friendlessness

Children with bipolar disorder often behave in ways that others interpret as mean, rude, or weird. They may have poor social skills, including impulsive and sometimes aggressive behavior. Many end up as outcasts at school.

At the start of the year or when changing schools, check into how your child's school is handling this common problem. If they don't have a plan, you might suggest they connect with Beyond Differences, a national nonprofit that identified social isolation as a problem many years before the pandemic and has come up with well-reviewed programs to combat it. The group offers a social and emotional learning curriculum, starting in middle school, that helps kids develop better relationship skills.

Your child's teacher may recommend that your child attend a school-based social-skills group. Make sure to find out what that would entail, including the credentials of whoever is leading it, and ask your child's clinician if it makes sense. Some programs may be beneficial, but they aren't right for every child, and sometimes the sheer stigma of being pulled out of class and publicly identified as socially awkward should be a deal-breaker.

When Your Child Just Says No

Many kids with mood disorders are so stressed at school that they end up refusing to go.

> "My daughter is refusing to go to school one to two days out of every week," says Janet. "She has told me that sometimes she feels so stressed there that it's like a knife stabbing her in the back all day. Every morning she has

physical symptoms, which sometimes she can overcome and sometimes not. And of course the more school she misses, the more overwhelmed and stressed she gets and it spirals into a nice tornado. We're still trying to figure out what to do about this."

As children's mental health problems have grown more prevalent, so has "school refusal." In recent years, up to 5% of students have been balking in the morning or ducking out, AWOL, later in the day, according to studies published at this writing. But school refusal is yet another problem that COVID-19 has recently made worse. Many shy students got used to attending in their jammies. Once the lockdowns ended, they resisted going back to an environment they found stressful.

"School refusal" isn't a diagnosis, but the *DSM-5* includes it as a symptom of various disorders, including major depression, anxiety disorders, and posttraumatic stress disorder. This is more than a request for a "mental health day"; quite often a child is sending a distress signal. Unfortunately, the longer it goes on, the harder it is for the child to return.

This behavior can easily throw family life into chaos, especially when one or two parents need to leave the house on time for work and can't afford to stay home to supervise a rebellious or potentially self-harming child. Raising the stress levels for all concerned is that some schools will report parents to Child Protective Services for abetting truancy.

How should a parent respond if a 15-year-old who may already weigh more than his mother or father refuses to get out of bed? What do you do if you've watched your child have a genuine panic attack, with shortness of breath, at the thought of going to class? Some parents end up in exhausting cycles of bribery and threats. Quite a few, in desperation, have even called police to escort kids to school—although we don't recommend this outside of a genuine emergency.

> "I felt so sorry for Matt, because I knew how much he was hurting and how much he hated school," recalls his mother, Beth. "But I knew he was digging a hole for himself, so when his counselor suggested I call the cops, I did. It felt awful, but I only had to do it once."

School refusal can sneak up on parents. It may start with a stomachache one day and ramp up slowly to the point where your child wants to stay home every day. Pay close attention and do your best to figure out the reasons. Often the problem is social: He or she is being bullied or ostracized. Or maybe there's a learning issue you haven't yet identified. Frequently, a student who can't master material falls behind and loses hope of catching up.

Whatever the reason, a parent in most cases should resist setting a precedent for kids to avoid school, advises Katrina Southard, a licensed clinical social worker and coordinator of the Wellness Center at Archie Williams High School. "What starts as a loving intention can be a habit that's hard to break," she says. "You want to be nurturing but you're digging a deeper ditch, and I've seen a lot of kids spiral down from there. The only way to move through anxiety is to move through the stressor, not avoid it."

Ideally your child has a therapist by now with whom you can address this problem. If not, this is a clear sign you need one. Sometimes the school psychologist, if your school is fortunate enough to have one, can help. The prescribed treatment may be for the student to attend just one class to start with, gradually increasing the exposure to the stressor (in this case school), as you would do with someone experiencing a high level of anxiety in other situations, until he or she is more comfortable staying all day. If the school can't help, you may need to consider a change of environment, an option we describe below. In extreme cases, it may be wise to consider a partial-hospitalization program.

"Kids tell me they cannot be reasoned out of school refusal," writes the psychologist John Duffy. "This is not a practical matter for them, but an emotional one, based in crippling fear and sometimes sadness."

Not Making the Grade?

There's no correlation between severe bipolar disorder and intelligence. It's well-known that geniuses can—and often do—suffer from mental illness. Yet bipolar disorder can easily prevent a student from succeeding or even staying in school, by thwarting the capacity to focus and follow rules.

Kids with bipolar disorder are more likely than others to have cognitive problems, including impaired concentration and memory. The way the illness interferes with sleep can also sabotage focus. And when manic, kids may simply not be able to sit still or to focus beyond the thoughts crowding their heads.

Added to all this, new medications may cause side-effects that confound learning. Kids may also fall behind in class due to time spent away due to suspensions and hospital stays, both of which are unfortunately not uncommon when a child has bipolar disorder.

Three Choices for Serious Problems

If for whatever reason your son or daughter is failing at school, academically or behaviorally, your first step should be to consult with the clinician. You may need to review the treatment plan, adjusting the medication and possibly increasing or adding psychotherapy. If that doesn't work, you essentially have three choices: change the school, homeschool, or work with what you've got.

Change Schools

Environment can make a big difference to anyone's frame of mind. Consider what happened with Sally Greenberg, who went from her first manic episode and hospitalization at 15 to four years of success in high school.

> "It was a small school where a certain level or range of eccentricity among the students was tolerated—and even expected," recalls Sally's father, the journalist and author Michael Greenberg. "Children of artists, actors, and such. We were lucky to have this school for her." Greenberg stresses that Sally was also in an outpatient program at the time and being carefully monitored at home. "It's not as if those years of high school were easy for her," he adds. "But she managed to avoid a full-blown manic attack. It was touch and go, but the school environment certainly helped, in the sense that Sally's linguistic and literary talents were recognized, encouraged, and able to blossom."

Still, changing schools may take a lot of time and energy you may not reasonably have. If you're looking at private schools, it can also be unaffordable, unless you can get the child's original school to pay—an option we discuss below.

You may also end up simply trading one set of problems for another.

> "We changed school literally every year in high school," says Charlene. "At each one there was a different set of

problems that would emerge after a few weeks or months. But mostly the story was the same: She couldn't make friends and couldn't keep up with the work, and she got more and more depressed."

Still, the evidence from research is what you might expect. Several studies suggest that adolescents attending schools with better social climates experience less depression, drug use, and bullying. How do you find these islands of quality? Start with the counselor at your child's school, but you may also want to contract with a private educational counselor, whose job it is to know how to find the right fit. They aren't cheap, but the right one can make a big difference.

Homeschool

Let's acknowledge right away that homeschooling a child with bipolar disorder is *not* for the faint of heart. It may also require one parent to stay home to supervise, which can lead to resentment if you're not careful. Children with bipolar disorder can sometimes be so irritable that it's a truly big ask for a parent to give up those hours of freedom. And of course it's not just time and tolerance that's required: Giving your child a good or even adequate experience will take a lot of research, networking with like-minded friends and maybe homeschooling consultants, and planning activities with other kids so your child isn't totally isolated. Are you honestly ready to take on these challenges? If so, the bright side is you'll be joining a trend that was well underway before the pandemic and has been growing even faster ever since. At this writing, roughly 5 million US students are going to school at home.

COVID-19 has given parents the world over a crash course in modified homeschooling, and many found it a good alternative to the social pressures and conformity of regular school. By October 2020, the US Census Bureau reported that 11% of US households were homeschooling—more than double the rate at the start of the pandemic. (This was genuine homeschooling, not simply remote learning.)

For Black and other minority families, the growth has been considerably sharper. Whereas roughly 3% of Black students were homeschooled before the pandemic, that number had risen to 16% by the end of 2020. Many parents have told researchers that they made the choice to protect their kids from the racism and lower expectations in public schools.

While the quality of homeschooling varies from home to home, at least some homeschooled students perform just as well or better academically as their peers. Kids who are markedly different—especially those with concentration problems that make it hard to sit still—may in fact thrive from being free of the negative feedback and social pressures while also able to explore and develop their own interests.

Work With What You've Got

Most parents—meaning those can't find a public-school nirvana or afford to pay private-school tuition or quit their day jobs to homeschool—will need to work with their kids' current school to try to make sure it doesn't sabotage their mental health. There's a bright side to this, however, which is that once you've learned the system you may find that public schools offer all sorts of support that you may not get anywhere else. Under federal law, public schools must provide a "free and appropriate public education" to all students, including those with mental and physical disabilities. That's true regardless of your income level.

Winning Strategies for Wherever You Are

Forge Alliances

During these crucial years, consider yourself the ambassador and even sometimes translator for a child who may be all too easily misunderstood. That means making friends, or at least alliances, with other parents, teachers, and school administrators. Even if you're holding down a job (or two) and raising other kids, try to find time to reach out.

Enlist Your Peers

Other parents of children with mental health issues will often be your best resources at school. Some will have already figured out solutions to problems you're facing and can steer you to the most sympathetic teachers, clinicians, and programs. Not least, other parents who know what you're going through can serve as stress-relieving antidotes to all those other parents who're so much quicker to judge, gossip, and ostracize.

> "My son was a wrestler," says one mother. "Before he went into the hospital, I'd go to his practices, and all the parents would talk to me. After he got out of the hospital and went back to wrestling, there was suddenly nobody to talk to. They all went to sit on the other side of the room. I think they just didn't know what to say."

It's easy to find online forums for parents of children with specific disorders. But since real-life friendships can be so much more fulfilling, here are some ways to forge them:

- Look for a special-education parent–teacher association (PTA)—known as SEPTAs—in your district.
- If your district lacks a SEPTA, find tips for launching one on the national PTA website.

- Ask school administrators if they might confidentially contact other parents in your boat for an initial coffee meeting to see if you click.
- Look for a local chapter of the Depression and Bipolar Support Alliance (DBSA), further details of which are in our Resources section.

Sometimes groups that began as coffee klatches morph into powerful lobbyists for school-wide and local change.

> "It's amazing how many people you meet when you are open about this issue—how many people will say, my child was just diagnosed, or my nephew or my neighbor," says a mother who became a local education activist. She began by joining a local support group and eventually created her own. "Unless somebody starts the conversation," she says, "everyone walks around not talking."

Polish Apples

Connecting with teachers is one of the best ways you can improve your child's daily life at school. We understand this may be hard. In grade school, teachers and your kid wanted you on campus, and volunteering may have been a breeze. Now your child has many different teachers and may be embarrassed by seeing you anywhere in public.

You're going to have to be more tactful and subtle than you were in those early years. Don't do your hobnobbing in front of your child. But seize whatever opportunities you can.

> "At the open house at the beginning of the year, I go up to the teachers and shake their hands," says one mother. "I look them right in the eye, and I hold their hand so they remember my face. I say, 'Hi, I'm Roberta Smith. I'm Jake's mom.' And then I say, 'Listen, if you have any

problems, can you call me right away? Because we can chat about these things.' I make myself very approachable, and they call me."

Reach out as well to the school counselor or psychologist, assuming the school has one or both. This contact may end up being more important than the teachers, especially if there's a problem.

After the initial meeting, stay in touch throughout the year. And don't just email. Write a note or call. Teachers are busy, but you may be surprised by their willingness to communicate, if you reach out with skill and compassion.

"More and more, parents just aren't talking to teachers," says Brian. "We've moved everything online, so if anything, they'll email. But some never reach out. In the past, maybe 30 parents out of 120 kids would contact me directly. These days it's down to four! But the more a parent communicates with the teachers and gets to know them, the more the teacher can help that kid."

Don't forget to let teachers know when things are going *right*. An occasional thank-you note or small gift, like fruit or cookies, can go a long way. Some parents have won teachers' hearts by writing an appreciative letter to the principal. If you have the time, you might try to establish yourself as an asset to the school by participating in fundraising efforts or volunteering in the office. All of this is a down payment for the time when you'll need to ask for support.

Manage Your Fear

It's now time for a note about emotions—starting with yours. We absolutely get that you may be stressed out, exhausted, panicked, and angry. Your human instinct is to do all you can to protect your child, and if you suspect your child is being mistreated by adults or other kids, you may quite understandably arrive at school in a fury. You'll need to control that urge, however, if you truly wish to help your child. No one responds well to anger, blame, or threats.

Pick a time when both you and the teacher are reasonably relaxed—and make an appointment; don't just drop by. It may also help you to bring notes of the points you want to get across.

Then, pay attention to the way you communicate. Use those classic "I statements" rather than "you statements"; that is, "I noticed Johnny staying up all night trying to finish his project," rather than "You're giving the kids too much homework." To convey respect, try "reflective listening," in which you subtly echo what the other person says so that he or she knows you care and are paying attention. You can say something such as "I'm hearing you say that Johnny has been distracting the class." Or even, "It sounds like you've got a lot to manage." Don't waste time talking about all the problems your Johnny has had in the past; focus on the issue at hand.

If you're sending an email, read it aloud to yourself, at very least, before pushing "send." At times when your emotions are running high, it may even help to send it first to a sympathetic friend, since in the heat of the moment it may be hard for you to catch yourself being subtly or not-so-subtly aggressive.

"The other day I looked back on all my emails to Matt's sixth-grade teacher during a single week, and it was really embarrassing," says Beth. "I somehow lost track of just how many I was sending and how furious they sounded.

I'm not sure I can blame her for not answering after the first three."

Try giving the teacher the benefit of the doubt. Most want to do a good job for every student yet were under unusual stress long before the pandemic played havoc with their lives, and in most cases must manage scores of students a day. If your child is acting out or sloughing off, even if it's due to illness or medication side-effects, you can't expect 100% tolerance—especially if the teachers don't understand what's going on. You'll get the best results if you arrive with an attitude that says, "We're all in this together."

If you learn that a teacher is being unreasonably intolerant with your child, it's perfectly appropriate for you to express your concerns to the teacher or the principal. Once again, try to avoid sounding accusatory. Instead, project an attitude that you're on the same team. That may be all it takes to enlist the teacher's cooperation. But if all else fails, insist on a change. Some teachers are exceptionally skilled at dealing with "difficult" kids and can make a huge difference in your child's attitude about school. But others lack the wherewithal and may even do serious damage to a vulnerable child.

When you do find an understanding teacher, be open about your child's challenges and strengths. Share all the relevant information, including about medication, to the extent your child is comfortable with that, and show the teacher you're willing to hear suggestions about the best way to work together.

Know Your Rights

It may seem like ancient history today, but until 1975, millions of US kids with disabilities—from being deaf or blind to having serious behavioral problems—couldn't attend public schools. (A child who used a wheelchair was considered a fire hazard!) Those who did go to school did so at institutions far from home, at their parents' expense, and in many cases were simply warehoused.

This was all before two landmark lawsuits on behalf of excluded children, which helped lead to two sweeping federal laws. The first, in 1973, was Section 504 of the Rehabilitation Act, a 1973 civil rights law prohibiting schools receiving federal funding from discriminating against students with disabilities. Two years later, the Education for All Handicapped Children Act—later renamed the Individuals with Disabilities Education Act (IDEA)—provided funding to remove barriers to mainstream education and give qualified students an individualized education program (IEP). We'll elaborate on each of these laws below, and there's a chart in the Appendix that lays out the differences. In a nutshell: 504 accommodations are significantly more informal and assume less involvement by parents.

Under the IDEA, schools must involve parents in every step of the process, whereas a 504 plan simply requires schools to notify parents if they decide to evaluate a student to determine if he or she qualifies for special consideration. The rules for 504 plans vary across school districts, which determine who may qualify for accommodations. Often the plan doesn't even need to be in writing, as is required under the IDEA.

A 504 plan may work just fine for students whose symptoms are mild to moderate. But kids with bipolar disorder may need more help than it can provide.

"The school doesn't think the IEP is needed, because my daughter is a very smart kid, but the 504 was not enough," says Jeanne. "Megan has missed so much school with her hospitalizations that she has barely attended one full week this year. If she's stressed out and having bad anxiety, it can trigger her, and I need the school to understand this might happen. It's important that Megan stay in school now but also that she not be too pressured."

If you're seeking any sort of special help for your child, we have three specific recommendations: Find a lawyer—at least for an initial consultation. Put all serious requests in writing. And keep records of all relevant documents.

Find a Lawyer

In any serious conflict with your child's school, consult with a special-education attorney. Many won't charge for an initial meeting. Find one in your area or state in the directory for the Council of Parent Attorneys and Advocates (https://www.copaa.org/). If your state lacks attorneys with this specialization, you may want to look in a neighboring state. Use caution if you choose to hire an advocate, however; some are quite good, but they aren't held to formal standards. Ask for references or find other ways to get a sense of the track record.

Write It Down

"I remember my 15-year-old granddaughter and I were having a discussion about bullying," says Howey. "She had witnessed someone being bullied and said she went to the school counselor, and nothing happened, so she'd never do that again. I said: 'That's because you didn't put it in writing. It didn't happen if it isn't in writing.'"

Thanks, Granma, right? This may be a lot to expect from a teenager. But Howey has a good point for you, personally, to keep in mind. Say your child has been bullied and tells you about it. The natural thing for you to do is call the teacher or principal. And maybe something will get done. But there is something about a letter. It adds a sense of conferring responsibility a phone call simply can't match.

In particular, we want you to know about a kind of notification known as a "Gebser letter," a sample of which we provide in the Appendix. "Gebser" refers to a 1998 Supreme Court case that wasn't about special education or bullying—it dealt with a lawsuit by the mother of a high school student who was having an affair with a teacher. But through the years, it has become a way to refer to a letter that puts a school on notice that bullying—or any other sort of discrimination or wrong treatment of a student with special needs—has occurred. School administrators pay attention to these kinds of letters, which remind them that they are responsible to see that the behavior stops—or possibly risk a lawsuit.

As a general rule, it's also a good idea to keep notes of telephone conversations with teachers and school leaders, which leads us to our third main suggestion.

Keep Records

As soon as you know you'll be requesting special help from your child's school, start keeping track of all relevant documents and notes. Consider maintaining a binder to keep copies of the following:

- Medical documents, including those relating to symptoms of your child's disorder and any side-effects of your child's medications
- Progress reports or report cards
- Results of standardized or proficiency tests

- Any formal letters and notices, informal notes, and emails from medical providers, teachers, and other school staff
- Notes on verbal communications, including phone conversations and face-to-face meetings
- Representative samples of schoolwork
- Financial records, including invoices and receipts, for services you pay for privately to advance your child's education

Make a list of the documents and arrange them in chronological order.

504 Accommodations: School Services "Lite"

If your child isn't too impaired to handle the normal challenges of public school, with a few exceptions, you may want to ask for help under Section 504. It's easier for students to qualify, since it merely requires that they have a physical or mental impairment that substantially limits one or more major life activities—a standard that any student with major depression is likely to meet. Many parents seek 504 modifications while waiting to see if their child qualifies for IDEA support.

This may be all-around a quicker, easier process than the one provided under the IDEA. Work with your child's mental health provider to see if the supports offered are adequate, or if you need to move up to the next level. Remember, a 504 plan guarantees merely a "free, appropriate public education" for students with disabilities—meaning an education comparable to students without disabilities, but not one designed to meet the student's unique needs.

The student may receive easy-to-manage supports such as sitting in front of the class, being allowed extra time to complete tests, and getting a break on homework or classwork. You might also enlist a teacher or counselor to help your child take medication—just be careful how you do this, to reduce the risk of shaming.

If you've chosen the 504 route, start by sending a written request to the school. (Remember, avoid the phone if possible and put things in writing!) You don't need a formal evaluation, but any medical records supporting your child's diagnosis may help. You may also want to ask your child's clinician to write a letter explaining how your child's disability limits his or her functioning. Once the 504 coordinator receives your request, the school may invite you to meet with a team of teachers and staff to see if your child is eligible, and if so, review a proposed plan. Most schools do this, although there's no formal requirement. Note that even as these federal laws exist, states have sometimes dramatically different ways of interpreting them, so you can't assume practices will be the same throughout the country.

IDEA: The Heftier Choice

If 504 assistance isn't enough, you can request special services paid for under the IDEA and provided for your child through an IEP. IEPs cover students meeting the criteria for one or more of more than a dozen categories of disabilities, including being deaf, blind, or autistic, or having brain injuries or disabling orthopedic problems.

The IDEA categories relevant to depression are "emotional disturbance" and a catch-all known as "other health impairment." You may prefer to seek a classification of "other health impairment," which doesn't carry the stigma of labeling someone as emotionally disturbed.

"Emotional Disturbance"

To qualify for an "emotional disturbance" under the IDEA, a student must have at least one of the following problems "over a long period of time and to a marked degree that adversely affects educational performance":

- An inability to learn that cannot be explained by intellectual, sensory, or health factors
- An inability to build or maintain satisfactory interpersonal relationships with peers and teachers
- Inappropriate types of behavior or feelings under normal circumstances
- A general pervasive mood of unhappiness or depression
- A tendency to develop physical symptoms or fears associated with personal or school problems

("Emotional disturbance" also includes schizophrenia.)

"Other Health Impairment"

In contrast to "emotional disturbance," "other health impairment" doesn't specifically mention depression, but the criteria will easily apply:

1. The student has limited strength or vitality or altered alertness, which results in limited alertness with respect to the educational environment.
2. The cause is a chronic or acute health problem, such as attention-deficit/hyperactivity disorder (ADHD), asthma, diabetes, epilepsy, a heart condition, hemophilia,

lead poisoning, leukemia, nephritis, rheumatic fever, or sickle cell anemia.

3. The student's educational performance is adversely affected.

The Evaluation

If you're seeking help under IDEA, your child has the right to a free evaluation of his or her learning impediments, paid for by the school. Either you or the school may request this. If you initiate the request, be sure to put it in writing. It's best to send the letter by certified mail or get a receipt when you hand-deliver it. Be specific about what you see as problems, but don't ask for a specific test or diagnosis. Maybe your fifth grader is still counting on his fingers. Or your daughter has turned in only 6 of 30 homework assignments that year.

Once you've made your request, the school must either complete a full evaluation or notify you in writing of the refusal and the reasons for it and advise you of your rights. If your child has been refused, ask to meet with school officials to make sure you understand the reasons and the appeal process.

You may want to get your own evaluation even if the school is willing to do one. The law says the school evaluator(s) should be "a multi-disciplinary team" with "trained and knowledge-able" personnel who use "technically sound instruments," but this is sometimes more aspirational than real. If you can show that the school ignored the concerns in your letter or is unable to do an adequate evaluation, you may be able to get it to pay. Also check if your insurance will reimburse you. Most won't, but Medicaid may.

Assuming the school agrees to evaluate your child, you must give your consent in writing and the evaluation must take place within 60 days, unless the law in your state says otherwise. The evaluation should determine whether your child qualifies as disabled and what his or her educational needs must be.

Note that this can be a drawn-out process. If you feel like the clock is ticking and your child is losing valuable time, consider writing a letter requesting that the school expedite the evaluation.

The Individualized Education Program

Once evaluation results are available, your school must invite you to an eligibility meeting where you and the other members of your child's team will decide whether your child is eligible for special education and related services. Consider asking your child's doctor or therapist to attend this meeting, perhaps by teleconferencing to save on travel time (and costs).

If your child is eligible, your school must develop an IEP within 30 days and must invite you to a meeting to help write it. The resulting written statement must include, at minimum:

- An assessment of your child's level of functioning
- A description of the special education and related services to be provided—including *where* the services will be provided, if the school can't offer them
- A statement of academic and functional goals to be assessed each year
- A description of how progress will be measured

It must then be reviewed at least once a year and revised as needed.

If you don't agree with the plan, state this at the meeting, write down that you do not agree, and give your note of disagreement to whomever is in charge of the meeting. As with all documents, sign and date it and keep a copy in your files.

Consider requesting another meeting to try to work out a compromise. In some states, you can ask for a meeting chaired by a neutral party, or for mediation. Before choosing either of these routes, consider talking to an experienced attorney.

The IEP may list relatively minor strategies, such as more time on tests, or being able to sit in the front row, but also may determine that your child needs intensive care at a setting outside the school. The guiding principle is that a student should be placed in the "least restrictive" learning environment. Your child shouldn't be sent to a separate special education class if his or her needs can be met in a regular classroom. But if your child needs round-the-clock residential care, the school may be required to pay for at least part of it. So while IEPs take time and energy, they do more than help prepare a student for "further education, employment, and independent living," as is the law's mission. They've also saved many parents a considerable amount of money.

As we've noted, your child may qualify for some psychological services, including school-based counseling, under this law. Another possibility is that the school might pay for placement in a therapeutic day program or even a long-term residential facility. These more extreme measures usually require a due process hearing or sometimes also an appeal to a state or federal court. Don't expect immediate relief.

> "If your child gets an IEP through a school district, they can be required to provide therapy," says Dorothy O'Donnell. "This was something I wish I'd known early on in this journey but unfortunately only realized after we'd been paying for therapy for years and finally consulted a lawyer. He was the one who told us that based on the severity of the mental problems the school

assessment found in my daughter, they should have provided therapy."

The Functional Behavioral Assessment

If your child's bipolar disorder is resulting in disciplinary problems, you need to know about the functional behavioral assessment (FBA), which is part of the IDEA law. This could be part of the IDEA evaluation, but any parent may request one if there's reason to believe a student is misbehaving because of mental illness. Asking for an FBA in writing as soon as you recognize the risk is also a strategic tactic to reduce the chance that your child will be punished, suspended, or expelled because of behavior beyond his or her control.

The assessment should be led by someone trained in understanding behavior, and it should look at where and when misbehavior is occurring.

"I used to do my best to get kicked out of math class, because I have dyscalculia, and knew it was more socially acceptable to be a troublemaker than be branded 'stupid,'" says Howey.

All Sorts of Support

Regardless of IEPs or 504s, teachers should still expect students to make their best efforts each day. The supports should be designed only to help them make the most of their capabilities.

The accommodations aim to address two main groups of problems that can interfere with academic success: stress and poor communication. Stress relief is especially important, given that stress at school can destabilize a student who is emotionally fragile. Kids with bipolar disorder may need extra help with transitions and unstructured periods during the day. Kids with common coexisting issues, such as ADHD and anxiety, may need more time with tests and assignments. As you develop a list of accommodations, ask your child for his or her input, which if nothing else may help get initial buy-in. Ideally, however, your child should take ownership of his or her plan over time, honing those important self-advocacy skills.

Following are some common accommodations that might fit into either a 504 plan or an IEP.

Relieving Stress
Scheduling

- Allow for a later start or a shorter day, to improve sleep and reduce stress.
- Schedule the most stimulating classes early in the day to get the student interested.
- Schedule the hardest classes for the time of day when the student is usually most alert.

"I arrange it so my son never has two classes in a row where he has to sit still," says one parent. For instance, her son might follow a math class with PE.

Classroom Activities

- Provide movement breaks at regular intervals.
- Allow a water bottle at the desk (some bipolar disorder medications make kids extra-thirsty).
- Permit frequent bathroom breaks (more frequent urination is another potential side-effect of medication)

and self-imposed "time-outs" if the student is feeling overwhelmed.

- Use alternative discipline tactics for behavior problems. Traditional approaches to discipline don't work well when kids have bipolar disorder. Some alternatives could include giving a student more time to comply with a request or writing up a list of options from which a student may choose.

Testing

- Break long tests into smaller segments.
- Simplify test instructions.
- Allow extra time for tests.
- Provide a test room away from other students and distractions.
- Offer other assignments as an alternative to high-stress tests.

One mother, whose son was in a drug rehabilitation program for two hours a day, three days a week, persuaded his school to give him high school credit for attending, arguing that this experience would help him more in life than any history class or English class.

Homework

- Simplify homework instructions.
- Extend deadlines for projects.

Improving Communication

- Have the student meet with a teacher on arriving at school each day to gauge his or her ability to succeed in certain classes. Potentially provide alternatives to stressful activities on difficult days.

- Conduct regular and frequent meetings or phone calls between teachers and parents about the student's classroom performance.

Be a Squeaky Wheel

Don't make the mistake of assuming that once an IEP is in place, you can check out. Many parents say they've had to bird-dog schools to make sure they're following the law, implementing a plan that's working well for their child.

Dorothy O'Donnell described this learning curve, after a couple years of assuming that her daughter Sadie was getting the help she needed. After all, Sadie's IEP provided several supports, such as preferential seating, reductions in classwork, and an hour a week of one-on-one tutoring. By fourth grade, however, these accommodations seemed like "Band-Aids on someone with a severed limb," O'Donnell decided.

"With the bigger class size and less time for her teacher to check in on her, the solution seemed to be to just let her skip assignments. This got much worse in fifth grade. Assignments I knew she'd completed because either I or her tutor helped her with them, and literally watched her put them in her backpack, were never making it into her teacher's hands. I was shocked at how many assignments the teacher said she was missing and never heard a thing about this until I requested a meeting with her. I told her that with Sadie's executive function and emotional problems, there was no way she was just going to put her assignments in the right place without some kind of reminder or check in from the teacher. My daughter was also unable to participate in events she liked, like reading in the garden, because she either forgot her book or couldn't find it. And the teacher just didn't have the time or desire to figure out a solution, like having an extra book on hand for her. Her teacher said she often just spent her time in class doodling or writing herself negative notes. I was furious because I didn't see how that could possibly be acceptable. It was clear she wasn't learning anything and was actually regressing."

O'Donnell ended up hiring a lawyer who helped move Sadie to a private school, at the public school's expense, which she believes vastly improved her daughter's education. You might also have to take extreme measures to make sure your child doesn't get lost in the shuffle.

At the same time, keep in mind that your child's teacher may be trying his or her hardest, but overwhelmed with the increasing numbers of students whose families are demanding accommodations.

"Ten years ago, maybe 10% of my students had an IEP or 504 plan," says Brian. "Now it's 30 to 40%. In many cases, they do need support, but in some cases you'll have these savvy parents who are simply trying to get their child an edge. The result is I've got 30 to 40 reports I have to read, all with different sorts of accommodations. Honestly, I don't read them. I don't have that kind of time. I try instead to get to know the kid."

Brian has a smart tip for kids coping with mood disorders in school.

"When I reflect on the students who've had the most success despite their challenges, it's really been those who've had a clear sense of their disorder—without denying it— and could talk about it with me," he says. "I'm thinking in particular of one girl who would occasionally get triggered by something and then fly out of the room wailing in emotional agony, but who would then return later in the day and apologize, and talk about it, without shame or frustration. She was also an incredible student, so maybe was special in that way, but her ability to establish that clear, trusting dialogue was key to her being so successful."

More COVID-19 Chaos

The pandemic has had a particularly disruptive impact on students receiving special services. In many cases, schools that shut down simply suspended provisions of IEPs. In several states, parents filed lawsuits complaining that their children had been unfairly harmed. In early 2020, then-US Education Secretary Betsy DeVos said students who missed out should be re-evaluated on return to school and receive "compensatory services." At this writing, schools were still struggling to catch up.

We recommend that you avoid getting mired in legal conflicts if possible. But do keep insisting on high-quality support—whether or not your school is physically open.

Chapter Eight

Life After High School

So your son or daughter has just turned 18.

In the past few years, you've done a great job tracking down effective clinicians, finding ways to afford them, keeping stress down at home, and working diligently with the schools. Your child may still be struggling but feels ready to launch—and you cautiously agree.

Now there's one more major task on your plate in this last year of adolescence.

It's time to help prepare your child for life outside the nest.

Make a Plan

You may be justifiably anxious about this next step. Both you and your teen may be feeling overwhelmed by the choices ahead. Transitions can be stressful for anyone, especially when they're as big as graduating school and possibly moving away from home. Yet as always, learning about your options may help calm you down. You and your child can create a plan to help both of you sleep better at night. Happily, it's by now more likely that your son or daughter has matured to the point that you'll now have a genuine partner in this project.

Remember—and remind your child—that taking a job or signing a lease is not an irrevocable step. For any Plan A, make a Plan B. Focus on keeping the stress as low as possible. If your child is moving out, be clear that he or she has a safe base with you and can return home if needed.

Manage Expectations

Now's a good time for you to listen more than talk, and to restrain any impulse to push. When you do offer your opinion, you'll want to walk the line between optimism and realism. Be mindful of the messages you've sent in the past. Even without saying it, your teen may feel he or she has let you down by not enrolling in your alma mater. Find a noncondescending way to communicate that you're proud your child has graduated—and is going to community college, taking a creative gap year, finding a job, or whatever else is in the works. There will be time for course corrections, if needed. Right now, you need a plan for the next year.

Lay the Foundation

Assuming your son or daughter is moving out, this is a good time to go over some fundamentals: reminders of all you've both learned about self-management and care. Consider relaying the suggestions below in a few, spaced-out heart-to-hearts, instead of a single, scary data dump.

Talk about the importance of adequate sleep, good nutrition, regular exercise, and avoiding impulsive behavior, including drugs, alcohol, and ill-advised hookups. Review the value of reliable routines and regular check-ins with parents. In our age of increasingly remote work and school, stress the value of real-life close friends, seen regularly, in person.

Impress on your child, if you haven't already done so enough, the importance of staying on any needed medication. Untreated mania can blow up work relationships and lead to other serious mistakes at school or on the job. But make a plan together in the event of a mental health emergency away from home. This could include a rule that you're allowed to call a friend of theirs if you haven't heard from them as expected.

If you haven't already done so, now is also a good time to talk about managing money responsibly, much as you would with any other teenager, but with some gentle extra emphasis on curbing impulsivity. People with bipolar disorder, as you surely know by now, are prone to risky behavior, including gambling and overspending, including unaffordable online "retail therapy." You might set up a credit card with a low limit to start out, with the condition that you, your partner, or another trusted adult monitor the spending.

Is College in the Cards?

Consider With Care

Even if your teen is set on college, you'll need to proceed carefully. Higher education isn't the best choice for everyone, especially for someone who is emotionally fragile and straight out of high school. The writing has been on the wall about this for several years; a recent study found that nearly 40% of students who enroll in four-year colleges still don't have a degree six years later. Many of them return home, lost, discouraged, and even traumatized.

If your teen is still struggling emotionally, give serious thought to alternatives, even if it means letting go of a dream.

"Sally is brilliant, but she couldn't take the stress of college," says the writer Michael Greenberg. "She kept trying and trying and always dropping out, and sometimes that led to her being hospitalized."

If you believe your child is ready for more independence and challenge, you should still set some limits. By no means send your kid to school across the country if he or she has no experience living alone.

> Meg set two conditions in the three months before she agreed to pay for her son's college deposit. He had to stop drinking and smoking marijuana, meaning he had to agree to be tested. He also had to choose a school close to home. "I just knew I wasn't going to be able to travel 3,000 miles to go get him if something went wrong," says Meg. She and Jason's stepfather chose not to have him drug-tested on campus, even though she knew parents who had done that. "I felt that he had to be responsible for himself," she says. "If he got into trouble at college he'd experience natural consequences of his decision-making," she says. Unfortunately, Jason did start drinking again in college, but quit smoking marijuana, and managed to graduate.

Your child may fare best by living at home and attending a community college for the first year or two. If that works out well, you might both feel more confident to move on to the bigger challenge, which could include a four-year school farther from home.

Fill the Gap

Taking a "gap year" has been an increasingly popular option in recent years. Whether you sign up for a formal program, which can be expensive, or design one of your own, the trick is to make sure you're not wasting time and money. It will take some thought and research to decide on a good use of the year. The plan could include volunteering, working as an intern, or taking a low-skill job to save up money. Talk to your child's high school counselor and carefully vet programs. The Gap Year Association offers accreditation and its website is a good early guide to programs, costs, and financial aid. Check out the array of enviable choices, including learning Mandarin in Taipei, conversing with national intellectual leaders at the School of the *New York Times*, mastering white-water rafting in the American Southwest, or interning with community organizations in Argentina. Internships are a particularly wise choice for students with or without specific emotional challenges. It's always a good idea to investigate what a job entails before deciding on a career.

When choosing a program, pay special attention to the structure it provides, since that can be a helpful guard against anxiety and depression.

> "After one serious episode, Sally spent about six months on a farm in Vermont where we had connections," says Michael Greenberg. "It wasn't a survive-in-the-wilderness kind of program, but you had to work. That was a good thing: The work engaged her; she was attached to the animals, and she was proud of the maple syrup they produced."

You may want to consider a "gap" program specifically designed to prepare students for adult life. Since 2014, hundreds of students with mental disabilities have graduated from NITEO, at Boston College, a six-month program aimed at helping kids develop the skills and resilience to go on to higher education or a job. NITEO is a small program trying to fill a big need, but similar efforts are emerging. Fountain House, a national nonprofit, runs a 14-week college re-entry program for students aged 18 to 30 who left school due to mental illness.

Vocational training is another good option to ease the transition into the working world. Many colleges also now have co-op programs, in which students can work part-time, which helps reduce financial stress and provides structure. For low-income families, the US Job Corps provides eight months to two years of academic and career training plus housing to kids aged 16 to 24.

Investigate the Angles

If you're helping with your high school senior's college application (and what parents aren't doing that these days?) don't hesitate to seek consideration of time lost to bipolar disorder, assuming your child agrees.

> "It was only after my daughter's freshman year that she tried medication," says Julie. "After that, she got all A's. So I'm writing a letter asking them to ignore the grades she got in her first year."

And when researching potential scholarships, check out the specially designated aid for children with disabilities, including mental illness, offered by organizations such as Google and Wells Fargo. Scholarships.com is a good first place to look, but you can also check with your child's high school counselor or contact the financial aid department of the college your child may attend.

College Mental Health Resources

Just as there is a significantly increased need for mental health providers throughout the country, there is also increased need for mental health services on college campuses—partly because kids who in previous generations would not have made it to college due to struggles with their mental health are now able to attend because of great advances in treatment. What this means, though, is that the use of college counseling centers is on the rise, having increased 30% between 2009 and 2015—and it continues to increase.

> "In my son's freshman year he became so depressed that he checked into the psychiatric hospital off-campus," says Beth. "I kept calling the mental health clinic and couldn't get any straight answers, so I flew across the country to get him out. When I arrived, I learned there were seven other kids in the hospital from the same school."

If your child does go away to school, it's important to know that a medical leave of absence may be necessary if a crisis occurs. There is no shame in taking a break from school in order to get healthy. As such, you will want to find out what your child's school's policy and protocol are for medical leaves of absence due to mental health issues, as well as re-entry into the institution once they've recovered.

When considering schools with your child, ask about the ratio of therapists to students. What is the school's policy for mental health crises? How effective is its disability office? What classroom accommodations are available? Some schools are better resourced than others in this regard; some even use their "wellness" services in their marketing. Assuming things look good, encourage your child to self-advocate, seek accommodations, and make use of the disability office and other resources as needed—but only as needed, and discreetly. Not every professor or even fellow student will be sensitive to learning about another student's mental health struggles.

Go with your son or daughter to check out a couple of schools. Questions will arise on campus that might not occur at home, and it's a great way to show your teen that he or she is not alone in this decision.

Get It in Writing

Don't forget to get your teen's written permission in advance to communicate with the school about health issues. Privacy rules are complicated, with sometimes different interpretations depending on the school. In some cases, colleges will make exceptions to their rules if a student is in crisis. Yet many a parent has been surprised, infuriated, and ready to sue by a college's refusal to share a student's health information, even in an emergency, citing HIPAA (the Health Insurance Portability and Accountability Act) or FERPA (the Family Educational Rights and Privacy Act) restrictions.

Sometimes a conscientious faculty member will reach out. And sometimes a parent can get answers even without a child's permission, by being sufficiently noisy and insistent. But you may not have the wherewithal to do that when you're panicked, so better to take simple precautions. Before your child leaves for school, call the campus information office and ask for any forms you and your student can sign in advance to ensure that officials can communicate with you.

The JED Foundation, a national mental health nonprofit group, gives this advice for parents worried about a faraway student's mental health:

- *Call the dean.* If you're concerned after speaking to your child, you can call the dean of students, the vice president of student affairs, or the counseling office for an independent check.
- *Report emergencies immediately.* If your child is talking about violence or self-harm or sounds markedly different from usual (such as speaking incoherently), let the counseling service or even campus security know immediately.
- *Get help if you're having trouble separating.* If you find yourself constantly worrying, despite reassurances from your child and campus professionals, you may need to talk it out with a professional.

There is some good news. Many colleges and universities around the country are now expanding and reshaping their student mental health services. For example, the JED Foundation has developed a rapidly expanding national program, called JED Campus, which consults with institutions of higher learning on how to improve their mental health systems and supports, as well as suicide prevention programs. As of this writing, there are more than 370 JED Campuses, and recent findings by the Foundation indicate that the ability of colleges and campuses to protect the mental health of their students has improved considerably.

Joining the Workforce?

Planning the Best Fit

Whether or not you have a college-bound student, now's a good time to brainstorm about future jobs with the best chance of preserving mental health. Satisfying work can be a major source of well-being, but choosing that work can be tricky. Best to anticipate some possible pitfalls.

Nearly 9 out of 10 people with bipolar disorder say the illness has affected their job performance, according to a survey by the Depression and Bipolar Support Alliance. Fifty-eight percent quit working outside their homes. More than 50% said they had to change jobs more often than others, and many felt they had been passed up for promotions.

Minimizing stress on the job should be a priority, and luckily there are ways to do that. Working at home—which has become a lot more common—is one way, although if that's alluring, you should also talk to your child about how to avoid the significant risks of social isolation.

A regular schedule with predictable tasks is preferable to shift work with changing hours or working on projects with intense deadlines. That way it's easier to avoid dangerous disruptions in sleep and healthy routines like getting enough exercise. Part-time, flexible work may be better than a full-time job, if that's possible. The gig economy is booming, but jumping from gig to gig can be stressful.

Self-awareness is a major contributor to success at work for *anyone*, so we hope by now your child has had enough counseling and practice to recognize his or her triggers and know how to manage anxiety. Consider jobs that are flexible enough to provide breaks when needed. Copywriting, technical writing, and computer programming may be good options for kids with relevant skills. Accounting is another skilled job that can be flexible and remote. Outside the home, low-stress, structured jobs include being an office receptionist, audiologist, or sonographer. Some easily stressed kids flourish by working with animals, and thanks to the pandemic, when so many families got new pets, there has never been a bigger demand for dog walkers. Landscaping and gardening are also low-stress and flexible jobs that don't entail a lot of interpersonal conflict.

There are lots of jobs available in caregiving of all kinds, but surveys show caregivers on average are extraordinarily stressed, with a high risk for depression. On the other hand, being unemployed—and uninsured—is also a major threat to mental health.

Talk to your teen about his or her strengths and passions. Encourage him or her to visit the high school career counselor and talk it over with the therapist. Look into internships to see if a certain job makes sense. And take it as slowly as you need.

If your child is considering a specific new job, look into the mental health benefits provided, as these can vary widely. What is the insurance coverage? Are there on-site resources? Many employers now offer such benefits, and younger generations, who've been more open about talking about mental illness, have been more outspoken in requesting them.

Even so, your child should think carefully about how much private information to share with the employer, at least at first. You can't predict the reaction, so the best plan may be to research the benefits independently and wait at least a few months before requesting any of the accommodations we describe below.

Rights on the Job

Your young adult should be aware of government support for people disabled by mental illness.

The Americans with Disabilities Act (ADA) protects people from discrimination if a physical or mental impairment "substantially limits one or more major life activities."

Reasonable accommodations could include flexible working hours, an option to work remotely, health insurance with mental health care, a workplace with reduced distractions, permission to drink water during the day or take mental health breaks, or time off with or without pay. Some employers may tap their disability insurance to pay at least a partial salary during this time.

These accommodations aren't automatic: Employees need to request them. You're not required to specify a psychiatric disorder. Saying you need time off to adjust to a new medication may be enough. But you may also need to provide some written documentation.

An employer can deny any accommodations that would cause the company undue hardship—for instance, by being excessively costly for a relatively small business.

For more information, call the US Department of Justice ADA Information Line at 800-514-0301 or go to www.ada.gov.

You and your child should also be aware of the following:

The US Equal Employment Opportunity Commission considers complaints by employees who believe they've been fired or denied accommodations unfairly. Claims must be filed within 180 days of the violation.

The Family and Medical Leave Act (FMLA) allows up to 12 weeks of unpaid leave during a year. For more information, call 866-487-9243 or visit the US Department of Labor website.

Social Security Disability Insurance (SSDI) provides income for qualified employees who can't work due to a documented mental or physical disability that is either intermittent or continuous.

Mood disorders may qualify for SSDI payments, and bipolar disorder is mentioned specifically in the law. But the requirements are strict, and applications are often rejected.

Call 800-772-1213 or visit the Social Security website for more information.

Chapter Nine

Coping With Crises

"I quickly became sensitive to the signs. In fact, I lived in terror of the signs," says Michael Greenberg, about his daughter's mania. "She had a certain way of talking: faster, and like there's a pressure in the speech, like, 'Yes. Yes. I do. Right. Yes.' A kind of pressured sort of falseness. She'd sit in a tense position, so deep in her own psyche that she couldn't really respond. And she'd stop sleeping. Sleep was really the biggest indicator. I'd hear her get up and I'd jump up and she'd be sitting out on the fire escape smoking a cigarette, or trying to leave our apartment."

Greenberg is describing something that millions of parents of children with bipolar disorder have sadly learned to recognize: the signs of a crisis brewing. Many such parents become hypervigilant, never able to predict what their kid will do next. One day might bring a mild argument, another a fist punched through a wall. Still another could produce a call from school or the police, an attempt to run away from home, a car crash, or—every parent's worst fear—a suicide. Until now, we've given you guidance on the day to day. This chapter is for when things fall apart.

Trigger alert: This chapter will deal with some of the scariest and hardest experiences you may have in caring for someone with serious mental illness. For many of you, it may never get this bad. But we want to arm you with the best possible information. Hope for the best, in other words, but make sure you never regret not preparing for the worst.

> "I continue to arraign and prosecute myself for every sign, every clue, I missed," writes Rep. Jamie Raskin (D-Md.), a former law professor who lost his 25-year-old son Tommy to suicide in 2020. Tommy had suffered from depression that his parents said in a remembrance had been "a kind of relentless torture in the brain for him" that became "overwhelming and unyielding and unbearable."

Sending Out an SOS

Many adolescents challenge authority and break rules. At some point, many lie, turn sullen, stay out late, keep secrets, and experiment with drugs. Yet it's common for kids who are struggling with bipolar disorder to go farther, sometimes becoming extraordinarily defiant, hostile, and aggressive. If your son or daughter is behaving this way, remind yourself that your child is not your enemy, determined to ruin your life. He or she needs help.

Remember what we told you earlier about not succumbing to shame. We've spoken with parents whose children have whacked them in the face, or stolen the car, or been caught selling drugs. You don't need to love their behavior, but loving them, as hard as it may sometimes be, may be the only thing that gets all of you through this.

"I could write a whole book about abandonment," says Greenberg. "Manic depression is annoying and exasperating. Most people end up just wanting to be left alone. People give up. But for Sally, I know my continuing to be there has helped her as much as anything. She knows there are relationships she doesn't want to lose."

Coping With Mania

Parents of children with bipolar disorder should learn to recognize the warning signs of an oncoming manic episode. Not all kids experience full-blown mania, but for those who do, there's a milder prelude, known as the "prodrome," which can last from a day or two to several weeks. This is when you have the most power to avert a potential disaster.

The author and psychologist David Miklowitz compares mania to a train leaving the station. If you catch it in time, you may prevent a crisis.

Become familiar with the sometimes-subtle signs that the train is about to accelerate. Is your adolescent suddenly sleeping less? Talking more? Seeming much more distractible?

If so, call the clinician to schedule an emergency appointment right away.

"I hate it when I hear about it a week later," says psychiatrist Kiki Chang, the bipolar disorder expert in California. Invested in his clients, Chang wants to do what he can for them when he can make the most difference.

Sometimes a higher dose of medication will do. A clinician may also prescribe a new drug temporarily. A high dose of a tranquilizing benzodiazepine such as Ativan (lorazepam) may avert full-blown mania. Or sometimes a clinician might recommend an antipsychotic, such as olanzapine, sold under the brand name Zyprexa. Olanzapine can be effective in the short term but is not a great candidate for longer periods since it tends to cause significant weight gain.

Short of changing meds, and, again, presuming you're catching the mania in time, you can take some precautions at home. Your priority should be to reduce any stress your child may be experiencing. Minimize conflict and arguments. Cancel any travel plans if possible. Double down on efforts to help your child get a good night's sleep, even if that means giving Benadryl or something stronger, prescribed by the doctor. Be sure to have a plan to get to the nearest hospital—that is, know where you're going and how you'll get there. If your child is out of control, you'll need to consider some options we describe below, because going in your car may be out of the question.

Flights From Reason

More than half of people diagnosed with bipolar disorder will at some point see, hear, or believe things that aren't real. This is known as psychosis. Hallucinations and delusions can range from hearing voices, most commonly, to seeing phantoms, to believing you have superpowers. Triggers can include stress, a new medication, recreational drugs, seizures, migraines, or infections.

Your child will likely be frightened and may be reluctant to tell you about these experiences. But if you see signs of this occurring, call your clinician right away. If you suspect your child has taken a hallucinogen, such as LSD or mushrooms, it's important not to behave aggressively, no matter how you feel about these substances. If the problem is not due to drugs, your child's doctor may want to prescribe a medication to treat the psychosis.

Michael Greenberg says it took him a few years to learn not to engage when Sally was in the grip of psychosis. "There were times when she felt she was being watched and kept closing the blinds in our apartment in New York," he recalls. "My instinct was to hear her out and protect her, but I realized that instead of asking, 'Who's watching us?' it was better to tell her she wasn't being watched, that it was a delusion. It felt like a defeat at first because it meant dismissing a large part of her psyche. And it made her very angry. But I came to see the best way I could help her was to be an island of sanity and rationality. I'm the place she can come back to, her reality check. This has turned out to be very important to her over the years."

Watch for Self-Harm

"I feel terrible. I have to make my feelings go away. I use very bitter medicine to make them go away," says "Juanita," a 20-year-old therapy patient quoted in *Cutting: Understanding and Overcoming Self-Mutilation*, by the psychiatrist Steven Levenkron. "When I do it, there's only the place on my skin that I'm looking at. There's nothing—no thoughts . . . I can take a nap after I finish looking at it and cover it with a bandage."

Self-harm is surprisingly common among adolescents at large. Some research suggests as many as one in five will have hurt themselves in a significant way (i.e., more than picking at a cuticle) at some point in their lives. The harm can include burning their skin or cutting it with razors, knives, glass shards, or safety pins. Many kids outgrow the behavior, but researchers have found that about 65% of youth who self-injure will go on to have suicidal thoughts, with a smaller group progressing to suicide attempts.

More girls self-harm than boys. The behavior is also more common among kids who have been bullied, have low self-esteem, or know a friend who has engaged in similar behavior. The frequency rises sharply when an adolescent has a mental disorder. Researchers have found that up to 60% of adolescent psychiatric patients overall injure themselves short of suicide. In kids with bipolar disorder, the behavior is most common during a "mixed phase," in which the child is experiencing simultaneous manic and depressive symptoms.

Inducing pain can help cope with emotions that are otherwise intolerable. It can also become addictive.

"It had a calming, centering effect," said Andy, describing his various techniques for self-harm. "You can't really have a crisis in your own head when you have a cut on your arm." At one point he figured out how to heat up the metal on a lighter by turning the flame upside down and then pressing the metal against his arm. "Then it kept escalating," he said, "until after three months, I poured a bunch of boiling water on my arm. That's when I had to go to the ER." When police arrested him for shoplifting, he told them he had done it to avoid cutting himself. They still put him in jail.

Self-harm can be easy for a parent to miss. For many kids, this behavior is a private way of dealing with otherwise intolerable emotions, so it's common for kids to try to hide their injuries from you, cutting and sometimes burning themselves on the shoulders, abdomen, or thighs in ways that can be covered by clothing. (One warning sign is if your child is suddenly favoring long-sleeved T-shirts or turtlenecks.) On the other hand, your child may have found friends who are also self-harming and is trading tips on techniques.

> "I try not to be obvious, but when his friends come over, I look them over stealthily and most of them are cutting," said Andy's mother. "You can see the scars in the summer when they wear shorts or short sleeves."

Most kids outgrow this behavior, but don't ignore it or dismiss it as a phase. Without overreacting, ask your child the reasons for the behavior, and don't fall into the trap of invalidating them ("It could be worse—you could be a Syrian refugee!"), which could make your child feel even worse. Intervene if the behavior continues. If your child doesn't yet have a therapist, now is the time to get one. You can also help by working together on a plan for what to do instead of cutting, when emotions feel intolerable. Talk about the ways you've learned to deal with your own stress.

Handling Violence at Home

A child with uncontrollable anger is crying out for limits, and he or she wants you to show you can keep everyone safe. Establish rules when things are calm. Make it clear that if anyone becomes physically violent, you will leave the house and call the police, and then stick to that rule the first time it happens: no freebies. It's also a good idea to prepare a list of emergency phone numbers and post it in a prominent place, reinforcing the fact that you mean business.

If you get any inkling that your child's illness could lead to violence, research the options in your community. You may be surprised by how much help is available. Some cities have crisis services that offer temporary, 24-hour care, short of hospitalization. But this may not be an option if your child is seriously aggressive.

One of the most important things you'll need to do if there's a threat of violence is to manage your own reactions. Revealing your fear, anger, or anxiety can fan the flames of your child's emotions, setting the two of you up for a dangerous feedback loop. A rule for doctors in Samuel Shem's book *House of God* is: "At a cardiac arrest, the first procedure is to take your own pulse." Check in with yourself and keep calm so that you can assess the situation, think clearly, and resist the impulse to yell or hit, which could frighten your child and escalate the danger. Recall the stress-management tips and do's and don'ts of dealing with conflicts we provided in Chapter 5, and practice telling yourself: *I am the adult here.* In the thick of things, you want to be able to scan the environment to make sure there aren't any dangerous items the child could grab and harm anyone. If you do see something, try to calmly remove it while keeping an eye on the child.

> "We have a mantra at home, which a wise friend once taught me," says Beth. "It's 'Don't let your lizard brain take over your wizard brain.'"

Beth makes a key point. If your adolescent flies into a rage, he or she is reacting with the most primitive part of the brain, the one involved in life-or-death struggles. The prefrontal cortex, involved in reasoning and good judgment, is the newest to evolve, and the one that separates us from most animals. It's still under construction in your child until about age 25. Sometimes you'll need to use your evolutionary advantage.

This may be a major test of your empathy. If things have reached this point, your child is telling you that he or she is out of control and needs you to keep things safe. You might say something like: "I see how upset you are and want to help.

I'm going to stay with you and make sure you stay safe. When you're ready, I want to know what is bothering you. Can you try to take some deep breaths and tell me what's wrong?"

If you can't get the behavior under control in a reasonable amount of time, don't hesitate to call for help. Sometimes your spouse or another adult close to the child may be better able to defuse the situation. If need be, however, call your child's doctor, a therapist, Child Protective Services, or a community mental health agency. Or if there's no other option, call 911, with the guidance we offer below.

Call the Cops?

In many parts of the country, local governments don't have sufficient funds for mental health response teams, meaning police are your only alternative for a response in a crisis. Sometimes all it takes to change a child's out-of-control behavior is for a uniformed cop to arrive and ask some pointed questions. Police can also transport a person who needs to go to the hospital, even if they are opposed.

You may have heard of a "5150," which refers to the part of the Welfare and Institutions code that allows police to detain someone with a mental challenge for up to 72 hours in a hospital psychiatric ward, with or without their consent. They can do so if a person is a danger to others (or himself or herself) or is "gravely disabled," meaning unable to provide for their own food, clothing, or shelter. (This usually won't apply if friends or family can provide that support.)

Section 5250 allows for the hold to be extended for up to two weeks.

Think carefully before enlisting local police in a mental health emergency. Sometimes officers can skillfully handle such crises. Yet at times they can make a volatile situation worse, and even deadly. In fact, about half of the people who are killed by police have some sort of mental disability, according to a Ruderman Family Foundation report analyzing incidents from 2013 to 2015. One of the cases investigated involved Kristiana Coignard, 17, who walked into the lobby of an East Texas police station asking for help. Coignard, who reportedly struggled with depression and bipolar disorder, had a knife in her waistband and "I have a gun" written on her hand. A scuffle with officers ended in her death.

If you have a child at risk of serious violence at home, we recommend that you waste no time in introducing yourself to local police in advance of any possible crisis and assessing whether or not you can depend on their help. If you can't, make sure you have another, better plan for a possible crisis.

If You Do Call 911 . . .

- Relay the information as calmly as you can.
- Use the phrase "mental health crisis" and explain the diagnosis.
- Ask if a crisis intervention team (CIT) is available. These are officers who have been specially trained to deal with this kind of emergency.
- When the officer arrives, repeat that you've called about a mental health crisis.
- Don't panic if you see your child escorted out in handcuffs. But make sure to get the name of the officer and follow the car if possible.

The 988 Alternative

Remember this number. It's designed to be easy to do so.

In July 2020, the Federal Communications Commission (FCC) designated 988 to replace the old 10-digit number for the National Suicide Prevention Lifeline. The service's new name is "988 Suicide & Crisis Lifeline," and calls are answered by staff trained in suicide counseling and other mental health and substance-use-related emergencies. 988 services are also available by SMS (just by texting, you guessed it, 988).

The switch was inspired by both the recent rise in suicide attempts and several incidents in which police were not prepared to respond. If you call or text 988, you may still be routed to the police, but in most cases it won't be necessary. A survey of Lifeline centers found police weren't required in about 98% of the calls, while in the remaining 2%, the caller was able to collaborate with Lifeline services to coordinate the response.

At this writing, it's too early to tell how this new program may work. Another alternative for advice by phone is Parents Anonymous's national helpline, at 1-855-4A PARENT (1-855-427-2736), with counselors available from 10 a.m. to 7 p.m. PST. Many states have other helplines.

Crises at School

One of the most appalling news stories of 2021 concerned 15-year-old Ethan Crumbley, arrested for shooting four people at a high school in Rochester Hills, Michigan. In a highly unusual move by authorities, Crumbley's parents were also arrested and charged in the crime, for giving their son a gun and ignoring signs of his mental distress. Teachers had caught the boy looking for ammunition online and drawing scenes of violence with the words "help me."

School shootings are rare, and Crumbley's parents were clearly outliers, as subsequent reporting established. They not only ignored signs of their child's mental illness and refused the school's request to take him home, but fled from police after being charged. So what lessons can more reasonable adults draw from the case?

Perhaps most importantly, understand that you can't count on every school to do the right thing when your child or someone else's child is in a crisis. (When Crumbley's teachers couldn't get the parents' cooperation, the boy returned to his classroom.) You should expect that if a student is clearly losing control that he or she will be removed from class, at least temporarily. If you get this kind of call from school, you should be ready to respond quickly and take your child to see a clinician ASAP. If not, you may risk having your child taken to the hospital in a police car, an obviously traumatic experience.

> "I got a call from my daughter's school in October, telling me she was planning to harm herself and that I was immediately required to remove her from school," says Janet in Nevada. "From that moment on, she was with another adult, a teacher or the school psychologist, at all times. But before I could get there, the school resource officer had stepped in and decided the right course of action was for her to go to a mental health facility. Had I not agreed, they would have transported her without my consent."

Trouble With the Law

It is—alas—not entirely unlikely that at some point you're going to be dealing with police. Your child may even end up incarcerated. Estimates vary widely, but one study suggested that up to 7 out of 10 youth in juvenile hall have some sort of diagnosable mental health problem.

There are some obvious reasons why kids with bipolar disorder land in jail. Mania can increase impulsivity and risk-taking, while diminishing concern about the consequences.

Juvenile justice in some ways is like the adult system, with parallel rules for arrests, hearings, and probation. But theoretically, at least, it operates on the premise that youth are less responsible for their actions and more responsive to rehabilitation than adults. We say "theoretically" because attitudes vary from place to place and even from person to person. No matter how ill your child may be, you can't count on universal understanding and tolerance.

If your child has been causing nonstop conflict at home, it may be tempting not to fight against detention for the sake of some relief. It's also true that some kids from chaotic home environments might benefit from the extra structure, rules, consequences, and regular meals. Yet for most adolescents with mental illnesses, you'll want to avoid or limit the time in detention as much as you can. Juvenile hall is no place for someone coping with bipolar disorder, as just one statistic makes clear: Incarcerated youth die by suicide two to three times more often than those in the general population.

Juvenile hall "counselors," who also serve as guards, are normally not well-trained to deal with mental illness, despite how common it is in that environment. They will often mistake mood disorder symptoms as defiance and punish it accordingly. Solitary confinement isn't uncommon, even as many states are challenging it, and no matter how traumatizing it can be to someone struggling with mental illness. There's also a risk that your child will receive psychotropic drugs that you or their doctor wouldn't want them to take. Finally, being around law-breaking and sometimes violent kids not only physically

218 If Your Adolescent Has Bipolar Disorder

endangers your kid but makes it more likely he or she will be influenced to continue antisocial behavior.

"About half of our juvenile hall is a mental health facility. And we don't have adequate services to keep up with that," Arthur L. Bowie, supervising assistant public defender of Sacramento County's juvenile division, told a reporter in 2014. "We're making criminals out of them."

Police have a lot of discretion if they arrest your child. Sometimes if you appear at the station as an obviously concerned and responsible parent, you can talk them out of a formal arrest. This unfortunately is one way the justice system penalizes the poor: Kids whose parents can't get time off their jobs to attend to them or find a good lawyer will likely face harsher treatment.

Know Your Rights

The juvenile justice system is large, complex, and constantly changing. We have room for just a few of the basics in this book. By now, however, we hope you've gotten good at googling. Many local communities and states have nonprofit organizations that will help you advocate for your child. The relevant words and phrases to find them are "juvenile justice," "advocacy," "mental illness," and the name of your state. We also list some online resources for you at the end of this book.

You should know that police must notify you if they are detaining your son or daughter and where that may be. They may decide to send your child home with you but with a notice to later appear at the station or in court. If your child is sent to juvenile hall, he or she has the right to make at least two phone calls, one of which must be to a lawyer.

Sometimes the stay will be brief, the charges minor, and for juveniles you can expect that the arrest record will later be expunged. But for anything more serious, you'll want to find an attorney, either for pay or pro bono—or you may be assigned one from the public defender's office. Make sure to notify your child's doctor ASAP and request that he or she attest to your child's mental health issues and alternatives to detention.

As soon as you can, find a contact person at the hall, and make that person aware of your child's mental health challenges. Advise them if your child is taking medication and get that medication to the hall without delay. You may find yourself needing to educate your child's lawyer, if there is one, about depression/bipolar disorder. It's also a good idea to provide psychiatric and educational evaluations to court personnel and your attorney. If your son or daughter has an individualized education program (IEP) or 504 plan, provide that to your contact at the hall and inform your child's attorney. Any existing accommodations should apply to any educational services provided in detention.

For serious charges, a juvenile court judge may decide on one of several possible outcomes:

- Your child may be sent back to live with you under court supervision.
- Your child may be sent to live in a group home or institution, or with foster parents, if it's found you can't adequately provide care.
- Your child may be put on probation and sent to a rehabilitative program, which may be out of state.
- Your child may be sent to a juvenile correctional facility.
- In the most serious cases, such as homicide, rape, and crimes with guns, and if your child is older than 14, he

or she may be tried as an adult and sent to prison. In that case, he or she will stay at a juvenile justice facility until at least age 18.

As the parent or guardian of your child, you may be financially responsible for any damages caused, including court-ordered payments to any victims.

Desperate Means

Now we come to that hardest of topics, the scariest for any parent to consider, but one you must face and prepare for if your child has bipolar disorder.

It's worth a reminder: People with bipolar disorder are more than 10 times as likely as others to attempt suicide, and as many as 15 to 20% (most of them untreated) will die that way. Whether or not your child has made a suicide attempt in the past or has talked about doing so, this is a danger you can't afford to ignore.

Attempts are most common during the first few episodes of illness, before a person has learned that the hopeless feelings and suicidal thoughts will eventually pass. This is one reason why adolescents, who don't yet have much life experience dealing with their symptoms, are at greater risk of acting on their suicidal impulses. Most suicidal adolescents desperately want to live but can't see another way out of their intolerable distress. Treatment can provide them with a life-affirming means of working toward getting well.

Risk Factors

Among older teenagers in general, girls are twice as likely as boys to make a suicide attempt but boys are four times more likely to die by suicide. A child is also more likely to attempt suicide if:

- There's a family history of such behavior.
- There are guns in the house (this is also a factor in *completed* suicides).
- The child is LGBTQ+ and has gotten negative feedback about "coming out."
- The child has an eating disorder.
- A girl has been a victim of dating violence.
- The child is abusing drugs.

Up to half of those who ultimately die by suicide have made previous attempts. In fact, most deaths from suicide are preceded by warning signs that survivors may recognize only after the fact.

Red Flags

Here are some warning signs that your child may be at risk of suicide:

- Withdrawal from friends, family, and activities
- Violent actions, rebellious behavior, or running away
- An increase in risk-taking behavior
- Drug or alcohol use
- Unusual neglect of his or her appearance
- Inability to tolerate praise or reward
- Describing himself or herself as a bad person
- Saying things like "Nothing matters anymore," or "I won't be a problem much longer"
- Giving away prized possessions, throwing out important belongings, or otherwise putting his or her affairs in order

- Becoming cheerful overnight after a period of depression
- Having hallucinations or bizarre thoughts

Preventing Suicidal Behavior

As we've noted throughout this book, it's crucial to have regular talks with your child and be aware of what's going on in his or her life. Without overdoing it, don't be afraid to address your worries. You might say something like "I can tell you've been under some stress lately" and ask if there's any way to help. You might also say "I worry because I love you" and ask if things ever get so hard that your child has thought about suicide. If your child is not already in treatment, this may be time to start. If your child insists that he or she is fine, gently leave the door open to talk again about this in the future. This is one of those occasions, however, when you don't want to be too subtle.

"Words gain strange and mystical powers when they are not spoken at times when they should be spoken," writes Rep. Raskin. "Not talking about suicide to a depressed person is like not talking about sex and birth control to a teenager. Verbal taboos create mystery, and people gravitate toward mystery . . . as uncomfortable and intrusive as it may seem, it is essential to use the word *suicide* itself in order to demystify and deflate it, to strip it of its phony pretense to omnipotence and supernatural force."

"When Sadie is struggling, I do ask if she's thinking about hurting herself," Dorothy O'Donnell said of her now college-student daughter. "And if she is, I remind her that the bad feelings will pass and try to get her to promise to call a hotline, me or her therapist—or someone she trusts—when she's really hopeless. And she's pretty good about doing that. I know she's called hotlines or her therapists a few times."

Don't be afraid to address the topic, especially if your child knows someone who has died by suicide or has seen related recent media coverage. Young people are vulnerable to "suicide contagion"—an increase in suicidal thoughts and behavior triggered by news, gossip, and idealization of a person who has just died by suicide. That's why Netflix changed the controversial suicide scene in the TV series *13 Reasons Why* two years after the show's 2017 premiere. Experts warned that the depiction of the lead actress cutting her wrist with a razor blade may have encouraged copycats.

You can't control everything your child watches or hears. But you can keep your ears open and use these occasions to have a frank conversation. You might ask what other action the friend or fictional character might have taken in response to adversity.

You've probably heard that saying about suicide being a permanent solution to a temporary problem. Many young people commit suicide impulsively after a stressful event such as losing a pet, being humiliated in some way, such as being ostracized at school, getting in trouble with the law, or breaking up with a girlfriend or boyfriend. If your child is open to talking about suicidal thoughts, suggest that you can collaborate to prevent it. Some parents and children have collaborated on a safety plan that stipulates some of the warning signs, coping strategies, and resources—including other adults your child can call. What activities always make your child feel better? Does he or she know you can be called at work or anywhere else?

If your child has bipolar disorder, don't delay doing the safety sweep we described in Chapter 5. It's essential and worth repeating that you should get rid of or lock up any guns and knives and prescription medications.

"While our daughter was still in the hospital, her therapist told us that as soon as she got back home we should walk through the house with her and remove anything that might be unsafe or triggering," says Sandy. "We locked up the knives. Scissors. Even the strings on hoodies. And we no longer let her sit in her room with the door shut anymore."

Hospitalization

"I came to appreciate hospitals, because I knew at least Sally was safe there—that she couldn't harm herself and that she would be able to sleep and reconstitute her psyche without pressure or interruption," says Michael Greenberg. "She would also be able to undergo changes of medication under professional observation without fear or serious ramifications if the new meds affected her badly, and she wouldn't be able to just wander out into the world and be taken advantage of by malicious strangers or be put in jail by police for some charge like disorderly conduct."

In any given year, about one in eight adolescents with bipolar disorder will need to be hospitalized due to their illness, according to the researcher David Miklowitz. It's also common for such kids to have to be hospitalized more than once.

Your child may be sent to a hospital after a crisis at school or a brush with police or after a clinician recommends it. You should also consider requesting hospitalization if your child can no longer function at school or in public. As Greenberg notes, a significant upside is that you can count on your child being physically safe for as long as it lasts. Moreover, on discharge, the staff should present you with a plan for continued outpatient care. Sometimes they will recommend community resources you didn't know existed.

Prepare a contingency plan for hospitalization as soon as you know your child has a serious mood disorder. Find the best available facility, based on what you can learn about its quality of care and whether it's in-network under your insurance plan. If possible, look for a teaching hospital, where you can count on an experienced psychiatrist overseeing the residents and other staff treating your child. Check whether the hospital is accredited by the Joint Commission on Accreditation of Healthcare Organizations (JCAHO) as a treatment facility for children.

Having your child be hospitalized can be frightening, especially if it's the first time and you have no idea what to expect. There's nothing like inpatient care, moreover, to press home the reality of your child's illness.

If your child needs a hospital stay, starting sooner rather than later may expedite treatment. Be sure to introduce yourself to not only the team that will be treating your child during the day but also to the evening staff. You should visit your child in the hospital during different times of the day so that as many of the staff as possible knows who you are and that they should call you with any problems.

Don't hesitate to press doctors to keep you informed. You have a right to information about the treatment being given to your child. Be clear with the hospital treatment team that you expect them to get your consent to any medication decision— even in the middle of the night.

It's crucial that you advocate for your child, and the doctors have a responsibility to tell you what is going on. If you're calling to check in on your child and can't get through, keep calling until you do. If need be, ask the operator for help in escalating your request. One option is to talk to the patient relations department, which every hospital should have.

If a time comes when you believe your child is stable and don't agree with continued hospitalization, and if your child agrees, you can ask to have your child released. But if the medical team disagrees with this, a court hearing may be necessary.

Either way, do your best to connect the inpatient team caring for your child with the outpatient team that will take up the work when your child is released. It's a good idea to ask that the two teams have a conference call, with you included, to discuss next steps.

Affording the Hospital Stay

Once again ideally, you should understand your insurance plan benefits *before* your child needs serious care. Call the number on your insurance card and get an explanation. Make sure to ask about what happens if your child needs repeated hospital stays. If the answer isn't satisfactory, look into other plans.

If your child has already been hospitalized, notify your plan right away and inquire about the cost. If the hospital is not in your plan's network, tell them you want them to negotiate a rate with your insurance company. If you don't have adequate insurance coverage at the time your child is hospitalized, consider applying for Medicaid.

The average length of a psychiatric hospitalization is between 7 and 13 days, and it can sometimes be longer, but in recent years it's becoming ever shorter. Your insurance company will likely push for the briefest possible stay, while the hospital staff may push back, if needed. Still, understand that the hospital's goal will be to stabilize the patient, solving the acute crisis. Don't expect intensive psychotherapy; medication, group therapy, and family crisis intervention will be the main tactics. Visits with the psychiatrist may last less than half an hour per day, if that.

What If Your Child Doesn't Consent to Hospitalization?

Many parents are surprised to learn that their child under age 18 has the right to refuse treatment, including hospitalization. The nature of the rights and the age at which they begin vary from state to state. Be aware that you may find yourself in a situation where your child's psychiatrist recommends hospitalization, and you agree, but your child doesn't consent.

In such cases, most states allow a physician to prescribe involuntary hospitalization for a short evaluation period, usually three days. After that time, if the evaluation team believes that a longer hospitalization is needed, a court hearing is required to determine whether the child can be forced to stay in the hospital. If the team recommends involuntary admission, the court can issue an order for a specific period.

"I've always tried to get her to the hospital before she's too far gone, when she's still scared about what's happening to her which is an indication she still has a grip on reality," says Michael Greenberg. "When you're manic you don't feel you're sick. You feel powerful and maximum aliveness, even though you've hit that point of mania when you've passed from the charming into the alarming . . . Somehow though we hit on this thing where she would act like she was going to prove to me she was okay by agreeing to go to the hospital. It was a way for her to allow herself to be in the hospital and allow herself to be treated. . . . It didn't always work. But there is always part of her that wants to be okay, to protect her life and relationships, that wants a life of predictability where mood swings are within the realm of manageableness."

The Lure of the "Troubled Teen" Industry

"Ellen left for a treatment program one month after her suicide attempt," says Charlene. "Faced with her depression, intrusive thoughts and constant suicidal ideations, and close to zero help from our health plan, I just couldn't do it at home anymore. . . . She stayed for four months, and we didn't get to speak to her for the first eight weeks . . . Combined with the medication, the program helped, overall, but we got a different kid back. It was as if she no longer quite trusted us."

Imagine your child is out of control: breaking rules, staying out all night, and maybe even violent. You fear that he or she is taking dangerous drugs and hanging out with dangerous people. As with Charlene, you may also feel the medical system has let you down.

You're at your wits' end. You're in trouble at work for all the time you've had to take off to care for your kid. Your other children may also be starting to act out. You're arguing with your partner . . . and then someone tells you that you can send your rebellious adolescent away somewhere—by force, if need be—for a few months for intensive treatment, discipline, and care. It may cost a fortune and insurance may not pay a dime, but you'll get a reprieve and your child may get life-changing therapy. Who wouldn't be tempted?

A growing and lucrative "troubled teen" industry, focused on problems including addiction, has emerged to respond to this yearning. More than 5,000 adolescents a year end up in "wilderness therapy" camps like the one Ellen attended, according to a 2020 investigative report on the industry in *Undark.*

In most cases, a child will move on from three months or more in a wilderness camp to a longer period in a residential treatment center (RTC) or boarding school that is often run by the same company. At last count there were more than 170 "therapeutic boarding schools," and many hundreds of "residential treatment centers" and private and government-run camps including the one Ellen attended. (Precise numbers aren't available, since not all facilities are licensed.) There's also a parallel transport business, sometimes staffed by buff military veterans, to escort resistant patients to their new quarters.

The camps, many of which are located in Utah and other western states, have drawn inspiration from the Outward Bound youth adventure program founded in Wales in 1941, while adding therapy and boot-camp-style discipline to address serious adolescent behavorial problems. Ellen had to learn to sew her own backpack and carve her own spoon before she could eat. The *Undark* report quoted other kids who had to remove their shoes and yell out their names while using the toilet, to prevent them from running away.

Some families have been lucky to find well-run programs that fill a desperate need.

After Claire's third hospitalization before her 14th birthday, her mother Sandy was relieved to find a RTC bed in a facility that specialized in mood disorders and accepted her insurance. "So far, I really like the treatment plan," Sandy said. "My husband and I are more involved than we were at the previous facility. They hold parent groups three times a week and we work on emotional coaching with a family therapist, doing verbal and written exercises. Those appointments have been very helpful for me, and I have used some of their techniques when talking to Claire on the phone."

"I watched several students turn their lives around," says the journalist David Marcus, who spent 18 months observing a group of adolescents attending a wilderness camp and boarding school for his book, *What It Takes to Pull Me Through: Why Teenagers Get in Trouble—and How Four of Them Got Out.* "These programs don't work miracles, but some kids just need a chance to reflect, to confront themselves and their demons, while their parents do the same," Marcus says.

At the same time, Marcus and other observers worry about the overall industry tendency to regard teens as a revenue stream. What's more, staff turnover, uneven curriculums, and patchy state standards have led to programs of vastly varying quality. The staff issues, aggravated by pandemic labor turmoil, could undermine children's safety.

Most of the programs are also extremely expensive. Wilderness camps can cost more than $500 a day for several weeks on top of several thousand dollars more for admission fees, plus at least a couple thousand dollars more for an "escort." RTCs and therapeutic boarding schools may cost as much as $10,000 a month. Educational counselors who direct parents to programs tack on another couple of thousand.

Insurance coverage is iffy at best, although you'll most likely be reimbursed if you choose a more conventional RTC, like the one Sandy found, offering short-term (six months or less) intensive therapy in a locked facility. For boarding schools, insurance plans may cover only the hours spent in therapy. For wilderness camps, plans rarely if ever reimburse, and sometimes specifically exclude them. That's largely due to the lack of strong scientific evidence that they make a difference. At this writing, wilderness therapy had yet to be subjected to a randomized controlled trial, with replicable results.

> "It's hard to make a case for spending a lot of money on a program for which there is no strong evidence," John Weisz, a professor of psychology at Harvard University who specializes in mental health interventions for children and adolescents, told *Undark*, adding, "From the state of the evidence that I've seen, we really don't know whether wilderness therapy has beneficial effects or not."

Wilderness programs in particular have a dark recent history. In 2007, a General Accounting Office report investigated thousands of allegations of abuse, including some fatalities, at programs throughout the country. These included the deaths of a 16-year-old girl who fell while rock climbing and a 14-year-old boy who died from dehydration.

Again, we do understand the fear and sense of urgency that would push a parent to opt for these programs. But at this writing, we're concerned about both the risks and expense.

If you feel there's no alternative, consider these suggestions:

- *Don't cut off communication with your child.* The best programs include parent participation. Choose one that allows you to visit at will and which guarantees regular updates on your child.
- *Make sure the program is licensed by the state in which it's based.* Then ask to see that license or contact the licensing agency. You can also check with the Better Business Bureau.
- *Do even more due diligence.* Ask your child's doctor about the program and request references from successful graduates.
- *Vet the staff.* The clinical director should have stellar credentials and experience treating bipolar disorder, and the program should have qualified and licensed therapists on board. Don't sign up with any facility that won't provide information on background checks of staff.
- *Investigate the academic curriculum if you're looking at more than three months.* Avoid having your child fall behind in school if possible.
- *Visit the site.* And ask for a tour. Ensure that the facility is safe—with adequate security—and sanitary, and if possible observe staff interactions with the kids.

We can probably assume most readers of this book haven't reached this point of urgency, and we hope none of you do. But however desperate you may feel at this moment, keep in mind that it will pass. If you stick to evidence-based treatment and have a loving, supportive relationship, the odds are good that your child will emerge from this phase and grow into adulthood with reliable tools to cope with difficult emotions.

Conclusion

Where's the Hope?

W e've spent much of this book telling you hard truths about bipolar disorder. But the message we most hope you'll keep in mind is that this illness does not spell doom for your child. Plenty of adults with this diagnosis are leading lives that give them joy and fulfillment, even amid hard times. David Sheff writes, "We increase our pain because we compare our insides with other people's outsides. It looks as if everyone else is doing great, that their kids are sailing through—but no one is sailing through. When we choose not to hide our struggles, there is tremendous relief. We can be supported. We can get help. We learn that we aren't alone. And we aren't. We are in this together."

In the time we've spent working on this book, we've learned of many young lives that have changed for the better.

Chamique Holdsclaw, the professional basketball star who struggled with depression at age 11, was diagnosed with bipolar disorder in 2011, seven years before being inducted into the Women's Basketball Hall of Fame. At this writing, she is devoting her time to mothering her two young children and speaking about mental health in schools and other venues. Part of her mission is to counter the resistance she still sees in Black and Brown communities to get help. "I say, listen, there's no need to walk around in pain; there are resources and organizations to help you. Let's do some digging. You can move through this." Public speaking isn't easy for her, she says, "but I'm passionate about this. If I can help give kids a foothold, I'm all for it."

Andy, the 18-year-old swimmer whose life was unmoored by the pandemic, had started psychotherapy and was working out at the gym. He still faced court hearings for his felony charge, but he was no longer cutting or feeling suicidal, and he was giving serious thought to life after high school. "I used to want to be an engineer because I love math, but it's too much sitting at a desk," he said. "So now I'm thinking I want to go to either cosmetology or fashion school."

Jason had graduated college, been sober for two years, and found a career passion in directing environmentally sustainable investments. "Roommates who used drugs have been a stressor, but Jason has been very disciplined," reports his mother. "He works out with weights and regularly cross-trains with running and cycling. His sleep hygiene is excellent."

Nic Sheff, who was addicted to drugs as a teen, had at last report stayed sober since 2011. He was also married, had written two memoirs and several novels for young adults, and was a co-producer on the Netflix series 13 Reasons Why. His father David writes: "Nic was staying with us recently and I went into the bathroom he uses and there was an arsenal of prescription medications on the counter. My first thought was, 'How sad it is that my son needs to take all these medications to be ok.' But that was quickly replaced with the opposite revelation: How lucky we are that he was diagnosed and is in treatment; how lucky we are that he's on these life-saving drugs!"

Claire was going to school and continuing with her medication and talk therapy, while Sandy, her mother, keeps learning more about coping with her daughter's disorder. "I know she will probably need at some point to return to the hospital—and in the past when that happened I'd be very upset, crying and not being able to function," she said. "But I've come to realize that this is ever-changing. Somehow it makes it easier."

Jenny, who was 13 when her pediatrician saw she had been cutting herself and who at one point required electroconvulsive therapy, returned to community college at 28 during the pandemic. "It has been a 12-year journey, and a rough ride for a while, but she finally found a good psychiatrist and the right balance of the meds and therapists," says her father, adding, "we keep our fingers crossed."

Not all of these stories end well. Some kids never recover. Some lives are lost. And some parents mourn the loss of their children's early potential.

"It is a privilege to be a parent to a young woman like Claire; she just needs to find her way right now," says Sandy. "She has such low self-esteem, and is so identified with wanting to die, even though I look at her as one of the most amazing people I know, truly she is incredible. Smart, beautiful, funny, and so caring."

"Sally is brilliant," says her father, Michael Greenberg, "but she never got very far in college because it was just too stressful. Now she's 40 years old and can't really hold down the kind of highly demanding job she would handle with ease if she didn't have bipolar disorder, because of her low tolerance for stress. There are also times when she has to return to the hospital."

Greenberg nonetheless is one of several parents we spoke to who counts his blessings and stays hopeful.

"She is married to a really good guy, and the two of us are very close," he said. "Whenever she calls, I drop what I'm doing to answer her. I reiterate my love for her and never let her feel that she can alienate me. These are the things in the end that I can do for her and that make a difference."

"Sadie" O'Donnell, who was diagnosed with bipolar disorder as a child, had a difficult end of 2021. While struggling with her medication and some suicidal thoughts, she failed one of her community college classes and dropped another. She stabilized with better treatment in January but was still feeling fragile and considering dropping out of school to pursue a career as an actor and musician. "Right now, I'm trying not to stress about her plans for the future," says Dorothy, her mother. "I just want her to focus on her mental health at the moment. I am proud of her for being able to live on her own and with the way she's been handling her mental health care and treatment—she refuses to let me participate in any of her psychiatrist appointments! After dealing with this stuff for so long, she is very in tune with her mental state and when she needs extra help."

Reflecting on the past several years, Dorothy says: "I guess one of the biggest broad lessons I've learned is to be the best parent to the child you actually have instead of the child you envisioned having, or wished you had. Another lesson I've been thinking about a lot lately is that you can't fix another person's pain or stop them from struggling no matter how hard you try and how much you love them. Obviously that one is really hard to accept, and it is my daughter who often has to remind me of this."

There's no way to ignore the fact that sometimes sheer luck can make all the difference in a child's life path. A parent may move heaven and earth and still lose a child to the illness. Still, your child's odds of surviving, and even flourishing—as well as those of millions of others affected by bipolar disorder—are getting better all the time, for many reasons.

For many years now, kids with all kinds of mental illness are on average being identified and treated earlier, offering hope that they can be helped before their brains get into harmful ruts. The pandemic did unquestionable damage to many US children's mental health, disrupting routines, increasing social isolation, and for some, robbing them of beloved family members. But by worsening a crisis already underway, it may lead to a tipping point in which society finally rises to the long-simmering challenge of protecting young people's mental health.

Progress With Policies

Urged on by advocates, legislators have been seeking ways to better regulate social media firms purveying emotionally harmful content. And new initiatives are starting to address the nationwide shortage of psychotherapists, including school psychologists.

In December 2021, the US Surgeon General, Vivek Murthy, issued a rare public advisory, calling on parents, researchers, social media executives, philanthropists, employers, and journalists to combat the "devastating" epidemic.

"We cannot overlook the escalating mental health crisis facing our patients," American Academy of Pediatrics President

Lee Savio Beers said around that same time. "We must treat this mental health crisis like the emergency it is."

Some state governments have gotten on board, with new laws pushing insurance firms to shorten wait times for mental health care. Some have also tried to tackle the adolescent sleep deficit, which can be such a serious stressor for kids with bipolar disorder. In 2022, California became the first state to mandate that high schools start no earlier than 8:30 a.m. and middle schools no earlier than 8 a.m.

To address the shortage of child psychiatrists, four US medical centers recently unveiled a new program allowing pediatricians to become board-certified adult and child psychiatrists in just three years instead of the usual five. Insurance companies, while still falling far short of abiding by the spirit of mental health parity, have been expanding access to mental health care in at least some ways, such as by approving reimbursements for phone and computer-based therapeutic sessions.

News From the Labs

Scientists are working on several fronts. In 2015, US researchers launched the ABCD Study, the nation's largest-ever long-term inquiry into children's brain development and health. The federally funded project enrolled nearly 12,000 students of diverse races, ethnicities, and education and income levels. Research tools will include brain scans and extensive, repeated interviews to try to understand the relationship between factors such as sleep, substance use, and physical activities with mental health. By observing brain development through adolescence and beyond, the study may identify risk factors for mood disorders and lead to improved diagnosis and treatment.

Other researchers are exploring new treatments for depression, including psychedelic substances such as psilocybin and LSD which have shown initial promise in adults. Scientists are also excited by new clues about the role of the immune system and systemic inflammation as the origin of many psychiatric disorders.

Building on the promise of transcranial magnetic stimulation (TMS), described in Chapter 2, scientists are seeking more sophisticated ways of stimulating brain regions to ease depression. In 2021, the *American Journal of Psychiatry* published results of a small study in which 80% of participants had their depression go into remission after treatment with SAINT, for Stanford Accelerated Intelligent Neuromodulation Therapy. The treatment is a type of TMS that delivers "theta burst stimulations," lasting three to four minutes, typically applied several times a day for five days.

Geneticists are hot on the trail of genes that increase the risk of bipolar disorder. In the largest genome-wide study of bipolar disorder at this writing, involving data from 41,000 people, researchers found about twice as many genetic locations associated with bipolar disorder as previously reported. The 2021 study could help improve understanding of the biological origins of the disorder. Treatment providers hope that one day not too far in the future they might use genetic tests and brain scans to prescribe the combination of therapy and medication to target the precise cause of someone's depression.

The Slow Revolution in Our Schools

It can be hard to recognize historic change when you're right in the middle of it, but these past several years have brought steady change in the field of education. Much of this progress could make life much easier for kids with bipolar disorder—as well as all other kids and their families.

We've told you about the federal laws that provide accommodations for students who need them. There are also important societal changes underway, including an increasing questioning of the value of higher education. The pandemic accelerated this attitude adjustment when most colleges turned to remote learning. But the questioning has been going on for many years.

One signpost of the change was the 2008 bestseller *The Price of Privilege*, in which the psychologist Madeleine Levine investigated what she characterized as an epidemic of emotional problems, including skyrocketing rates of depression, substance use, and anxiety disorders, sabotaging America's most privileged young people. Levine contended that upper-class and upper-middle-class materialism, intrusive parenting, and pressure to achieve had created a toxic brew resulting in the highest rates of adolescent mood disorders in any socioeconomic sector. As we've noted, these sorts of stressors don't create bipolar disorder, but they can certainly aggravate it.

Two years later came the breakout popular success of *Race to Nowhere*, a documentary that touched on the same themes. Tens of thousands of Americans throughout the country crowded into school auditoriums to hear its messages, hanging around afterward for public discussions of the damage done by pressuring kids into unrestrained résumé-building. First-time filmmaker Vicki Abeles said she resolved to investigate the problem after a doctor told her that her 12-year-old daughter was having stress-induced stomachaches. She interviewed students who told her about their insomnia, anxiety, and prevalent cheating. The film's basic message is that kids' mental health suffers when success is defined by high grades and test scores.

The nonprofit Challenge Success, which we mentioned in Chapter 7, arose in the wake of the reaction to Levine's book and Abeles's movie. It has since worked with hundreds of schools and families, championing reforms such as:

- *New attention to students' schedules*, including later start days, limits on homework, and moving finals to before winter break
- *Modified grading systems*, such as using narrative assessments and eliminating student rankings, while implementing stronger policies against cheating
- *Adult education*, including "dialogue nights" in which students share concerns with parents and faculty, and efforts to "de-bunk the myth that there is only one path to success."

All over the United States, individual schools and school districts have been paying more attention to students' emotional well-being. One small example is the new Wellness Center at Archie Williams High School in San Anselmo, California: a cozy room with sofas, tea, fidgets, and two welcoming full-time staff. The center provides temporary respite for kids who are feeling overwhelmed, while attempting to reduce the rising rates of "school refusal." "There was some pushback when the idea for this came up six years ago, as we were in the midst of budget cuts," says assistant principal Chad Stuart. "But it has been a terrific investment and now other schools in the county are looking into doing this as well."

Still Needed: More Focus on the Big Picture

Even with all the new progress in labs, schools, and even legislatures, we all need to think harder about broader, structural issues that have huge and inequitable impacts on mental health. Better health insurance won't be much use to a parent who can't get time off from a job to drive a child to therapy. Improved telehealth won't help a family that can't afford WiFi. A new "wellness" center is of limited support for a child who can't sleep in a crowded, noisy apartment. These are just some of the long-festering problems that will take enormous political will to improve, yet which would surely deliver huge benefits for everyone's mental health.

How to Hang in There

You may be using every bit of energy you have right now to help your child manage this serious illness. Yet you may want to consider, now or later, extending your efforts to support some of the progress being made in mental health. Maybe you'll create a small parents' support group at your school. Maybe you'll send money to an advocacy group you admire. Maybe you'll write your congressional representative to champion a mental health bill. Maybe you'll run for office yourself. You've learned so much about this illness, and humans in general, by caring for your child. At some point you may want to devote your experience to helping support others.

If you're still in the thick of it, however, here are three final messages to keep in mind.

Remember that you're not alone, and that there are many resources out there to support you and your family. We offer a list at the end of this book, and we encourage you to be relentless in taking advantage of them.

Remember, too, that your child is so much more than any issues he or she may have.

In her best selling memoir, Hope Jahren describes her life as an award-winning scientist, wife, and mother, with her bipolar disorder playing only a small part.

Winston Churchill, who was reportedly diagnosed with bipolar disorder in middle age, famously referred to his long periods of depression as the "black dog," yet also famously boosted British spirits with his exuberant speeches during World War II.

Your son or daughter doesn't need to write bestsellers or lead a nation for you to find something to celebrate. One of the best things you can do as a parent will be to reflect back the bigger picture you see, highlighting the gifts your unique child brings to the world, while remembering Churchill's motto: "Never give in, never give in, never, never, never."

Appendix

Medications for Bipolar Disorder With FDA Approval

Medication(s)	Indication for Youth				Indication for Adult			
	Mania	Mixed	Bipolar Depression	Maintenance	Mania	Mixed	Bipolar Depression	Maintenance
Aripiprazole (Abilify)	X	X			X	X		X
Asenapine (Saphris)	X	X			X	X		X
Carbamazepine (Tegretol, Epitol, Equetro, Teril, Carbatrol)					X	X		
Caripazine (Vraylar)					X	X	X	
Chlorpromazine (Thorazine)					X			
Divalproex (Depakote)					X			
Valproic Acid (Depakene)					X			
Lamotrigine (Lamictal)								X

Medication(s)	Indication for Youth				Indication for Adult			
	Mania	Mixed	Bipolar Depression	Maintenance	Mania	Mixed	Bipolar Depression	Maintenance
Lithium Carbonate (Eskalith, Lithobid, Lithane, Lithonate, Lithotabs) Lithium Citrate (Cibalith-S)	X				X			X
Lurasidone (Latuda)			X				X	
Lumateperone (Calypta)							X	
Olanzapine/Samidorphan (Lybalvi)						X	X	X
Olanzapine (Zyprexa)	X				X	X		X
Olanzapine/Fluoxetine (Symbyax)			X				X	
Oxcarbazepine (Trileptal)					X			
Quetiapine (Seroquel)	X				X		X	
Risperidone (Risperidal)	X	X			X	X		
Ziprasidone (Geodon)					X	X		

X = Medication is indicated for that use.

Education

504 or IDEA: What's the Difference?

Who's Covered?
IDEA

- All school-aged children meeting criteria for 1 or more of 14 conditions, including "emotional disturbance" and depression
- Children whose disabilities adversely affect educational performance

SECTION 504

- Students meeting the definition of physically or mentally "handicapped" in ways that "substantially limit" a life activity, such as walking, seeing, hearing, speaking, and learning

How Are Students Evaluated?
IDEA

- Requires that the child be fully and comprehensively evaluated by a multidisciplinary team
- Requires informed and written parental consent
- Requires a re-evaluation of the child at least once every three years, or if conditions warrant or if the child's parent or teacher requests it

SECTION 504

- Requires a variety of documented sources
- Parents need to be notified, but written consent isn't required

- Requires "periodic" re-evaluation
- No provisions made for independent evaluation at school's expense
- Requires re-evaluation before a significant change in placement

What Services Are Guaranteed?

IDEA

- Requires an individualized education program (IEP)
- Provides any combination of special education and general education classrooms
- Provides related services, if required, which might include speech and language therapy, occupational therapy, physical therapy, counseling services, psychological services, social services, and transportation

SECTION 504

- Does not require an IEP, but it does require a plan
- Provides an education comparable to that provided to those students who are not disabled
- Placement is usually in a general education classroom. Children can receive specialized instruction, related services, or accommodations within the general education classroom.
- Provides related services, if needed

What If Parents and Schools Disagree?

IDEA

- Must provide impartial hearings for parents who disagree with the identification, evaluation, or placement of the student

- An impartial appointee selects a hearing officer
- The student's current IEP and placement continues to be implemented until all proceedings are resolved
- Parents must receive 10 days' notice prior to any change in placement
- Enforced by US Department of Education, Office of Special Education

Section 504

- Must provide impartial hearings for parents who disagree with the identification, evaluation, or placement of the student
- Requires that parents have an opportunity to participate and be represented by legal counsel
- A hearing officer is usually appointed by the school
- Enforced by US Department of Education, Office of Civil Rights

Source: deBettencourt, L. U. (2002). Understanding the differences between IDEA and Section 504. *TEACHING Exceptional Children, 34*(3), 16–23. https://doi.org/10.1177/004005990203400302. Reproduced with permission.

Sample Gebser Letter

Send individual letters to both the school principal and superintendent.

Your name

Date

Dear (name of school principal and school district superintendent):

I am writing you on behalf of my child, (name and birthdate), who is a student attending (name of high school) in the (name of school district).

My son/daughter, who has been diagnosed with (insert name of the disability), is being repeatedly discriminated against (or bullied), prohibiting him/her from being able to access his/her education. (Detail how the student is not able to access education—school refusal, unable to ride the bus, etc.) We have already alerted the following school personnel to the issue: (list of names). But it has not been addressed.

The (name of school district) receives federal funds in return for which it contracts to not discriminate. It is your legal requirement to investigate and correct this discrimination. School administrators have control over the site and personnel involved. If you do not investigate and correct the problem, you and the district are acting in a way that implies you are deliberately indifferent to the discrimination. You and the school district may be liable personally and officially for damages.

I request that you (insert what you think will solve the problem for your child).

Optional bullying language:

The (name of school district) has an anti-bullying policy that states: (insert specifics that have been violated).

As you can see from the examples I have given you, this anti-bullying policy is not being upheld.

I would appreciate your written notification, of when I can expect the investigation to be complete and what steps you will be taking, within 10 days. Please put a copy of this letter in my child's cumulative file.

Sincerely,

(Your name)

Note: Thanks to Catherine Michael of the CMK Law Firm in Carmel, Indiana, for this wording.

Glossary

504 plan A set of classroom accommodations to support students who need help short of special education.

adrenal glands Glands located just above the kidneys. Their hormones help regulate many physiological functions, including the body's stress response.

adrenocorticotropic hormone (ACTH) A hormone released by the pituitary gland.

anticonvulsant A medication that helps prevent seizures. Many anticonvulsants have mood-stabilizing effects as well.

antidepressant A medication used to prevent or relieve depression.

antipsychotic A medication used to prevent or relieve psychotic symptoms. Some newer antipsychotics have mood-stabilizing effects as well.

anxiety disorder Any of several mental disorders that are characterized by extreme or maladaptive feelings of tension, fear, or worry.

attention-deficit/hyperactivity disorder (ADHD) A disorder characterized by a short attention span, excessive activity, or impulsive behavior. The symptoms of the disorder normally begin early in life.

atypical antipsychotic One of the newer antipsychotic medications. Some atypical antipsychotics are also used as mood stabilizers.

bipolar disorder not otherwise specified (BP-NOS) A term used for any form of bipolar disorder that doesn't meet the diagnostic criteria for bipolar I, bipolar II, or cyclothymia.

bipolar I disorder A form of bipolar disorder characterized by the occurrence of at least one manic or mixed episode, often preceded by an episode of major depression.

bipolar II disorder A form of bipolar disorder characterized by an alternating pattern of hypomania and major depression.

Children's Health Insurance Program (CHIP)   A partnership between the federal and state governments that provides reduced-cost health coverage to children in families earning too much money to qualify for Medicaid.

cognitive-behavioral therapy (CBT)   A form of psychotherapy that aims to correct ingrained patterns of thinking and behavior that may be contributing to a person's mental, emotional, or behavioral symptoms.

comorbidity   The simultaneous presence of two or more disorders.

conduct disorder   A disorder characterized by a repetitive or persistent pattern of having extreme difficulty following rules or conforming to social norms.

corticotropin-releasing hormone   A substance released by the hypothalamus.

cortisol   A hormone released by the adrenal glands that is responsible for many of the physiological effects of stress.

crisis residential treatment services   Temporary, 24-hour care in a nonhospital setting during a crisis.

cyclothymia   A mood disorder characterized by cycling between hypomania and relatively mild depressive symptoms. This pattern lasts for at least a year, and any intermittent periods of normal mood last no longer than two months at a time.

day treatment   *See* partial hospitalization.

delusion   A belief that is seriously out of touch with reality.

depression   A feeling of being sad, hopeless, or apathetic that lasts for at least a couple of weeks. *See* major depression.

***Diagnostic and Statistical Manual of Mental Disorders*, 5th edition (*DSM-5*)**   The manual that mental health professionals use for diagnosing all kinds of mental illnesses.

dopamine   A neurotransmitter that is essential for movement and also influences motivation and perception of reality.

dysthymia   A mood disorder that involves being either mildly depressed or irritable most of the day. These feelings occur more days than not for 12 months or longer and are associated with other symptoms.

eating disorder   A disorder characterized by serious disturbances in eating behavior. People may severely restrict what they eat, or they may go on eating binges and then attempt to compensate by such means as self-induced vomiting or misuse of laxatives.

electroconvulsive therapy (ECT)   A treatment that involves delivering a carefully controlled electrical current to the brain, which produces a brief seizure. This is thought to alter some of the electrochemical processes involved in brain functioning.

endorphins   Protein-like compounds in the brain that have natural pain-relieving and mood-elevating effects.

family therapy   Psychotherapy that brings together several members of a family for therapy sessions.

frontal lobes   Part of the brain involved in planning, reasoning, controlling voluntary movement, and turning thoughts into words.

gamma-amino butyric acid (GABA)   A neurotransmitter that inhibits the flow of nerve signals in neurons by blocking the release of other neurotransmitters.

group therapy   Psychotherapy that brings together several patients with similar diagnoses or issues for therapy sessions.

hallucination   The sensory perception of something that isn't really there.

health maintenance organization (HMO)   A type of managed care plan in which members must use health care providers who work for the HMO.

hippocampus   Part of the brain that plays a role in learning, memory, and emotion.

home-based services   Assistance provided in a patient's home to improve family coping skills and avert the need for more intensive services.

hospitalization   Inpatient treatment in a facility that provides intensive, specialized care and close, round-the-clock monitoring.

hypomania   A somewhat high, expansive, or irritable mood that lasts for at least four days. The mood is more moderate than with mania but also clearly different from a person's usual mood when not depressed.

hypothalamic-pituitary-adrenal (HPA) axis   A body system comprising the hypothalamus, pituitary gland, and adrenal glands along with the substances these structures secrete.

hypothalamus   Part of the brain that serves as the command center for the nervous and hormonal systems.

indicated prevention program   A program that targets individuals who have some symptoms of a disorder but don't yet meet all the diagnostic criteria for the full-fledged illness.

individual therapy   Psychotherapy in which a patient meets one on one with a therapist.

individualized education program (IEP)   A written educational plan for an individual student who qualifies for services under IDEA.

Individuals with Disabilities Education Act (IDEA)   A federal law that applies to students who have a disability that impacts their ability to benefit from general educational services.

interpersonal therapy (IPT)   A form of psychotherapy that aims to address the interpersonal triggers for mental, emotional, or behavioral symptoms.

Katie Beckett option   *See* TEFRA option.

kindling hypothesis   A theory stating that repeated episodes of mania or depression may spark long-lasting changes in the brain, making it more sensitive to future stress.

learning disorder   A disorder that adversely affects a person's performance in school or ability to function in everyday situations that require reading, writing, or math skills.

light therapy   A therapeutic regimen of daily exposure to very bright light from an artificial source.

lithium   A mood-stabilizing medication.

maintenance therapy   Any treatment that is aimed at preventing a recurrence of symptoms.

major depression   A mood disorder that involves either being depressed or irritable nearly all the time, or losing interest or enjoyment in almost everything. These feelings last for at least two weeks, are associated with several other symptoms, and cause significant distress or impaired functioning.

managed care   A system for controlling health care costs.

mania   An overly high or irritable mood that lasts for at least a week or leads to dangerous behavior. Symptoms include grandiose ideas, decreased need for sleep, racing thoughts, risk taking, and increased talking or activity. These symptoms cause marked impairment in functioning or relationships.

Medicaid   A government program, paid for by a combination of federal and state funds, that provides health and mental health care to low-income individuals who meet eligibility criteria.

medical necessity   A standard used by managed care plans in determining whether or not to pay for a health care service. To satisfy this standard, the service must be deemed medically appropriate and necessary to meet a patient's health care needs.

melatonin   A hormone that regulates the body's internal clock, which controls daily rhythms of sleep, body temperature, and hormone secretion.

mental health parity   A policy that attempts to equalize the way that mental and physical illnesses are covered by health plans.

mental illness   A mental disorder that is characterized by abnormalities in mood, emotion, thought, or higher-order behaviors, such as social interaction or the planning of future activities.

mixed episode   A bipolar episode that is characterized by a mixture of mania and depression occurring at the same time.

monoamine oxidase inhibitor (MAOI)   An older class of antidepressant.

mood   A pervasive emotion that colors a person's whole view of the world.

mood disorder   A mental disorder in which a disturbance in mood is the chief feature.

mood stabilizer   A medication for bipolar disorder that reduces manic and/or depressive symptoms and helps even out mood swings.

neuron   A cell in the brain or another part of the nervous system that is specialized to send, receive, and process information.

neurotransmitter   A chemical that acts as a messenger within the brain.

norepinephrine   A neurotransmitter that plays a role in the body's response to stress and helps regulate arousal, sleep, and blood pressure.

omega-3 polyunsaturated fatty acids—A substance found in foods including cold-water fish, such as salmon and tuna, flaxseed, walnuts, and pecans. Omega-3s have anti-inflammatory properties, which may help with symptoms of depression.

oppositional defiant disorder   A disorder characterized by a persistent pattern of unusually frequent defiance, hostility, or lack of cooperation.

partial hospitalization   Services such as individual and group therapy, special education, vocational training, parent counseling, and therapeutic recreational activities that are provided for at least four hours per day.

phototherapy   *See* light therapy.

pituitary gland   A small gland located at the base of the brain. Its hormones control other glands and help regulate growth, metabolism, and reproduction.

placebo   A sugar pill that looks like a real medication but does not contain an active ingredient.

point of service (POS) plan   A type of managed care plan that is similar to a traditional HMO or PPO, except that members can also use providers outside the HMO organization or PPO network in exchange for a higher copayment or deductible.

preferred provider organization (PPO)   A type of managed care plan in which members may choose from a network of providers who have contracts with the PPO.

prefrontal cortex   Part of the brain involved in complex thought, problem-solving, and emotion.

primary prevention   Activities that aim to keep a disorder from ever occurring in people who are free of symptoms.

protective factor   A characteristic that decreases a person's likelihood of developing an illness.

psychiatrist   A medical doctor who specializes in the diagnosis and treatment of mental illnesses and emotional problems.

psychosis   A state of severely disordered thinking characterized by delusions or hallucinations.

psychotherapy   The treatment of a mental, emotional, or behavioral disorder through "talk therapy" and other psychological techniques.

randomized controlled trial   A study in which participants are randomly assigned to a treatment group or a control group. The control group receives either a placebo or standard care. This study design allows researchers to determine which changes in the treatment group over time are due to the treatment itself.

rapid-cycling bipolar disorder   A form of bipolar disorder in which four or more mood episodes occur within a single year.

receptor   A molecule that recognizes a specific chemical, such as a neurotransmitter. For a chemical message to be sent from one nerve cell to another, the message must be delivered to a matching receptor on the surface of the receiving nerve cell.

recurrence   A repeat episode of an illness.

relapse   The re-emergence of symptoms after a period of remission.

remission   A return to the level of functioning that existed before an illness.

residential treatment center   A facility that provides round-the-clock supervision and care in a dorm-like group setting. The treatment is less specialized and intensive than in a hospital, but the length of stay is often considerably longer.

resilience   The ability to adapt well to stressful life events and bounce back from adversity, trauma, or tragedy.

respite care   Child care provided by trained parents or mental health aides to give the usual caregivers a short break.

reuptake   The process by which a neurotransmitter is absorbed back into the sending branch of the nerve cell that originally released it.

risk factor   A characteristic that increases a person's likelihood of developing an illness.

S-adenosyl-L-methionine (SAM-e)   A natural compound that is sold as a dietary supplement.

schizoaffective disorder   A severe form of mental illness in which an episode of either depression or mania occurs at the same time as symptoms of schizophrenia.

schizophrenia   A severe form of mental illness characterized by delusions, hallucinations, or serious disturbances in speech, behavior, or emotion.

second messenger   A molecule inside a nerve cell that lets certain parts of the cell know when a specific receptor has been activated by a neurotransmitter.

secondary prevention   Activities that aim to keep the full-blown disorder from developing in people who have risk factors or early symptoms.

selective serotonin reuptake inhibitor (SSRI)   A widely prescribed class of antidepressants.

self-efficacy   The belief in one's own ability to perform effectively in a particular situation.

serotonin   A neurotransmitter that plays a role in mood and helps regulate sleep, appetite, and sexual drive.

side-effect   An unintended effect of a drug.

social rhythm therapy   A therapeutic technique that focuses on helping people regularize their daily routines.

St. John's wort   (*Hypericum perforatum*) An herb that is sold as a dietary supplement.

stress response   The physiological response to any perceived threat—real or imagined, physical or psychological.

substance use disorder   The continued use of alcohol or other drugs despite negative consequences, such as dangerous behavior while under the influence or substance-related personal, social, or legal problems.

suicidality   Suicidal thinking or behavior.

switching   The rapid transition from depression to hypomania or mania.

synapse   The gap that separates nerve cells.

system of care   A network of mental health and social services organized to work together to provide care for a particular patient and his or her family.

TEFRA option   A funding option, authorized by the Tax Equity and Financial Responsibility Act of 1982, that allows states to provide community- and home-based services for children with disabilities who are living at home and need extensive care.

temperament   A person's inborn tendency to react to events in a particular way.

transcranial magnetic stimulation (TMS)   An experimental treatment in which a special electromagnet is placed near the scalp, where it can be used to deliver short bursts of energy to stimulate the nerve cells in a specific part of the brain.

utilization review   A formal review of health care services by a managed care plan to determine whether payment for them should be authorized or denied.

Resources

Books

General Information for Parents

Treating and Preventing Adolescent Mental Health Disorders: What We Know and What We Don't Know
Editors: Dwight L. Evans, Edna B. Foa, Raquel E. Gur, Herbert Hendin, Charles P. O'Brien, Daniel Romer, Martin E. P. Seligman, and B. Timothy Walsh
Publisher: Oxford University Press; 2nd edition, 2017

Straight Talk About Your Child's Mental Health: What To Do When Something Seems Wrong
Author: Stephen V. Faraone
Publisher: The Guilford Press, 2003

The Explosive Child: A New Approach for Understanding and Parenting Easily Frustrated, Chronically Inflexible Children.
Author: Ross W. Greene, PhD
Publisher: Quill, 2001

The Stressed Years of Their Lives: Helping Your Kid Survive and Thrive During Their College Years
Authors: B. Janet Hibbs, PhD, MFT, and Anthony Rostain, MD, MA
Publisher: First St. Martin's Griffin edition, 2020

Mood Prep 101: A Parent's Guide to Preventing Depression and Anxiety in College-Bound Teens
Author: Carol Landau
Publisher: Oxford University Press, 2020

Depression for Dummies
Authors: Laura L. Smith and Charles H. Elliott
Publisher: For Dummies; 2nd edition, 2021

The Brain
Neuroscience for Dummies
Author: Frank Amthor
Publisher: For Dummies; 2nd edition, 2016

The Teenage Brain: A Neuroscientist's Survival Guide to Raising Adolescents and Young Adults
Authors: Frances E. Jensen with Amy Ellis Nutt
Publisher: Harper Paperbacks; Reprint edition, 2016

The Three-Pound Enigma: The Human Brain and the Quest to Unlock Its Mysteries
Author: Shannon Moffett
Publisher: Algonquin Books, 2006

Bipolar Disorder and Depression
If Your Adolescent Has Depression: An Essential Resource for Parents
Authors: Dwight L. Evans, MD, Moira A. Rynn, MD, and Katherine Ellison
Publisher: Oxford University Press, 2023

Bipolar Disorder for Dummies
Authors: Candida Fink and Joe Kraynak
Publisher: For Dummies; 3rd edition, 2015

The Bipolar Teen: What You Can Do to Help Your Child and Your Family
Authors: David J. Miklowitz and Elizabeth L. George
Publisher: The Guilford Press, 2007

Personal Accounts of Bipolar Disorder and Related Mental Illnesses
Hurry Down Sunshine: A Father's Memoir of Love and Madness
Author: Michael Greenberg
Publisher: Bloomsbury Publishing PLC, 2010

Monochrome Days: A First-Hand Account of One Teenager's Experience With Depression
Authors: Cait Irwin, Dwight L. Evans, MD, and Linda Wasmer Andrews
Publisher: Oxford University Press, 2007

Lab Girl
Author: Hope Jahren
Publisher: Knopf, 2016

Mind Race: A Firsthand Account of One Teenager's Experience With Bipolar Disorder
Authors: Patrick E. Jamieson, PhD, and Moira A. Rynn, MD
Publisher: Oxford University Press, 2006

Night Falls Fast: Understanding Suicide
Author: Kay Redfield Jamison
Publisher: Knopf, 1999

Touched With Fire: Manic-Depressive Illness and the Artistic Temperament
Author: Kay Redfield Jamison
Publisher: The Free Press, 1993

An Unquiet Mind: A Memoir of Moods and Madness
Author: Kay Redfield Jamison
Publisher: Vintage, 1996

The Thought That Counts: A Firsthand Account of One Teenager's Experience With Obsessive-Compulsive Disorder
Authors: Jared Kant, Martin Franklin, PhD, and Linda Wasmer Andrews
Publisher: Oxford University Press, 2008

Acquainted With the Night: A Parent's Quest to Understand Depression and Bipolar Disorder in His Children
Author: Paul Raeburn
Publisher: Broadway, 2004

Tweak: Growing Up on Methamphetamines
Author: Nic Sheff
Publisher: Atheneum Books for Young Readers, 2009

The Golden Ticket: A Life in College Admissions
Author: Irena Smith
Publisher: SheBooks, 2023

His Bright Light: The Story of Nick Traina
Author: Danielle Steel
Publisher: Delacorte Press; Book Club edition, 1998

Just Like Someone Without Mental Illness Only More So: A Memoir
Author: Mark Vonnegut, MD
Publisher: Bantam, 2011

Especially for Adolescents
When Nothing Matters Anymore: A Survival Guide for Depressed Teens
Author: Bev Cobain
Publisher: Free Spirit Publishing; revised and updated edition, 2007

Conquering the Beast Within: How I Fought Depression and Won . . . and How You Can, Too
Author: Cait Irwin
Publisher: Three Rivers Press, 1999

Wide Awake: A Buddhist Guide for Teens
Author: Diana Winston
Publisher: TarcherPerigee, 2003

ADHD
Buzz: A Year of Paying Attention
Author: Katherine Ellison
Publisher: Hachette Books, 2010

Driven to Distraction
Authors: Edward M. Hallowell and John J. Ratey
Publisher: Anchor, 2011

ADHD: What Everyone Needs to Know
Authors: Stephen Hinshaw and Katherine Ellison
Publisher: Oxford University Press, 2015

If Your Adolescent Has ADHD
Authors: Thomas J. Powers, PhD, and Linda Wasmer Andrews
Publisher: Oxford University Press, 2018

What Your ADHD Child Wishes You Knew: Working Together to Empower Kids for Success in School and Life
Author: Dr. Sharon Saline
Publisher: TarcherPerigee, 2018

The Essential Guide to Raising Complex Kids With ADHD, Anxiety, and More
Author: Elaine Taylor-Klaus
Publisher: Fair Winds Press, 2020

Anxiety
You and Your Anxious Child: Free Your Child From Fears and Worries and Create a Joyful Family Life
Authors: Anne Marie Albano and Leslie Pepper
Publisher: Avery, 2013

If Your Adolescent Has an Anxiety Disorder: An Essential Resource for Parents
Authors: Edna B. Foa, PhD, and Linda Wasmer Andrews
Publisher: Oxford University Press; Illustrated edition, 2006

What You Must Think of Me: A Firsthand Account of One Teenager's Experience With Social Anxiety Disorder

Authors: Emily Ford, Michael Liebowitz, and Linda Wasmer Andrews
Publisher: Oxford University Press, 2007

Eating Disorders
Next to Nothing: A Firsthand Account of One Teenager's Experience With an Eating Disorder
Authors: Carol Arnold with B. Timothy Walsh
Publisher: Oxford University Press, 2007

Hungry: A Mother and Daughter Fight Anorexia
Authors: Sheila Himmel and Lisa Himmel
Publisher: Berkley; Original edition, 2009

Eating Disorders: What Everyone Needs to Know
Authors: B. Timothy Walsh, Evelyn Attia, and Deborah R. Glasofer
Publisher: Oxford University Press, 2020

If Your Adolescent Has an Eating Disorder: An Essential Resource for Parents
Authors: B. Timothy Walsh, MD, and Deborah R. Glasofer
Publisher: Oxford University Press; 2nd edition, 2020

Schizophrenia
If Your Adolescent Has Schizophrenia: An Essential Resource for Parents
Authors: Raquel E. Gur, MD, PhD, and Ann Braden Johnson, PhD
Publisher: Oxford University Press, 2006

Me, Myself, and Them: A Firsthand Account of One Young Person's Experience With Schizophrenia
Authors: Kurt Snyder, Raquel E. Gur, MD, PhD, and Linda Wasmer Andrews
Publisher: Oxford University Press, 2007

Self-Harm
Cutting: Understanding and Overcoming Self-Mutilation
Author: Steven Levenkron
Publisher: W. W. Norton & Company; Revised edition, 1999

Eight Stories Up: An Adolescent Chooses Hope Over Suicide
Authors: DeQunicy Lezine and David Brent
Publisher: Oxford University Press, 2008

Substance Use and Addictions
Chasing the High: A Firsthand Account of One Young Person's Experience With Substance Abuse
Authors: Kyle Keegan and Howard Moss
Publisher: Oxford University Press, 2008

Beautiful Boy: A Father's Journey Through His Son's Addiction
Author: David Sheff
Publisher: Mariner Books, 2018

Clean: Overcoming Addiction and Ending America's Greatest Tragedy
Author: David Sheff
Publisher: HarperCollins, 2013

High: Everything You Want to Know About Drugs, Alcohol, and Addiction
Authors: David Sheff and Nic Sheff
Publisher: HarperCollins, 2019

School
Special Education—Plain and Simple: A Quick Guide for Parents, Teachers, Advocates, Attorneys, and Others
Author: Patricia L. Johnson Howey
Publisher: Beyond the Sunset Publisher; 2nd edition, 2021

Wrightslaw: From Emotions to Advocacy: The Special Education Survival Guide
Authors: Pamela Wright and Peter Wright
Publisher: Harbor House Law Press; 2nd edition, 2006

Books on Wilderness Camps, Residential Treatment, and Boarding Schools
What It Takes to Pull Me Through: Why Teenagers Get in Trouble—and How Four of Them Got Out
Author: David L. Marcus
Publisher: Harper Paperbacks; Reprint edition, 2006

Help at Any Cost: How the Troubled-Teen Industry Cons Parents and Hurts Kids
Author: Maia Szalavitz
Publisher: Riverhead Books, 2006

Additional Resources
Parenting Helplines
National: https://www.nationalparenthelpline.org/
State Lists: https://www.nationalparenthelpline.org/find-support/state-resources
Parents Anonymous national helpline: 1-855-4A PARENT
(1-855-427-2736)

Foundations
National and International Advocacy and Research Groups
American Academy of Child and Adolescent Psychiatry
3615 Wisconsin Avenue, N.W.

Washington, D.C. 20016-3007
202-966-7300
http://www.aacap.org

American Foundation for Suicide Prevention
AFSP National Office
199 Water Street
11th Floor
New York, NY 10038
(888) 333-AFSP (2377)
https://afsp.org/

American Psychiatric Association
800 Maine Avenue, SW, Suite 900
Washington, DC 20024
(202) 559-3900
https://www.psychiatry.org/

American Psychological Association
750 First Street NE
Washington, DC 20002-4242
(800) 374-2721
https://www.apa.org/

Depression and Bipolar Support Alliance
55 E Jackson Blvd, Suite 490
Chicago, IL 60604
(800) 826-3632
https://www.dbsalliance.org/

Activist Groups
Bring Change to Mind
https://bringchange2mind.org/

Families for Depression Awareness
https://www.familyaware.org/

Kicking the Stigma
https://www.colts.com/community/kicking-the-stigma/

Make It OK
https://makeitok.org/

One Mind
https://onemind.org/
National Alliance on Mental Illness
4301 Wilson Blvd., Suite 300
Arlington, VA 22203

1-800-950-6264
http://www.nami.org

International Bipolar Foundation
IBPF offers programs and information that educate the public and raise awareness regarding this mental health condition.
https://ibpf.org/

Mental Health America—Bipolar Disorder
https://www.mhanational.org/conditions/bipolar-disorder

Mental Health America—Depression
https://www.mhanational.org/conditions/depression

JED Foundation
530 7th Avenue, Suite 801
New York, NY 10018
212-647-7544
https://jedfoundation.org/

LGBTQ+
The Trevor Project
Call 1-866-488-7386 toll-free.

Helping Families Support Their Lesbian, Gay, Bisexual, and Transgender (LGBT) Children
Author: Caitlin Ryan, PhD, ACSW
https://nccc.georgetown.edu/documents/LGBT_Brief.pdf

People of Color
The Steve Fund
P.O. Box 9070
Providence, RI 02940
info@stevefund.org
(401) 249-0044
https://www.stevefund.org/

Online Information for Parents
AACAP Facts for Families
https://www.aacap.org/AACAP/Families_and_Youth/Facts_for_Families/Layout/FFF_Guide-01.aspx

Adolescent Brain Cognitive Development
https://abcdstudy.org/

Beyond Differences
https://www.beyonddifferences.org/

Centers for Disease Control and Prevention
The CDC offers a broad array of health information, including a page about Positive Parenting Practices: www.cdc.gov/healthyyouth/protective/positivepa renting/index.htm

Columbia University Clinic for Anxiety and Related Disorders
https://www.anxietytreatmentnyc.org/specialized-programs.cfm

Effective Child Therapy—Evidence-based mental health treatment for children and adolescents
https://effectivechildtherapy.org/

Employee Assistance Programs
https://www.workplacementalhealth.org/mental-health-topics/employee-assista nce-programs

Food and Drug Administration: The site includes material on vaping, smoking, cannabis, CBD, COVID, and dietary supplements.
www.fda.gov

MedlinePlus: Bipolar Disorder
https://medlineplus.gov/bipolardisorder.html

National Institute of Mental Health
https://www.nimh.nih.gov/

Parents' Medication Guides (American Academy of Child and Adolescent Psychiatry)
https://www.aacap.org/AACAP/Families_and_Youth/Family__Resources/ Parents_Medication_Guides.aspx?hkey=c5ad9d72-b5db-4994-b3ab-96fe5350439a

Protecting Youth Mental Health
The US Surgeon General's Report, 2021
https://www.hhs.gov/sites/default/files/surgeon-general-youth-mental-health-advisory.pdf

Society for Adolescent Mental Health and Medicine
https://www.adolescenthealth.org/Resources/Clinical-Care-Resources/Mental-Health/Mental-Health-Resources-For-Parents-of-Adolescents.aspx

Find a Provider

The National Alliance on Mental Illness (NAMI) has a helpline for free assistance Monday through Friday, 10 a.m. to 10 p.m. EST. You can reach the helpline at 1-800-950-6264. NAMI also offers a free, 24/7 crisis text: just text 988.

The Substance Abuse and Mental Health Services Administration (SAMHSA), a government agency, provides a treatment locator for low-cost facilities.
https://findtreatment.gov/

The National Association of Free & Charitable Clinics, Mental Health America, and the Open Path Psychotherapy Collective also provide online tools to find affordable mental health services.
https://nafcclinics.org/
https://mhanational.org/finding-help
https://openpathcollective.org/find-a-clinician/

Psychology Today—probably hands-down the easiest way to locate a therapist or psychiatrist; you can search by insurance, location, etc.
https://www.psychologytoday.com/us

Find a CBT Therapist (Association for Behavioral and Cognitive Therapies)
https://services.abct.org/i4a/memberDirectory/index.cfm?directory_id=3&pageID=3282

Child and Adolescent Psychiatrist Finder (American Academy of Child and Adolescent Psychiatry)
https://www.aacap.org/AACAP/Families_and_Youth/Resources/CAP_Finder.aspx

Talkspace
https://www.talkspace.com/

BetterHelp
https://www.betterhelp.com/

NATSAP—The National Association of Therapeutic Schools and Programs provides information on licensed facilities.
https://natsap.org/

Health Insurance
The Children's Health Insurance Program (CHIP)
https://www.healthcare.gov/medicaid-chip/childrens-health-insurance-program/

Employee Benefits Security Administration: Ask EBSA
https://www.dol.gov/agencies/ebsa/about-ebsa/ask-a-question/ask-ebsa

HealthCare.gov
https://www.healthcare.gov/

HealthSherpa
https://www.healthsherpa.com/

Medicaid: Managed Care
https://www.medicaid.gov/medicaid/managed-care/index.html

Reimbursify
https://reimbursify.com/

Internet Management

Children's Online Privacy Protection Rule ("COPPA")
https://www.ftc.gov/legal-library/browse/rules/childrens-online-privacy-protect
ion-rule-coppa

ConnectSafely—Up-to-date information for parents on the latest online platforms
kids are using.
https://www.connectsafely.org/parentguides

Parenting, Media, and Everything in Between (Common Sense Media)
https://www.commonsensemedia.org/articles

A Parent Guide to Teens, Technology, & Social Media
Author: Karen Hamilton, LMFT, CATC
A useful guide for parents regarding teens, tech, and social media:
https://karenhamiltontherapy.com/wp-content/uploads/2018/09/A-Parent-
Guide-to-Teens-Technology-Social-Media-2018-new.pdf

Cyberbullying Research Center
https://cyberbullying.org/
They have handouts with tips for parents and teens, and a resource section that also
includes advice for parents about sexting.

Wait Until 8th
https://www.waituntil8th.org/

Suicide Prevention

988 Suicide & Crisis Lifeline
Offers free and confidential emotional support in crisis. National network local
crisis centers answer calls 24-7.
https://988lifeline.org/
988

American Foundation for Suicide Prevention
AFSP National Office
199 Water Street
11th Floor
New York, NY 10038
(888) 333-AFSP (2377)
https://afsp.org/

JED Foundation
530 7th Avenue, Suite 801
New York, NY 10018

212-647-7544
https://jedfoundation.org/

The Steve Fund
P.O. Box 9070
Providence, RI 02940
info@stevefund.org
(401) 249-0044
https://www.stevefund.org/

Substance Use Disorders
Alcoholics Anonymous
(212) 870-3400 (check your phone book for a local number), www.aa.org

American Council for Drug Education
www.acde.org

Beautiful Boy Fund
https://www.beautifulboyfund.org/about-us

Leadership to Keep Children Alcohol Free
(937) 848-2993, www.alcoholfreechildren.org

Narcotics Anonymous
(818) 773-9999, www.na.org

National Council on Alcoholism and Drug Dependence
www.ncadd.us

National Institute on Alcohol Abuse and Alcoholism
(301) 443-3860, www.niaaa.nih.gov

National Institute on Drug Abuse
(301) 443-6441, https://nida.nih.gov/

Partnership to End Addiction
(212) 841-5200, https://drugfree.org/

Substance Abuse and Mental Health Services Administration
(800) 662-4357, www.samhsa.gov

Education
Wrightslaw
https://www.wrightslaw.com/
You can also contact a Parent Training and Information Center in your state, which offers free information on special-needs education.

Matrix Parent Network and Resource Center for families of children with special needs.
https://www.matrixparents.org/

Academic Accommodations for Students With Psychiatric Disabilities
https://www.washington.edu/doit/academic-accommodations-students-psychiatric-disabilities

Boston University's NITEO Program
https://cpr.bu.edu/wellness-and-recovery-services/niteo/

Challenge Success
https://challengesuccess.org/

Fountain House College Re-Entry
https://collegereentry.org/

Road2College: College Co-Op Programs: What You Need to Know
https://www.road2college.com/colleges-with-coop-programs/

Scholarships.com: Clinically Depressed Scholarships
https://www.scholarships.com/financial-aid/college-scholarships/scholarship-directory/physical-disabilities/clinically-depressed

Homeschooling
https://www.highschoolofamerica.com/
Learn more about homeschooling and how your child can earn a recognized diploma from High School of America today.

Job Corps
https://www.jobcorps.gov/parents

Gap year programs:
The Gap Year Association
https://www.gapyearassociation.org/

Bullying
StopBullying.gov
https://www.stopbullying.gov/

Beyond Differences
https://www.beyonddifferences.org/

Juvenile Justice
Youth.gov
https://youth.gov/youth-topics/juvenile-justice

Navigating the Juvenile Justice System in New Jersey: A Family Guide
https://www.njjn.org/uploads/digital-library/NJ-Parents-Caucus_Navigating-JJ-System-Family-Guide_2014.pdf

ADHD
Children and Adults with Attention-Deficit/Hyperactivity Disorder (CHADD)
4221 Forbes Blvd, Suite 270
Lanham, MD 20706
(301) 306-7070, http://www.chadd.org

Learning Disorders and Disabilities
International Dyslexia Association
(410) 296-0232, www.interdys.org

LD OnLine
www.ldonline.org

Learning Disabilities Association of America
(412) 341-1515, www.ldaamerica.org

National Center for Learning Disabilities
(301) 966-2234, www.ncld.org

YAI—Seeing Beyond Disability
https://www.yai.org/
This organization along with affiliate agencies offers support and services for children and adults with intellectual and developmental disabilities.

US Department of Justice ADA Information Line For information on government support, call 800-514-0301 or go to www.ada.gov

Eating Disorders
National Association of Anorexia Nervosa and Associated Disorders
(888) 375-7767, www.anad.org

National Eating Disorders Association
1-800-931-2237, www.nationaleatingdisorders.org

Free Apps to Chart Moods
Note: Before using any app . . .
1. Check for price changes; these are all free, but there are "premium" paid options.
2. Make note of the free trial period's duration, if applicable.
   • T2 Mood Tracker
     Monitors moods for anxiety, stress, depression, brain injury, posttraumatic stress, and general well-being.

- eMoods
  eMoods can help identify triggers for a relapse of bipolar disorder.
- Moodpath
  After an initial screening, this app provides a "scientifically validated" assessment every two weeks.

Mental Health Law
Americans With Disabilities Act
https://www.ada.gov/

Colorado General Assembly: Children and Youth Mental Health Treatment Act
https://leg.colorado.gov/bills/hb18-1094

Council of Parent Attorneys and Advocates
https://www.copaa.org/

US Equal Employment Opportunity Commission: Questions and Answers on the Final Rule Implementing the ADA Amendments Act of 2008
https://www.eeoc.gov/laws/guidance/question-and-answers-final-rule-implementing-ada-amendments-act-2008

US Department of Labor: Family and Medical Leave Act
https://www.dol.gov/agencies/whd/fmla

Parity
The Mental Health Parity and Addiction Equity Act (MHPAEA)
https://www.cms.gov/CCIIO/Programs-and-Initiatives/Other-Insurance-Protecti ons/mhpaea_factsheet

To check your health plan's compliance with parity, call or go to the following:

US Department of Labor Employee Benefits Security Administration (EBSA)
https://www.dol.gov/agencies/ebsa—check page on consumer information on health plans or contact EBSA toll-free at 1-866-444-3272

US Department of Health and Human Services: 1-877-696-6775

National Association of Insurance Commissioners
https://content.naic.org/
Contains your state's department of insurance website and contact information.

To learn more about benefits and the appeals process, go to:

The National Conference of State Legislatures: Mental Health Benefits: State Laws Mandating or Regulating. https://www.ncsl.org/research/health/mental-health-benefits-state-mandates.aspx

The HealthCare.gov page on health insurance rights and protections.

The US Department of Labor maintains a parity resource webpage with links to the federal parity regulations, "Frequently Asked Questions" and other agency guidance, educational fact sheets, videos, reports, and links to other websites and organizations with helpful parity information. https://www.dol.gov/agencies/ebsa/laws-and-regulations/ laws/mental-health-and-substance-use-disorder-parity

Community Catalyst and Health Law Advocates post a wide range of health care resources, including resources for substance use disorders advocates and resources for health care consumers. www.communitycatalyst.org, www.healthlawadvocates.org

Helpful handout on parity: https://www.communitycatalyst.org/resources/publi cations/document/parity-issue-brief-FINAL-12-9-14.pdf?1418154547

Bibliography

Abeles, V., & Congdon, J. (Directors). (2010). *Race to nowhere* [Film]. Reel Link Films.

American Academy of Child and Adolescent Psychiatry. (n.d.). *Post pediatric portal programs.* https://www.aacap.org/AACAP/Medical_Students_and_Residents/Triple_Board_Residency_Training/Post_Pediatric_Portal_Programs.aspx

American Academy of Child and Adolescent Psychiatry. (2019, October). *Marijuana and teens.* https://www.aacap.org/AACAP/Families_and_Youth/Facts_for_Families/FFF-Guide/Marijuana-and-Teens-106.aspx

American Academy of Pediatrics. (2014). School start times for adolescents. *Pediatrics, 134*(3), 642–649. https://doi.org/10.1542/peds.2014-1697

American Academy of Pediatrics, the American Academy of Child Adolescent Psychiatry, & the Children's Hospital Association. (2021). *Pediatricians, child and adolescent psychiatrists and children's hospitals declare national emergency in children's mental health.* https://www.aap.org/en/news-room/news-releases/aap/2021/pediatricians-child-and-adolescent-psychiatrists-and-childrens-hospitals-declare-national-emergency-for-childrens-mental-health/

American Foundation for Suicide Prevention. (n.d.). *An introduction to firearms and suicide prevention.* https://afsp.org/an-introduction-to-firearms-and-suicide-prevention

American Psychiatric Association. (2018). *Position statement on the risks of adolescents' online activity.* https://www.psychiatry.org/getattachment/fb0fcd5b-45d5-4177-9756-47a35f389048/Position-2018-Risk-of-Adolescents-Online-Activity.pdf

American Psychiatric Association. (2022). *Diagnostic and statistical manual of mental disorders* (5th ed., text revision). American Psychiatric Association.

American Psychological Association. (2017, June). *Parenting styles*. https://www.apa.org/act/resources/fact-sheets/parenting-styles

Axelson, D. (2019). Meeting the demand for pediatric mental health care. *Pediatrics, 144*(6), Article e20192646. https://doi.org/10.1542/peds.2019-2646

Bahji, A., Zarate, C. A., & Vazquez, G. H. (2021). Ketamine for bipolar depression: A systematic review. *International Journal of Neuropsychopharmacology, 24*(7), 535–541. https://doi.org/10.1093/ijnp/pyab023

Bailey, R. K., Mokonogho, J., & Kumar, A. (2019). Racial and ethnic differences in depression: Current perspectives. *Neuropsychiatric Disease and Treatment, 15*, 603–609. https://doi.org/10.2147/NDT.S128584

Berge, J. M. (2009). A review of familial correlates of child and adolescent obesity: What has the 21st century taught us so far? *International Journal of Adolescent Medicine and Health, 21*(4), 457–483. https://doi.org/10.1515/ijamh.2009.21.4.457

Beyond Differences. (n.d.). *What is social isolation?* https://www.beyonddifferences.org/social-isolation/

Bipolar Network News. (2019, July 19). *Lithium FDA-approved for bipolar disorder in children 7–17*. http://bipolarnews.org/?p=4748

Bogost, I. (2018, October 29). The fetishization of Mr. Rogers's "look for the helpers." *The Atlantic*. https://www.theatlantic.com/technology/archive/2018/10/look-for-the-helpers-mr-rogers-is-bad-for-adults/574210/

Boston Children's Health Physicians. (2019, August 12). *Growing trend of school refusal*. https://www.childrenshospital.org/bchp/news/growing-trend-school-refusal

Brody, D. J., & Gu, Q. (2020, September). Antidepressant use among adults: United States, 2015–2018. *NCHS Data Brief, 377*. https://www.cdc.gov/nchs/products/databriefs/db377.htm

Brown, B. (2019, August 7). *What Toni Morrison taught me about parenting*. https://brenebrown.com/articles/2019/08/07/what-toni-morrison-taught-me-about-parenting/

Cagle, J. (2018, April 11). Mariah Carey: My battle with bipolar disorder. *People*. https://people.com/music/mariah-carey-bipolar-disorder-diagnosis-exclusive/

Campbell, D. (2018, December 11). Study finds high levels of depression among LGB teenagers. *The Guardian*. https://www.theguardian.com/world/2018/dec/12/study-finds-high-levels-of-depression-among-lgbt-teenagers

Caron, C. (2021, September 21). Worried about your teen on social media? Here's how to help. *The New York Times*. https://www.nytimes.com/2021/09/21/well/family/teens-social-media-help.html

CBS News. (2021, November 7). *SAINT: Hope for new treatment of depression*. https://www.cbsnews.com/news/saint-treatment-for-depression/

Centers for Disease Control and Prevention. (n.d.). *CDC healthy schools: Obesity*. https://www.cdc.gov/healthyschools/obesity/index.htm

Centers for Disease Control and Prevention. (n.d.). *Sexual risk behaviors can lead to HIV, STDs, & teen pregnancy*. https://www.cdc.gov/healthyyouth/sexualbehaviors/index.htm

Centers for Disease Control and Prevention. (n.d.). *Sleep and sleep disorders: Data and statistics.* https://www.cdc.gov/sleep/data_statistics.html

Centers for Disease Control and Prevention. (2022, June 8). *Sleep and sleep disorders: Schools start too early.* https://www.cdc.gov/sleep/features/schools-start-too-early.html

Chalasani, R. (2018, April 11). *Famous people with bipolar disorder.* CBS News. https://www.cbsnews.com/pictures/famous-people-celebrities-bipolar/

Clegg, N. (2021, September 18). *What the Wall Street Journal got wrong.* Meta. https://about.fb.com/news/2021/09/what-the-wall-street-journal-got-wrong/

Cole, E. J., Phillips, A. L., Bentzley, B. S., Stimpson, K. H., Nejad, R., Barmak, F., Veerapal, C., Khan, N., Cherian, K., Felber, E., Brown, R., Choi, E., King, S., Pankow, H., Bishop, J. H., Azeez, A., Coetzee, J., Rapier, R., Odenwald, N., . . . Williams, N. R. (2022, February). Stanford neuromodulation therapy (SNT): A double-blind randomized controlled trial. *The American Journal of Psychiatry, 179*(2), 132–141. https://doi.org/10.1176/appi.ajp.2021.20101429

Curtin, S. C. (2020). State suicide rates among adolescents and young adults aged 10–24: United States, 2000–2018. *National Vital Statistics Reports, 69*(11). https://www.cdc.gov/nchs/data/nvsr/nvsr69/nvsr-69-11-508.pdf

Davenport, S., Gray, T. J., & Melek, S. P. (2019, November 20). *Addiction and mental health vs. physical health: Widening disparities in network use and provider reimbursement.* Milliman. https://www.milliman.com/en/insight/addiction-and-mental-health-vs-physical-health-widening-disparities-in-network-use-and-p

Dembosky, A. (2021, November 18). *Americans can wait many weeks to see a therapist. California law aims to fix that.* NPR. https://www.npr.org/sections/health-shots/2021/11/18/1053566020/americans-can-wait-many-weeks-to-see-a-therapist-california-law-aims-to-fix-that

Dickson, C. (2015, February 5). *Bipolar teen's death in police station highlights rift between cops, mentally ill.* Yahoo! News. https://www.yahoo.com/entertainment/news/bipolar-teen-s-death-highlights-frequency-of-violent-encounters-between-police--mentally-ill-014049696.html?guccounter=1

Duffy, J. (2021, August 23). *Here's how to prevent your children from refusing to go to school.* CNN. https://www.cnn.com/2021/08/23/health/school-refusal-psychology-wellness/index.html

Dunayevich, E., & Keck, P. E. (2000). Prevalence and description of psychotic features in bipolar mania. *Current Psychiatry Reports, 2*(4), 286–290. https://doi.org/10.1007/s11920-000-0069-4

Dwyer, J. B., Landeros-Weisenberger, A., Johnson, J. A., Londono Tobon, A., Flores, J. M., Nasir, M., Couloures, K., Sanacora, G., & Bloch, M. H. (2021). Efficacy of intravenous ketamine in adolescent treatment-resistant depression: A randomized midazolam-controlled trial. *The American Journal of Psychiatry, 178*(4), 352–362. https://doi.org/10.1176/appi.ajp.2020.20010018

Eggleston, C., & Fields, J. (2021, March 22). *Census Bureau's Household Pulse Survey shows significant increase in homeschooling rates in fall 2020.* United States Census Bureau. https://www.census.gov/library/stories/2021/03/homeschooling-on-the-rise-during-covid-19-pandemic.html

Ellison, K. (2020, March 28). E-therapy apps see booming business since corona-virus pandemic. I gave one a try. *The Washington Post*. https://www.washingtonp ost.com/healthinclude/e-therapy-apps-see-booming-business-since-coronavi rus-pandemic-i-gave-one-a-try/2020/03/27/985682c4-6d20-11ea-a3ec-70d 7479d83f0_story.html

Ellison, K. (2021, March 27). Sleep-deprived kids have gotten a break with remote learning's later start times. Some hope it's a wake-up call for schools. *The Washington Post*.   https://www.washingtonpost.com/health/teenage-sleep-remote-learn ing-school-time/2021/03/26/29d3c004-898b-11eb-8a8b-5cf82c3dffe4_ story.html

Fischer, C. (n.d.). *15 honest quotes about bipolar disorder*. National Alliance on Mental Illness. https://namimtsanjacinto.org/carrie-fisher-15-honest-quotes-bipolar-disorder/

Gentile, D. A., Reimer, R. A., Nathanson, A. I., Walsh, D. A., & Eisenmann, J. C. (2014, May). Protective effects of parental monitoring of children's media use: A prospective study. *JAMA Pediatrics*, *168*(5), 479–484. https://doi.org/10.1001/ jamapediatrics.2014.146

Goldstein, T. R., Ha, W., Axelson, D. A., Goldstein, B. I., Liao, F., Gill, M. K., Ryan, N. D., Yen, S., Hunt, J., Hower, H., Keller, M., Strober, M., & Birmaher, B. (2012). Predictors of prospectively examined suicide attempts among youth with bipolar disorder. *Archives of General Psychiatry*, *69*(11), 1113–1122. https:// doi.org/10.1001/archgenpsychiatry.2012.650

Goldstein, T. R., Krantz, M., Merranko, J., Garcia, M., Sobel, L., Rodriguez, C., Douaihy, A., Axelson, D., & Birmaher, B. (2016). Medication adher-ence among adolescents with bipolar disorder. *Journal of Child and Adolescent Psychopharmacology*, *26*(10), 864–872. https://doi.org/10.1089/cap.2016.0030

Goodman, L. (n.d.). *Guidance for advocates: Identifying parity violations & taking action*. Health Law Advocates. https://www.communitycatalyst.org/resources/ publications/document/parity-issue-brief-FINAL-12-9-14.pdf?1418154547

GoodTherapy. (2014). *How much does therapy cost?* https://www.goodtherapy.org/ blog/faq/how-much-does-therapy-cost

Greenberg, M. (2010). *Hurry down sunshine: A father's memoir of love and madness*. Bloomsbury Publishing.

Griswold, B. (2015, June 8). *Blue Shield of California and Magellan: A deceptive arrangement*. Navigating the Insurance Maze. https://theinsurancemaze.com/ articles/magellan/

Hall-Flavin, D. K. (2018, November 17). *Antidepressants and weight gain: What causes it?* Mayo Clinic. https://www.mayoclinic.org/diseases-conditions/depress ion/expert-answers/antidepressants-and-weight-gain/faq-20058127

Harman, G., Kliamovich, D., Morales, A. M., Gilbert, S., Barch, D. M., Mooney, M.A., Ewing, S. W. F., Fair, D. A., & Nagel, B. J. (2021). Prediction of suicidal ideation and attempt in 9 and 10 year-old children using transdiagnostic risk features. *PLoS ONE*, *16*(5), Article e0252114. https://doi.org/10.1371/journal. pone.0252114

Harvard Health Publishing. (2021, February 2). *Exercise is an all-natural treatment to fight depression*. https://www.health.harvard.edu/mind-and-mood/exercise-is-an-all-natural-treatment-to-fight-depression

Harvard Health Publishing. (2021, March 30). *Sour mood getting you down? Get back to nature*. https://www.health.harvard.edu/mind-and-mood/sour-mood-getting-you-down-get-back-to-nature

Heilmann, A., Mehay, A., Watt, R. G., Kelly, Y., Durrant, J. E., van Turnhout, J., & Gershoff, E. T. (2021). Physical punishment and child outcomes: A narrative review of prospective studies. *The Lancet, 398*(10297), 355–364. https://doi.org/10.1016/S0140-6736(21)00582-1

Hevesi, D. (2012, May 22). Katie Beckett, who inspired health reform, dies at 34. *The New York Times*. https://www.nytimes.com/2012/05/23/us/katie-beckett-who-inspired-health-reform-dies-at-34.html

Hosseini, R. F. (2014, November 27). How Sacramento turns at-risk kids into criminals. *Sacramento News & Review*. https://www.newsreview.com/sacramento/content/how-sacramento-turns-at-risk-kids-into-criminals/15590372/

Howell, B. A., Wang, E. A., & Winkelman, T. N. A. (2019). Mental health treatment among individuals involved in the criminal justice system after implementation of the Affordable Care Act. *Psychiatric Services, 70*(9), 765–771. https://doi.org/10.1176/appi.ps.201800559

Jacobson, R. (2022, July 28). *How to talk to your teen about substance use*. Child Mind Institute. https://childmind.org/article/talk-teenager-substance-use-abuse/

Jahren, H. (2016). *Lab girl*. Knopf.

JED Foundation. (n.d.). *Supporting mental health from a distance: When should a parent intervene?* https://jedfoundation.org/set-to-go/supporting-mental-health-from-a-distance-when-should-a-parent-intervene/

Jick, H., Kaye, J. A., & Jick, S. S. (2004, July 21). Antidepressants and the risk of suicidal behaviors. *JAMA, 292*(3), 338–343. https://doi.org/10.1001/jama.292.3.338

Joly, V. (2017, February 23). *Single case agreement (SCA) with insurance companies*. Vinodha Psychotherapy and Consultation. https://vinodhatherapy.com/blogs/2017/2/23/single-case-agreement-sca-with-insurance-companies

Kaplan, A. (2020, January 29). Does science support the "wilderness" in wilderness therapy? *Undark*. https://undark.org/2020/01/29/does-science-support-the-wilderness-in-wilderness-therapy/

Kaplan, K. (2018, November 8). A lot more Americans are meditating now than just five years ago. *Los Angeles Times*. https://www.latimes.com/science/sciencenow/la-sci-sn-americans-meditating-more-20181108-story.html

Keane, D. (2021, 25 October). Molly Russell's father meets Facebook whistle-blower Frances Haugen. *Evening Standard*. https://www.standard.co.uk/news/uk/molly-russell-dad-teenager-suicide-facebook-whistblower-frances-haugen-b962289.html

Kowatch, R. A., Sethuraman, G., Hume, J. H., Kromelis, M., & Weinberg, W. A. (2003, June 1). Combination pharmacotherapy in children and adolescents

with bipolar disorder. *Biological Psychiatry, 53*(11), 978–984. https://doi.org/
10.1016/s0006-3223(03)00067-2

Krantz, M., Goldstein, T., Rooks, B., Merranko, J., Liao, F., Gill, M. K., Diler, R., Hafeman, D., Ryan, N., Goldstein, B., Yen, S., Hower, H., Hunt, J., Keller, M., Strober, M., Axelson, D., & Birmaher, B. (2018, February). Sexual risk behavior among youth with bipolar disorder: Identifying demographic and clinical risk factors. *Journal of the American Academy of Child and Adolescent Psychiatry, 57*(2), 118–124. https://doi.org/10.1016/j.jaac.2017.11.015

Lambert, K. (2015). Do or diy. *RSA Journal, 161*(5561), 20–23. https://www.jstor.org/stable/26204384

Lambert, K. (2018). Building the brain's contingency circuit. In *Well-grounded: The neurobiology of rational decisions* (pp. 73–94). Yale University Press.

LaMotte, S. (2020, July 29). *Spanking has declined in America, study finds, but pediatricians worry about impact of pandemic.* CNN. https://www.cnn.com/2020/07/27/health/spanking-decline-us-wellness/index.html

Lee, A. M. I. (n.d.). *What is a functional behavioral assessment (FBA)?* Understood. https://www.understood.org/en/articles/functional-assessment-what-it-is-and-how-it-works

Lee, S., Rothbard, A. B., & Noll, E. L. (2012). Length of inpatient stay of persons with serious mental illness: Effects of hospital and regional characteristics. *Psychiatric Services, 63*(9), 889–895. https://doi.org/10.1176/appi.ps.201100412

Levenkron, S. (1998). *Cutting: Understanding and overcoming self-mutilation.* Lion's Crown.

Levine, M. (2008). *The price of privilege: How parental pressure and material advantage are creating a generation of disconnected and unhappy kids.* HarperCollins.

Lewis, S. (2017, December 14). *Neuropsychologist: Your brain & human behavior specialist.* Healthgrades. https://www.healthgrades.com/right-care/brain-and-nerves/neuropsychologist-your-brain-human-behavior-specialist

Libby, B. (2022, July 26). *Even in his youth.* HealthDay. https://consumer.healthday.com/encyclopedia/depression-12/depression-news-176/even-in-his-youth-644949.html

Maayan, L., & Correll, C. U. (2010). Management of antipsychotic-related weight gain. *Expert Review of Neurotherapeutics, 10*(7), 1175–1200. https://doi.org/10.1586/ern.10.85

MacPhee, J., Modi, K., Gorman, S., Roy, N., Riba, E., Cusumano, D., Dunkle, J., Komrosky, N., Schwartz, V., Eisenberg, D., Silverman, M. M., Pinder-Amaker, S., Watkins, K. B., & Doraiswamy, P. M. (2021, June 21). *A comprehensive approach to mental health promotion and suicide prevention for colleges and universities: Insights from the JED campus program.* National Academy of Medicine. https://nam.edu/wp-content/uploads/2021/06/A-Comprehensive-Approach-to-Mental-Health-Promotion-and-Suicide-Prevention.pdf

Makin, S. (2019, April 12). Behind the buzz: How ketamine changes the depressed patient's brain. *Scientific American.* https://www.scientificamerican.com/article/behind-the-buzz-how-ketamine-changes-the-depressed-patients-brain/

Manelis, A., Soehner, A., Halchenko, Y. O., Satz, S., Ragozzino, R., Lucero, M., Swartz, H. A., Phillips, M. L., & Versace, A. (2021). White matter abnormalities in adults with bipolar disorder type-II and unipolar depression. *Scientific Reports*, *11*, Article 7541. https://doi.org/10.1038/s41 598-021-87069-2

Marcus, D. L. (2006). *What it takes to pull me through: Why teenagers get in trouble—and how four of them got out*. Harper Paperbacks.

Martini, R., Hilt, R., Marx, L., Chenven, M., Naylor, M., Sarvet, B., & Ptakowski, K. K. (2012, June). *Best principles for integration of child psychiatry into the pediatric health home*. American Academy of Child & Adolescent Psychiatry. https://www.aacap.org/App_Themes/AACAP/docs/clinical_practice_center/ systems_of_care/best_principles_for_integration_of_child_psychiatry_into_ the_pediatric_health_home_2012.pdf

Marylanders to Prevent Gun Violence. (n.d.). *Maryland safe storage map*. https:// mdpgv.org/safestoragemap/

Mayo Clinic. (2020, February 7). *Compulsive sexual behavior*. https://www.may oclinic.org/diseases-conditions/compulsive-sexual-behavior/symptoms-causes/ syc-20360434

Mayo Clinic. (2020, November 18). *SAMe*. https://www.mayoclinic.org/drugs-supplements-same/art-20364924

Mazza, M., Di Nicola, M., Della Marca, G., Janiri, L., Bria, P., & Mazza, S. (2007). Bipolar disorder and epilepsy: A bidirectional relation? Neurobiological underpinnings, current hypotheses, and future research directions. *Neuroscientist*, *13*(4), 392–404. https://doi.org/10.1177/10738584070130041101

McCallion, G., & Feder, J. (2013, October 18). *Student bullying: Overview of research, federal initiatives, and legal issues*. Congressional Research Service report. https://sgp.fas.org/crs/misc/R43254.pdf

Mental Daily. (2021, July 3). *Physical activity found to be more beneficial than previously known for brain health of children*. https://www.mentaldaily.com/arti cle/2021/07/physical-activity-found-to-be-more-beneficial-than-previously-known-for-brain-health-of-children

Mental Health America. (2018). *The state of mental health in America 2018*. https:// www.mhanational.org/issues/state-mental-health-america-2018

Miklowitz, D., & Chung, B. (2016). *Family-focused therapy for bipolar disorder: Reflections on 30 years of research*. Family Process, 55(3), 483–499.

Miklowitz, D, J., & George, E. L. (2007). *The bipolar teen: What you can do to help your child and your family*. The Guilford Press.

Miller, J. N., & Black, D. W. (2020). Bipolar disorder and suicide: A review. *Current Psychiatry Reports*, *22*(6). https://doi.org/10.1007/s11920-020-1130-0

Miller, L., Wickramaratne, P., Hao, X., McClintock, C. H., Pan, L., Svob, C., & Weissman, M. M. (2021, September 30). Altruism and "love of neighbor" offer neuroanatomical protection against depression. *Psychiatry Research: Neuroimaging*, *315*, Article 111326. https://doi.org/10.1016/j.pscy chresns.2021.111326

Morin, A. (n.d.). *9 steps to take if your request for evaluation is denied*. Understood. https://www.understood.org/en/articles/9-steps-to-take-if-your-request-for-eva luation-is-denied

Muzaffar, N., Brito, E. B., Fogel, J., Fagan, D., Kumar, K., & Verma, R. (2018). The association of adolescent Facebook behaviours with symptoms of social anxiety, generalized anxiety, and depression. *Journal of the Canadian Academy of Child and Adolescent Psychiatry, 27*(4), 252–260.

National Alliance on Mental Illness. (2022, June). *Mental health by the numbers*. https://www.nami.org/mhstats

National Institutes of Health. (2021, June 22). *Cannabis use may be associated with suicidality in young adults*. US Department of Health and Human Services. https://www.nih.gov/news-events/news-releases/cannabis-use-may-be-associa ted-suicidality-young-adults

National Institute of Mental Health. (n.d.). *Bipolar disorder*. https://www.nimh. nih.gov/health/statistics/bipolar-disorder

National Institute of Mental Health. (n.d.). *Suicide*. https://www.nimh.nih.gov/ health/statistics/suicide

National Institute of Mental Health. (2021, September 29). *Genomic data from more than 41,000 people shed new light on bipolar disorder*. https://www.nimh. nih.gov/news/research-highlights/2021/genomic-data-from-more-than-41000- people-shed-new-light-on-bipolar-disorder

Nivoli, A. M. A., Pacchiarotti, I., Rosa, A. R., Popovic, D., Murru, A., Valenti, M., Bonnin, C. M., Grande, I., Sanchez-Moreno, J., Vieta, E., & Colom, F. (2011). Gender differences in a cohort study of 604 bipolar patients: The role of predominant polarity. *Journal of Affective Disorders, 133*(3), 443–449. https:// doi.org/10.1016/j.jad.2011.04.055

O'Donnell, D. (2015, October 9). *A label for my daughter we can all love*. Scary Mommy. https://www.scarymommy.com/a-label-for-my-daugh ter-we-can-all-love

Office of Juvenile Justice and Delinquency Prevention. (2017, July). *Intersection between mental health and the juvenile justice system*. https://ojjdp.ojp.gov/ model-programs-guide/literature-reviews/intsection_between_mental_health_ and_the_juvenile_justice_system.pdf

Office of the US Surgeon General. (2021, December 7). *Protecting youth mental health: The U.S. Surgeon General's advisory*. https://www.hhs.gov/sites/default/ files/surgeon-general-youth-mental-health-advisory.pdf

Pandey, E. (2021, August 31). *Homeschooling reaches critical mass*. Axios. https:// www.axios.com/2021/08/31/homeschooling-pandemic-critical-mass

Parikh, T., & Walkup, J. T. (2021, April). The future of ketamine in the treatment of teen depression. *The American Journal of Psychiatry, 178*(4), 288–289. https:// ajp.psychiatryonline.org/doi/pdf/10.1176/appi.ajp.2020.21020172

Parks, C. (2021, June 14). The rise of Black homeschooling. *The New Yorker*. https://www.newyorker.com/magazine/2021/06/21/the-rise-of-black-homesc hooling

Pearson, D. G., & Craig, T. (2014, October 21). The great outdoors? Exploring the mental health benefits of natural environments. *Frontiers in Psychology, 5*. https://doi.org/10.3389/fpsyg.2014.01178

Perry, B. I., Stochl, J., Upthegrove, R., Zammit, S., Wareham, N., Langenberg, C., Winpenny, E., Dunger, D., Jones, P. B., & Khandaker, G. M. (2021, January 13). Longitudinal trends in childhood insulin levels and body mass index and associations with risks of psychosis and depression in young adults. *JAMA Psychiatry, 78*(4), 416–425. https://doi.org/10.1001/jamapsychiatry.2020.4180

Peru, G. (2022, January 20). *The best sunlight lamps for winter depression and light therapy*. MUO. https://www.makeuseof.com/tag/light-therapy-beat-winter-depression/

Pleat, T. A. (n.d.). *Katie Beckett waiver brings home care to kids with serious disabilities*. Special Needs Alliance. https://www.specialneedsalliance.org/blog/katie-beckett-waiver-brings-home-care-to-kids-with-serious-disabilities/

Potter, M. P., Liu, H. Y., Monuteaux, M. C., Henderson, C. S., Wozniak, J., Wilens, T. E., & Biederman, J. (2009). Prescribing patterns for treatment of pediatric bipolar disorder in a specialty clinic. *Journal of Child and Adolescent Psychopharmacology, 19*(5), 529–538. https://doi.org/10.1089/cap.2008.0142

ProCon.org. (2022, June 6). *State-by-state recreational marijuana laws*. https://marijuana.procon.org/legal-recreational-marijuana-states-and-dc

Rachamallu, V., Elberson, B. W., Vutam, E., & Aligeti, M. (2019). Off-label use of clozapine in children and adolescents: A literature review. *American Journal of Therapeutics, 26*(3), e406–e416. https://doi.org/doi: 10.1097/MJT.0000000000000894

Raeburn, P. (2004). *Acquainted with the night: A parent's quest to understand depression and bipolar disorder in his children*. Broadway.

Ratey, J. J., & Hagerman, E. (2008). *Spark: The revolutionary new science of exercise and the brain*. Little, Brown.

Ray, B. D. (2022, March 26). *Homeschooling: The research*. National Home Education Research Institute. https://www.nheri.org/research-facts-on-homeschooling/

Rey, C. M. (2003, May 6). *Study suggests bipolar disorder may cause progressive brain damage*. University of California San Francisco. https://www.ucsf.edu/news/2003/05/97207/study-suggests-bipolar-disorder-may-cause-progressive-brain-damage

Rivers, I., Poteat, V. P., Noret, N., & Ashurst, N. (2009). Observing bullying at school: The mental health implications of witness status. *School Psychology Quarterly, 24*(4), 211–223. https://doi.org/10.1037/a0018164

Rudgard, O. (2018, November 6). The tech moguls who invented social media have banned their children from it. *Independent*. https://www.independent.ie/life/family/parenting/the-tech-moguls-who-invented-social-media-have-banned-their-children-from-it-37494367.html

Russell, D. O. (Director). (2012). *Silver linings playbook* [Film]. Weinstein Company.

Ryan, C. (2009). *Helping families support their lesbian, gay, bisexual, and transgender (LGBT) children*. Georgetown University. https://nccc.georgetown.edu/docume nts/LGBT_Brief.pdf

Ryan, C., Huebner, D., Diaz, R. M., & Sanchez, J. (2009). Family rejection as a predictor of negative health outcomes in white and Latino lesbian, gay, and bisexual young adults. *Pediatrics, 123*(1), 346–352. https://doi.org/10.1542/peds.2007-3524

Second Nature. (2019, October 10). *Is it time for wilderness therapy?* https://www.second-nature.com/blog/is-it-time-for-wilderness-therapy

Serna, J., & Winton, R. (2017, June 19). Carrie Fisher's autopsy reveals cocktail of drugs, including cocaine, opiates and ecstasy. *Los Angeles Times*. https://www.latimes.com/local/lanow/la-me-ln-carrie-fisher-autopsy-report-20170 619-story.html

Sheff, D. (2017, May). *I thought addiction was my son's problem. But addiction is a family disease*. Partnership to End Addiction. https://drugfree.org/parent-blog/i-thought-addiction-was-my-sons-problem-but-addiction-is-a-family-disease/

Sheff, D. (2018). *Beautiful boy: A father's journey through his son's addiction*. Mariner Books.

Shem, S. (1978). *The house of God*. Penguin.

Shim, R. S. (2021). Dismantling structural racism in psychiatry: A path to mental health equity. *The American Journal of Psychiatry, 178*(7), 592–598. https://doi.org/10.1176/appi.ajp.2021.21060558

Singhal, A., Ross, J., Seminog, O., Hawton, K., & Goldacre, M. J. (2014). Risk of self-harm and suicide in people with specific psychiatric and physical disorders: Comparisons between disorders using English national record linkage. *Journal of the Royal Society of Medicine, 107*(5),194–204. https://doi.org/10.1177/0141076814522033

Sobowale, K., & Ross, D. A. (2018). Poverty, parenting, and psychiatry. *Biological Psychiatry, 84*(5), e29–e31. https://doi.org/10.1016/j.biopsych.2018.07.007

Spiegel, A. (2010, February 10). *Children labeled "bipolar" may get a new diagnosis*. NPR. https://www.npr.org/2010/02/10/123544191/children-labeled-bipolar-may-get-a-new-diagnosis

Stallard, P., Spears, M., Montgomery, A. A., Phillips, R., & Sayal, K. (2013). Self-harm in young adolescents (12–16 years): Onset and short-term continuation in a community sample. *BMC Psychiatry, 13*, Article 328. https://doi.org/10.1186/1471-244X-13-328

Steel, D. (1998). *His bright light: The story of Nick Traina*. Delacorte Press.

Stensland, M., Watson, P. R., & Grazier, K. L. (2012, July). An examination of costs, charges, and payments for inpatient psychiatric treatment in community hospitals. *Psychiatric Services, 63*(7), 666–671. https://doi.org/10.1176/appi.ps.201100402

Substance Abuse and Mental Health Services Administration. (n.d.). *Know the risks of marijuana*. https://www.samhsa.gov/marijuana

Thomas, K. C., Shartzer, A., Kurth, N. K., & Hall, J. P. (2018, February 1). Impact of ACA health reforms for people with mental health conditions. *Psychiatric Services, 69*(2), 231–234. https://doi.org/10.1176/appi.ps.201700044

Tohen, M. (n.d.). *Expert Q&A: Bipolar disorder.* American Psychiatric Association. https://www.psychiatry.org/patients-families/bipolar-disorders/expert-q-and-a

Typaldos, M., & Glaze, D. G. (n.d.). *Teenagers: Sleep patterns and school performance.* National Healthy Sleep Awareness Project. https://sleepeducation. org/wp-content/uploads/2021/04/teenssleeppatternsandschoolperforma nce.pdf

University of Oxford. (2010, January 5). *Combination therapy better than leading drug for bipolar disorder, study suggests.* ScienceDaily. https://www.sciencedaily. com/releases/2009/12/091231165336.htm

US Food and Drug Administration. (2018, February 5). *Suicidality in children and adolescents being treated with antidepressant medications.* https://www.fda.gov/ drugs/postmarket-drug-safety-information-patients-and-providers/suicidality-children-and-adolescents-being-treated-antidepressant-medications

Variety. (2019, July 16). *"13 Reasons Why" edits controversial suicide scene.* NBC News. https://www.nbcnews.com/pop-culture/tv/13-reasons-why-edits-contro versial-suicide-scene-n1030241

Wagner, K. D. (2018, August 28). Treatment of bipolar depression in children and adolescents. *Psychiatric Times, 35*(8). https://www.psychiatrictimes.com/view/ treatment-bipolar-depression-children-and-adolescents

Waldorf School of St. Louis. (n.d.). *Waldorf School of St. Louis media and technology philosophy.* https://www.waldorfstl.org/media-and-technology

Watson, J. (n.d.). *Wilderness therapy programs: A comprehensive guide for parents.* Aspiro Adventure Therapy. https://aspiroadventure.com/wilderness-therapy-programs/

Whitlock, J., & Lloyd-Richardson, E. (2019). *How are self-injury and suicide related?* Child Mind Institute. https://childmind.org/article/how-are-self-inj ury-and-suicide-related/

Whitmire, R. (2019, April 8). *Alarming statistics tell the story behind America's college completion crisis: Nearly a third of all college students still don't have a degree six years later.* The 74. https://www.the74million.org/article/alarming-statistics-tell-the-story-behind-americas-college-completion-crisis-nearly-a-third-of-all-coll ege-student-still-dont-have-a-degree-six-years-later/

Wozniak, J., Biederman, J., Mick, E., Waxmonsky, J. G., Hantsoo, L., Best-Popescu, C. A., Cluette-Brown, J., & Laposata, M. (2007). Omega-3 fatty acid monotherapy for pediatric bipolar disorder: A prospective open-label trial. *European Neuropsychopharmacology: The Journal of the European College of Neuropsychopharmacology, 17*(6–7), 440–447. https://doi.org/10.1016/j.eurone uro.2006.11.006

Wright, K. P., Linton, S. K., Withrow, D., Casiraghi, L., Lanza, S. M., de la Iglesia, H., Vetter, C., & Depne, C. M. (2020). Sleep in university students prior to and during COVID-19 stay-at-home orders. *Current Biology*, *30*, R797–R798. https://www.cell.com/current-biology/pdf/S0960-9822(20)30838-1.pdf

Yapıcı Eser, H., Taşkıran, A. S., Ertınmaz, B., Mutluer, T., Kılıç Ö., Özcan Morey, A., Necef, I., Yalçınay İnan, M., & Öngür, D. (2020, April). Anxiety disorders comorbidity in pediatric bipolar disorder: A meta-analysis and meta-regression study. *Acta Psychiatrica Scandinavica*, *141*(4), 327–339. https://doi.org/10.1111/acps.13146

Zakrzewski, C., & Lima, C. (2021, October 4). Former Facebook employee Frances Haugen revealed as "whistleblower" behind leaked documents that plunged the company into scandal. *The Washington Post*. https://www.washingtonpost.com/technology/2021/10/03/facebook-whistleblower-frances-haugen-revealed/

Index

For the benefit of digital users, indexed terms that span two pages (e.g., 52–53) may, on occasion, appear on only one of those pages.

Boxes are indicated by *b* following the page number